AN INTRODUCTION TO LINGUISTICS

Also by Stuart C. Poole

CATALAN IN THREE MONTHS

An Introduction to Linguistics

Stuart C. Poole

St. Martin's Press
New York

AN INTRODUCTION TO LINGUISTICS

St. Martin's Press, Scholarly and Reference Division, 175 Fifth Avenue, New York, N.Y. 10010

First published in the United States of America in 1999

This book is printed on paper suitable for recycling and made from fully managed and sustained forest sources.

Printed in Hong Kong

ISBN 0–312–22115–0 clothbound
ISBN 0–312–22116–9 paperback

Library of Congress Cataloging-in-Publication Data
Poole, Stuart C., 1947–
An introduction to linguistics / Stuart C. Poole.
p.   cm.
Includes bibliographical references and index.
ISBN 0–312–22115–0 (cloth). — ISBN 0–312–22116–9 (pbk.)
1. Linguistics.   2. Language and languages.   I. Title.
P121.P585   1999
410—dc21   98–47245
                                                                CIP

Contents

Preface

This book introduces the nature of language. It deals with the sounds that we make when we speak, with the way in which we construct sentences, with the ways in which our speech varies between social situations, and so on. It does so by the commonly adopted method of having chapters with such headings as phonetics, syntax, social variation. Less conventionally, it has a major chapter which, against the background of these aspects of linguistics, presents the principal features of the languages of western Europe.

You have at least one remarkable skill; you can speak a language. For at least one language you generally know what can and what cannot be designated by the everyday words, you know what is and what is not an acceptable way of combining words to form a sentence, you have a good idea of whether or not a particular statement would be acceptable in a particular social situation. As a skilled user, then, you already have a substantial foundation for the study of language. That foundation and an interest in language are all you need; given those, this introductory book can lead you to an understanding of what language consists of, of how it works. It serves as an introductory book for students of linguistics and as important background material for students of modern languages. Reflecting my work in continuing education, I have attempted to write in a readable style that will also make the book attractive to the many people who want to explore the fascinating world of language without entering full-time education.

I would like to thank my wife Beryl and a student, Arthur McIvor, for taking time to read and comment on my draft. I also thank Beryl for her support and tolerance while I was working on the book. I also thank Arthur as a representative of those students whose interest and enthusiasm help to inspire and reward my work. The facilities of the University of Edinburgh such as the library and word-processing facilities have been of great assistance.

1

What Is Language?

or
Why Can't Chimpanzees Build Power Stations?

1.1 The Significance of Language

For better or worse, the human race dominates life on Earth. If we want to consider why this should be so, we might usefully think about such features of our way of life as our use of things in the world around us to extend our capabilities, our complex social structure with its hierarchies and its division of labour, and our ability to conceptualise, to learn, to solve problems, and so on.

The human race is by no means unique in exhibiting these features. Chimpanzees use 'tools': they strip twigs and use them to extract termites from their nests. The chimpanzees and the termites both live in social groups. Chimpanzee females live on individual home ranges within a territory that is defended by a group of related males. Termites live in a colony with three castes: reproductives, workers and soldiers. Chimpanzees can be trained to respond in accordance with different symbolic gestures.

So if we can build power stations, why can't chimpanzees? A major reason is that they lack a larynx and a mouth that allow the articulation of a wide range of distinguishable sounds. Without these they are doomed to making little progress. One can scarcely imagine us building and operating power stations or implementing a system of justice as intricate as ours without us having an extremely complex system of communication like that provided by our speech. Far simpler tasks require language: language for learning, language for planning, language for co-operation. Without speech it is, indeed, difficult to refer to anything that is removed from us in space and time, anything that we cannot point to here

1

and now; this becomes clear as soon as you try to arrange to meet a friend outside the town hall at seven o'clock without saying or writing anything. Language allows human beings to learn and adapt to changing circumstances far more quickly than would be achieved by evolution; a word of warning passed from father to son is a much more direct and efficient way of adapting the species to its environment than is a process of natural selection whereby those not inclined to do the right thing are eventually weeded out. Human language is infinitely versatile; honey-bees have a remarkable way of letting others know the direction in which a source of nectar lies and how far away it is by means of a 'dance', but they could not begin to discuss the merits of other foodstuffs or alternative ways of constructing their homes.

The power that language gives us is, indeed, so great, the Bible tells us, that God felt obliged to restrict it; in Genesis, chapter 11, we read that our plans to build a tower, that of Babel, up to Heaven were countered by God putting an end to our common language because it gave such power:

> And the Lord said, Behold, the people is one, and they have all one language; and this they begin to do: and now nothing will be restrained from them, which they have imagined to do.

Some would even maintain that the very contemplation of building a tower reaching up to Heaven would be impossible without speech, arguing that even our thoughts are impossible without speech, that we cannot conceptualise without the framework that our language provides for perceiving the world around us.

In short, the nature and the dominance of the way of life that the human race leads is, despite any obstacles that God may have put in its path, due in very large part to the fact that human beings can speak.

1.2 What Is Language?

We have just seen that even chimpanzees lack the physiological equipment required for speech as we know it. That is, of course, not to say that animals cannot communicate. Animals have developed ways of letting others know that they have found a supply of food, of warning others of danger, of attracting a mate, and so on. Such communication may be by means of sight, smell or sound.

Given the huge range of forms of communication, it is important that before we embark on our study of language we have a clear understanding of what we mean by the term *language*. Our first response might be that language relates to communication between human beings and not to communication between animals, and that is certainly a useful first step towards a definition. But are applause in a theatre, an expression of friendship by means of a smile or attracting somebody's attention by means of a 'cough' any more a part of language than are the alarm calls of vervet monkeys which distinguish between snakes, leopards and eagles?

One attempt to define human language was made by the American linguist **Charles F. Hockett** (Hockett, 1958). He enumerated a number of features which, he argued, constitute human language. Other communication systems might exhibit one or more of these features but only human language has them all. The 'dance' of the honey-bee which informs other bees about the location of a source of nectar meets many of the criteria. It meets, for example, that of **interchangeability**: any creature that can transmit the information can also receive such information and vice versa. It meets that of **productivity**, the ability to vary a message to reflect differences in the circumstances concerned; this is clearly necessary in a case where the source of the nectar may be constantly changing. The dance does not, however, meet the criterion of **cultural transmission** for the bees are acting instinctively, not behaving in a way that they have learnt from others. This last criterion is particularly associated with human language for the one stimulates the other; we acquire our native tongue by cultural transmission and it is by means of our native tongue that we receive cultural transmissions, that we learn and adapt. This is the spiral that has driven human development.

So how, then, might we define the term *language*? An earlier American linguist, **Edward Sapir**, gave a definition in a book published in 1921 (Sapir, 1921, p. 8). He supported the hypothesis that language relates to communication between human beings. Just as Hockett was to associate human language with cultural transmission, so too Sapir considered that it is 'non-instinctive' and 'voluntarily produced'. Thus for him language does not include such instinctive forms of communication as smiling and cries of pain. His definition is as follows:

> Language is a purely human and non-instinctive method of communicating ideas, emotions, and desires by means of a system of voluntarily produced symbols.

He goes on to say that these symbols are, in the first instance, auditory; thus language is primarily a matter of speech as opposed to, say, sign language.

The element **'symbols'** reflects the fact that there is rarely an inherent association between a word and the object or concept that it denotes. Any sequence of sounds can serve to denote an object as long as the speakers of the language concerned make the same association; we could just as well denote a dog using the word *perro*, the word *chien* or the word *hond*, as the Spaniards, the French and the Dutch have shown. The element **'system'** reflects the fact that language provides us with the framework for generating appropriate utterances rather than providing us with an infinite store of ready-made utterances. We can create utterances never uttered before; this may possibly be the first time that anyone has ever written the following: 'An elderly mariner leading a monkey by a chain staggered into a bank and asked a teller for a glass of whisky and a banana'!

For comparison we may look at a definition given by a modern British linguist, **David Crystal**, who wrote the following (Crystal, 1989, p. 251):

> The discussion may be summarized by referring to language as human vocal noise (or the graphic representation of this noise in writing) used systematically and conventionally by a community for purposes of communication.

Thus this definition also proposes **communication** as the principal function of language. What it does not do is attempt to specify what is communicated; as the British linguist **John Lyons** points out (Lyons, 1992, p. 3), Sapir was too restrictive in this.

Nor is there any element corresponding to 'non-instinctive'; while any particular language is culturally transmitted – an infant acquires the language of the society in which it grows up, irrespective of the language of its parents – it is now generally accepted that humans inherit a predisposition towards acquiring language. Indeed the modern linguist and cognitive scientist **Steven Pinker** uses the word **instinct** to embody the essence of human language (Pinker, 1994, p. 18). Whether one considers language to be instinctive or not depends on precisely what one is talking about. Language is instinctive in so far as we are all born with a predisposition to speak, we all acquire a language without tuition and when we speak we do not consciously convert our thoughts into speech. Language is, however, non-instinctive in that we can choose what to say or whether to say anything at all; it is not instinctive in the way that removing one's hand from a very hot plate is, done before we are even aware of the situation.

Both definitions refer to the element of system and both allude to the fact that the association between the words used and the things that they denote is not inherent, Sapir by using the word *symbols* and Crystal by referring to the fact that the association is the result of **convention**. Crystal, in referring to **vocal noise**, is more specific about the principal way in which the message is physically transmitted.

While, as **R. H. Robins** suggests (Robins, 1990, p. 12), there is a danger of definitions of language being simplistic, it might help us to focus our study of language if we try to distil a definition. Such a definition might be something like the following: 'Language is a form of human communication by means of a system of symbols principally transmitted by vocal sounds.'

1.3 The Functions of Language

The term *communication*, then, can be used to cover most of the function of language. But the function of language is varied. *I've got a knife* could imply that it is now only necessary to find a fork before one can start eating or it could be a warning. *Do you have a knife?* could be an offer to lend a knife or a request to borrow one. If the person we are talking to has been ill we probably want an honest answer to the question *How are you?*; if we ask it simply as part of a greeting we may not want an honest answer. Linguists have different terms for the different functions of language. In the case of *How are you?* used just to be sociable, for example, they use the term

phatic communion, that being the use of speech with the aim of establishing or maintaining social relations. In such cases the important thing may be simply that one says something, as saying nothing might be taken as a sign of displeasure. An expression of emotion such as *That's fantastic!* or *Shit!* may be called an **emotive utterance**. When an utterance is an act in itself, the utterance being spoken by somebody with relevant authority, it may be called a **performative utterance**; a bridge, for example, may be officially opened by some dignitary saying *I declare this bridge open*. Such matters will be developed further in section 3.8.

1.4   What Is a Language?

Having considered what language is, let us briefly contrast what we have hitherto been considering with what we are concerned with when we talk about the Russian language or the Arabic language. The use of the word *language* in both cases clouds a very significant difference.

Language, the faculty for communication by speech sounds, is a universal characteristic of the human race. But we do not share one medium of communication; Russians and Arabs speak different languages. A language, then, is a medium of communication specific to a society; it forms part of the culture of that society. Being a feature of the human race, 'language' is inherited genetically, whereas we acquire 'a language' from the society in which we spend our first years. A child born in Russia of Russian parents will acquire Arabic if it is taken away from its parents and spends its earliest years in an Arabic environment in, say, Jordan or Algeria.

1.5   The Elements of Language

If a young child sees a dog he may draw it to his mother's attention by pointing to it and saying 'dog'.

Even such a simple utterance involves a number of facets of language. The speaker has to recognise which category of the world around him the animal concerned belongs to and he has to know the label that attaches to that category. He has then to transmit the sequence of sounds that convey that label to the hearer, thereby generating the thought of a dog in the mind of that person. The study of words is **lexis** and that of meaning, of the relationship between word and the real world, is **semantics**. The study of speech sounds is **phonetics** and, in the context of language systems, **phonology**. These facets of linguistics will be dealt with in chapters 2–5.

An older child may well say 'That dog is bigger than our dog.' This more complex utterance exhibits further facets. The word *bigger* is a complex word in that a modifying element has been added to the basic word *big* in order to express the idea of comparison. The words have to be assembled in a certain order to indicate the relationship between them; swapping round the phrases *that dog* and *our dog* would clearly completely change the sense of the sentence. The stucture of words, **morphology**, is dealt with in chapter 6 and the structure of phrases and sentences, **syntax**, is dealt with in chapter 7.

A person in Glasgow might pronounce the word *dog* in the same way as he pronounces the word *dug*. A Glaswegian dustman is more likely to do so than is a Glaswegian solicitor. Here we are touching on the fields of **regional variation** and **social variation** which are dealt with in chapters 8 and 9 respectively.

The Anglo-Saxons denoted a dog with the word *hund*, the precursor of the word *hound* that has now been relegated to a very restricted use. It is generally accepted that the word *hound* is related to, say, the Italian word *cane*, one of the distinctive features of the Germanic languages being the development of the phoneme /k/ into a fricative sound. The French equivalent of *cane* is *chien*, a feature of the phonological development of French being the development of /k/ before /a/ in Latin to /ʃ/. Such changes to language over time belong to the field of **historical linguistics**, the subject of chapter 10. Drawing on what has been presented in earlier chapters, chapter 11 outlines **the languages of western Europe**, giving a profile of the distinctive features of these languages and indicating the relationship between them. The final chapter, chapter 12, deals with how language is recorded on paper, with **writing systems**.

Summary

Speech has allowed human beings to develop in a completely different way from other animals. This is due in large part to the cultural transmission that our speech allows, which facilitates a faster adaptation to changes in our environment.

Language is generally considered to be a form of communication between human beings by means of a system of symbols which are principally transmitted by vocal sounds. While the faculty of speech is considered to be inherited, the system that we use, the specific language, is determined by the society in which we grow up, it being culturally transmitted.

Communicating by speech requires symbols to be transmitted orally in an order that shows the relationship between them. The form of utterance will be affected by geography and social factors.

Our utterances have a variety of functions in addition to communicating facts; we may speak to express our emotions, for example, or to reinforce a relationship with somebody.

Exercises

1.1 Write what you consider to be a good definition of the term *language*. Justify the choice of the elements that you have incorporated in your definition.

1.2 What do you consider to be the principal benefits to the human race of language?

1.3 How well, in your opinion, does the word *communication* represent the function of human language?

2

Lexis

or
Are Slithy Toves Smoothly Wet?

2.1 What Is a Word?

If we stripped language down to its barest essentials we would, we might intuitively feel, have to retain words. When a child shouts 'Dog' we have little material for a discussion of syntax or social variation. What we do have even in this simplest of utterances is a word and, as the nature of a word implies, an association with something in the real world and a sequence of sounds that conveys that something to other people. If we set aside exclamations of joy, fear, and so on we can communicate little verbally without words. It is words which, expressed as sounds, convey the thought of a thing, of a concept, from the mind of one person to the mind of another person, providing, of course, that these two people speak the same language. For speakers of English the word *dog*, conveyed by means of the sound sequence /dɔg/ or, in the case of many Americans, /dɑg/, transmits the concept of a particular kind of animal. The word *large*, conveyed by the sounds /la:dʒ/, refines the image.

But what idea is represented by the word *spick*? Very little. Only when that word is accompanied by two more words, *and span*, do we have a symbol that represents a concept, a concept similar to that represented by the word *clean* or the word *spotless*. The meaning of the phrase *kick the bucket* can, in the literal sense of striking one's foot against a pail, be arrived at by a summation of the meaning of the constituent words, but in the idiomatic sense of dying it cannot. The verb is variable for subject and for tense as is the verb *die*, but otherwise the phrase is set; we do not have the leeway that we have in the literal sense to say 'kick the pail', 'kick this bucket', and so on.

Thus the three words *kick the bucket* used idiomatically must, from a functional point of view, be regarded as a single unit, for this unit fulfils the same function as the single word *die*. Similarly, the more prosaic phrasal verbs of English are a lexical unit; *give in* is as much a unit as *concede*. Why do we have to use two words to denote a female singer when we can denote a female actor with one: *actress*?

Thus a unit of meaning may consist of more than one word. It may also consist of less than one word; the *un-* in *unhealthy* is a unit of meaning, a very significant one in so far as it completely inverts the sense of *healthy*. A unit of meaning can, then, range from an **idiom**, a phrase that has a meaning not apparent from its constituent words, to a **morpheme**, a minimal unit of meaning of which there may be several in a word.

Word, then, will not do as a term for a unit of meaning. Recognising that phrases like *give in* are no different functionally to single words like *concede*, linguists devised the term **lexeme** or **lexical item** to denote an item of vocabulary with a single referent whether it consists of one word or more than one word. The term *lexeme* also allows greater precision in that the forms *gives*, *gave*, and so on, can be considered to be different forms of the one lexeme: *give*. The lexeme, which one can equate to the form that one would look up in a dictionary, encompasses the set of forms that may be used to realise the lexeme in various environments.

So how can we define a word?

Useful tests might be indivisibility, insertion and substitutability. Words are indivisible and they can be inserted between other words; we can insert *large* between *the* and *dog* but not within *dog*. We can substitute the word *cat* for the word *dog*. But then much the same can be said of phrasal lexemes like *kick the bucket* and *give in*. Similarly, morphemes cannot be divided, can be inserted and can be substituted; the *un-* of *uninformed* can, for example, be replaced by *mis-*.

The American linguist **Leonard Bloomfield** (Bloomfield, 1933, p. 178) considered a word to be a minimum free form:

A word, then, is a free form which does not consist entirely of (two or more) lesser free forms; in brief, a word is a *minimum free form*.

The inclusion in this definition of the word *free* removes bound morphemes, morphemes that cannot stand independently as words, such as *un-*, from what might be allowed as a word. This definition does not seem to admit words that are compounds of other words; it would admit *fire* and *man* but not *fireman*. But elsewhere Bloomfield says that a free form which is not a phrase is a word, which would admit *fireman*.

We may find the sound system helpful in determining what is a word. In both *black bird* and *blackbird* the principal stress indicates where the noun starts. In Italian, morphemes that are word-final almost always end in a vowel; this is not so of other morphemes. Hockett turns to the sound system when he suggests that a word is 'any segment of a sentence bounded by successive points *at which pausing is possible*' (Hockett, 1958, p. 167).

In the end, however, we may have to accept that – setting aside the convention of leaving spaces between sequences of characters in the written language – it is difficult to define satisfactorily what a word is. The range of meaning or function encompassed by a word varies from language to language. The French equivalent of *I shall give* is represented by two words: *je donnerai*, the marker for the future tense being incorporated in the verb. In Spanish only one word is required, *daré*, the element *-é* being considered sufficient to indicate who is going to do the giving. The Swedish equivalent of *the house* is a single word: *huset*. Where we say *in my house* a Swede would also use three words, but a Finn, assuming that he was not a Swedish-speaking Finn, would use only one; in the agglutinative Finnish language the equivalent of *in my house* is *talossani*. How do we treat elided forms? How many words are there in the French *j'acheterai* or the English equivalent *I'll buy*? The sound system of French might suggest that *j'a-* constitutes one syllable; syntax, on the other hand, would argue for two separate words as an object pronoun can be inserted to give *je l'acheterai*. How do we treat separable verbs in German? *Aufstehen*, meaning *to get up*, would appear to be a single word, but then we find that in the equivalent of, say, *I get up at seven o'clock* it is split into two parts: *ich stehe um sieben Uhr auf*. In the Spanish equivalent there is a reflexive pronoun which is suffixed in the infinitive, *levantarse*, but freestanding in the present tense: *me levanto a las siete*.

This variability is reflected in Edward Sapir's description of a word as 'merely a form, a definitely molded entity that takes in as much or as little of the conceptual material of the whole thought as the genius of the language cares to allow' (Sapir, 1921, p. 32). This American linguist tells us that in some of the highly synthetic languages of the Native Americans it is not always easy to say whether a particular element of language is to be interpreted as an independent word or as part of a larger word (Sapir, 1921, p. 33). So, too, in the analytic or isolating language Chinese characters represent morphemes rather than words.

Perhaps, after all, it is not of such great significance how languages combine morphemes, units of meaning, into words. Perhaps the concept of the word is not as important as we may have thought.

2.2   Where Do Words Come From?

We speakers of English refer to a dog by means of the word *dog*. Why? What is the connection between the sequence of sounds /dɔg/ or /dɑg/ on the one hand and a particular kind of animal on the other? The spoken word does not sound like a dog, the written word does not look like a dog. There is no reason why a person who does not speak English should associate the word with a dog rather than with, say, a ship or the action of cooking.

There is only an association between word and object because the English-speaking community accepts that this is the case. The association is a matter of convention. Any sequence of sounds could serve just as well to denote a dog; as we have seen, the sounds /sjɛ̃/, the sounds produced by the word *chien*, do the job just as well for the French and the sounds /hɔnt/ serve just as well for the Dutch. As Juliet comments in Shakespeare's play *Romeo and Juliet*, 'that which we call a rose,/ By any other name would smell as sweet'. The nature of the association between word and object can be likened to that of the association between a red cross and medical services, the association between a red light and the requirement to stop.

So if words have no inherent relationship with objects in the real world, what determines their form?

Firstly, of course, some words do have something of an inherent relationship with the thing that they denote. This is clearly the case with **onomatopoeic** words, words which represent sounds or things which make a sound. The words *bang* and *crash* are clearly imitative of the sounds that they denote. While the word *dog* is arbitrary, the young child's equivalent *bow-wow* is basically imitative, although here, too, a conventional form has developed; a Danish child imitates a dog with *vovvov*. Indeed, the theory that human speech arose as the result of humans imitating animals has been given the light-hearted name of 'the bow-wow theory', as opposed to, say, the 'yo-he-ho' theory, the theory that speech arose out of man's co-operation with his fellows.

Other words, though not directly imitative, may also exhibit **sound symbolism**, may also reflect the nature of the object or concept that they denote. Which would you expect to be larger, a **geek* or a **gock*? Which would you expect to move more quickly, a **gish* or a **gump*? What is **bloviating*? (The use of an asterisk in conjunction with a word indicates that it is a hypothetical word, that it does not exist.)

It has been argued, for example, that high front vowels, those produced with the tongue raised towards the front of the mouth, tend to be indicative of smallness; cf. Scots *wee*, Swedish *liten*, French and Catalan *petit*, the diminutive suffixes of Italian (*-ino*), Spanish (*-ito*) and Portuguese (*-inho*). This may be imitative, the mouth being rounded, more voluminous, for the back vowels such as the /ɔ/ of *lot*. Thus, if you thought that a **gock* should be bigger than a **geek* you help to substantiate this view.

The initial cluster *sl-* of English, it has been suggested, is indicative of the condition that Leonard Bloomfield called 'smoothly wet' (Bloomfield, 1933, p. 245); cf. *slide, slippery, slimy*. This is one of a large number of associations between sound and characteristic listed by Bloomfield. The cluster *kr-* suggests noisy impact as in *crash* and *crunch*, the cluster *-omp* suggests clumsiness as in *clump* and *thump*, and so on. Thus he would surely agree if you felt that a **gump* would be slower than a **gish*.

So does Lewis Carroll's nonsense phrase *slithy toves* suggest something smoothly wet? If it does, is that indicative of a universal association between word and characteristic or are we simply drawing an analogy with other words that sound similar? To put it another way, is the association between word and characteristic or between word and word? After all, Carroll's word *slithy* is supposed to have been derived by fusing the words *lithe* and *slimy*.

The initial cluster *bl-*, it has been suggested, may imitate inflation, as in, for example, *blow, blast, bladder*. The equivalents of *blow* in the Germanic languages generally begin with the same cluster, as in German *blasen*, Dutch *blazen*, Swedish *blåsa*. By way of Latin *flare* we have similarly imitative initial sounds in such words as *inflate* and, dare we say, *flatulent*. But as etymologists would argue that all these words derive from the same Indo-European source, we can hardly use them to adduce some universal association between the form of the words and inflation. While there may have been an imitative source word, it proves nothing when one word derives from another. Warren G. Harding, a president of the United States of America, is said to have coined the word *bloviating* to denote speaking with gaseous eloquence; is this suggestive of a universal or simply of analogy with *blow*?

One case where we do find a widespread correlation is between the concept of mother and the sound [m]: Arabic uses the word (in transliteration) *umm*, Chinese uses the word *mā*. An Inca goddess of agriculture was called Pachamama, Mother Earth. It has been suggested that [m], one of the first consonant sounds that a child makes, has been widely associated with the mother because that is the sound that the child makes when its lips are seeking the breast. Indeed, the Latin word for a breast is *mamma*, that being the source of such English words as *mammal* and *mammary*.

Such speculation about inherent links between word and thing may be fascinating. But the fact remains that the vast majority of our words have no discernible link with the real world. So where have they come from? We have said that the English word *inflate* is derived from the Latin word *flare*. On shakier ground, because we are going beyond documentary sources, we can, on the basis of feasible sound changes, assume that the Latin word *flare* and the English word *blow* have a common ancestor and we can guess what form it might have taken. But eventually we lose any hint of a trail and we have to take the ancestors of our words for granted.

It is, then, more constructive to consider the different ways in which these ancestral elements have evolved into the words that we now use to denote the things around us, the different ways in which we acquire labels for new objects and concepts.

Let us imagine that the handkerchief was a new concept in the English-speaking world and that we therefore had no word for such an object. How might we go about getting a word?

We might refer to its form or its function. The Spanish word *pañuelo* refers to the object's form, *pañuelo* being a diminutive form of the word *paño*, meaning cloth. Similarly, the Portuguese word *lenço* is derived from a Latin word meaning linen cloth. The French word, on the other hand, refers to the function of the object, *mouchoir* being derived from the verb *moucher* which denotes the cleaning of the nose; they are cognates of – that is, they are from the same source as – the English word *mucus*. The Swedish word, *näsduk*, gives more of an indication of the function of the object than do the Dutch word *zakdoek* and the German word *Taschentuch*, for the Swedish word is a compound of the equivalents of *nose* and *cloth* while the Dutch and German words are compounds of the equivalents of *pocket* and *cloth*.

We might use English elements or borrow from other languages. Using our own elements, we might extend the use of an appropriate word such as *cloth* or *wiper* to denote this new item. Or we might be more specific and make a new compound word or phrase such as **nosecloth* or **nose wiper*. Alternatively, we might adopt a foreign word, possibly the word used by the society from which we acquired the object itself. If such a word did not readily fit in with the sounds or morphology of English it might be altered in the process. The process of popular etymology might even give the word a more apparent meaning; thus the French word *mouchoir* might conceivably become **musher*. Once in the language, the new label might change over time; it might, for example, become simplified in some way.

If we look at what has in fact happened, we see a number of these factors at work. The word *handkerchief* is a hybrid in that the element *kerchief* derives from Old French *covrechef*, literally **cover-head*, and the native element *hand* is prefixed to provide a word which denotes a variant that one holds in one's hand. The word has subsequently become slightly simpler in that the sound /d/ is no longer heard. In informal speech it has become significantly simplified, having contracted to *hankie*.

Having sampled a number of ways in which our words may be shaped, we shall now briefly look at them a little more systematically.

Firstly, we often fulfil a need for a new label simply by using a word in a different word class. The nouns *pocket* and *table* have, for example, come to be used as verbs as in *to pocket the money* and *to table a proposal*. This process is known as **conversion**.

One word can be formed on the basis of another by the addition of morphemes with a particular significance. The verb *cover* becomes the verb *discover* by the addition of a morpheme implying removal. This removal can be negated by the prefix *un-*: *undiscovered*. The verb *discover* becomes *discoverer* by the addition of a morpheme implying the person who does the action. This process of word formation is known as **derivation**.

Clearly, different languages form derivations in different ways. In the Romance languages, for example, it is common to derive a noun related to an activity from the feminine form of the past participle of the verb denoting that activity. In this way, for example, French has derived its words for an entrance, an exit and a view: *entrée, sortie* and *vue*. The German equivalents are a prefixed nominal form of the verb: *Eingang, Aussgang* and *Aussicht*.

Occasionally a word is coined on the false assumption that it was presupposed by an apparently derived form. In this way *edit* appeared on the assumption that an editor must be a person who edits. The words *pea* and *cherry* have evolved from a form that was assumed to be plural; cf. *pease pudding* and the French word *cerise*. This process is known as **backformation**.

Our label for some things is the result of analogy with something else; thus we talk of the *foot* of a mountain and the *mouth* of a river. These are metaphors. We are dealing here with **semantic extension**, a new concept being included within the semantic range of an existing word. In this way the word *coach*, originally denoting a horse-drawn vehicle, now denotes a long-distance bus or a railway vehicle. The range of the Italian word *carrozza* has been similarly extended, as has that of the German word *Wagen*. The German equivalent of *sky*, *Himmel*, was extended to cover the new concept of heaven when Christianity came along. The Swedish word for a telephone receiver, *lur*, had long before denoted a viking horn.

Semantic extension may reflect the society concerned. The Swedish word for a book, *bok*, is the same as the word for a beech tree, this reflecting the practice of inscribing the bark of the beech tree. A general term may be applied to a more specific item where that item is of particular significance to the society. In *The Italian Language* (1984), the Italian linguist Bruno Migliorini gave as an example the development of the Latin word *machina* into the Italian word *macina* with the more specific sense of a millstone because 'the machine *par excellence* was the miller's grindstone'. One might similarly explain the Italian word *macchina* in the sense of a car in terms of the car being a major machine of our age.

Alternatively, a new word may result from the **compounding** of existing elements in the language. In this way we acquired numerous words like *houseboat* and *boathouse*. Icelandic has generally done this. While other languages have derived their word for a kitchen from the Latin *coquina* (English *kitchen*, French *cuisine*, German *Küche*, and so on), Icelandic coined the word *eldhús* by compounding its equivalents of *fire* and *house*. Similarly, the Icelandic word for a volcano, *eldfjall*, is constructed from the words for fire and a mountain. Chinese does the same thing in this case; there, too, the word for a volcano, *huǒshān*, is constructed from the equivalents of *fire* and *mountain*.

Like other Germanic languages, English makes extensive use of compounding. It is, however, rather arbitrary about whether the elements should be written as one word, as two words or as a hyphenated word; the *New Shorter Oxford English Dictionary* (1993) has *fireman*, *fire station* and *fire-fighter*.

This all helps to justify the concept of the lexeme, but one is still left with a grey area: is *leather bag* a compound noun or do we simply have here a modified simple noun as we do with *big bag*?

The elements of a compound may be merged such that at least one element is abbreviated. In this way, for example, the phrase *motor cavalcade* became *motorcade*, *camera recorder* became *camcorder*. Such forms are **blend** words. *Slithy* would seem to be one of the many blend words coined by Lewis Carroll. The Swedish word for a sauna, *bastu*, is a blend of the compound word *badstuga*, literally *bathing hut*. When talking of a stationmaster the Swedes may use the full form *stationsinspektor* or the blend form *stins*.

As an alternative to using native elements to produce a new label, one can, of course, turn to other languages for material.

A language can form new compounds using elements taken from the classical languages. The word *television* is composed from a Greek element indicating distance and a Latin element indicating sight. In the field of medicine, terminology is generally based on classical elements; *hepatitis*, for example, is based on the Greek equivalent of *liver*. Such words are called **neo-classical compounds**. Like blend words, they are composed of elements that cannot exist by themselves.

A language can also, of course, acquire a word ready-made from another language. An object or concept acquired from another society may be given the label used by that society. Thus the word *sauna* – which is not, as we now know, Swedish – came to us from Finnish. The words *chocolate* and *tomato* came from a native language of what is now Mexico. The people of the Andes gave Europe the word *llama* and received from the Spaniards the word *kawallu*, the horse being previously unknown to them. Societies that are pioneers in a particular field often provide the labels for other societies. In this way Italy has exported musical terminology, France has provided terminology in the field of cooking – or cuisine! – and the German-speaking world has provided terminology in the field of psychology. Thus, from the Latin verb *crescere*, meaning *to grow*, we have by way of Italian the musical term *crescendo* and by way of French the word for a bakery item: *croissant*. In the seventeenth century the Dutch were a major maritime power and Dutch maritime terminology was adopted widely. The Dutch word for a sailor, *matroos*, for example, went into German as *Matrose*, into Russian as матрос; the Dutch word *jacht* went into German as *Jacht*, into Russian as яхта, into *English as yacht*. When a word is adopted by one language from another it is referred to as a **loanword**.

Loanwords may retain a pronunciation similar to that which they had in their language of origin or the pronunciation may be adapted to the phonology of the adoptive language. Some people retain the French pronunciation of the word *garage* with the sound /ʒ/ but others replace this rather alien sound with /dʒ/. So, too, the word may or may not retain its native morphology; *spaghetti* retains its Italian plural form, possibly because we do not recognize it as such – the word means *small pieces of string* – but musicians play *cellos*, not **celli*.

One might, of course, argue whether or not a foreign word has been adopted by the English language. The word *spaghetti* is so widely used in the English-speaking world that most people would accept that it has been adopted by the English language, but might not its retention of an Italian plural morpheme and the fact that it denotes a food so closely associated with Italy lead one to argue that it is an Italian word that may be inserted into an English sentence? Perhaps less likely to be deemed an English word, if only because its use is largely restricted to the people that it denotes, is *cognoscenti*. Also counting against its adoption is the fact that much of its function is already performed by a cognate of French origin, the word *connoisseur*.

How long can a word be in a language and still be considered a loanword? The word *connoisseur* has not come from modern French; the diphthong /oi/ was a feature of Old French; the modern French equivalent is *connaisseur*. The word *chef* would generally be accepted to be a loanword, but what about the cognate *chief* which, as the spelling and the original sound /tʃ/ show, was transferred from Old French? Is *take* to be considered a loanword because it was of Norse origin and ousted the Old English *niman*? We must conclude that such concepts as a loanword are useful guides to the processes involved but that there is a danger of oversimplifying what happens in the real world.

A Swedish book on the subject of the influence of English on Swedish by Magnus Ljung is entitled *Skinheads, Hackers & Lama Ankor* (1988). The first two words of the title are loanwords that have passed from English to Swedish. But what of *lama ankor*, a translation of *lame ducks*? Instead of borrowing, to use the usual term, or adopting, to use a more appropriate term, a word from another language, a society may take the principle of a foreign word but translate its constituent elements. In this way the literal sense of the English word *honeymoon* was imitated as *lune de miel* in French. The English term *skyscraper* gave rise to the literal equivalents *gratte-ciel* in French, *rascacielos* in Spanish, *Wolkenkratzer* in German, and so on. On the model of the French term for a railway, *chemin de fer*, literally *iron road*, German has *Eisenbahn*, Swedish has *järnväg* and Finnish has *rautatie*. Terms acquired in this way are called **loan translations** or **calques**.

Here, too, we do not have a category with distinct boundaries. It is relatively easy to identify a loan translation when the term is as idiosyncratic as *honeymoon*. But when the term is more prosaic, like *mousetrap*, it is quite feasible that different communities happen to have independently produced a term from the equivalent semantic elements. It is hardly likely that the Icelanders modelled their word for a volcano on that used by the Chinese!

A word may derive from the name of a place or person. The word *coach* may be derived from the name of a Hungarian town. The word *copper* derives from the name *Cyprus*. Items may be named after the person who invented or discovered them; thus the Italian Alessandro Volta gave his name to the volt and the Italian Luigi Galvani gave his name to the process of galvanization.

A new word or phrase in a language may be adopted in a modified form which makes it more acceptable, which makes it appear more meaningful. The word *crayfish* is derived from the Old French word *crevisse*; the element *fish* was considered to be more appropriate for the name of a creature that lives in water. The Spanish word for a bolt was once *berrojo* (cf. French *verrou*). It later became *cerrojo* by association with the function of a bolt, *cerrar* being the equivalent of *to close*. The Portuguese word *ferrolho*, on the other hand, was influenced by the material of which a bolt is made, namely iron. The alteration of words in this way is called **popular etymology**.

Other ways in which lexemes change once they are in a language will be looked at in chapter 10.

Summary

We commonly consider the word to be a fundamental building block of language, but as units of meaning may be expressed by more than one word, linguistics has the concept of lexeme.

Some lexemes arguably have some intrinsic association with the things that they denote, but the origins of most words are lost in the mists of time. What we can establish is how these elements subsequently provide the lexemes that we use. New lexemes can be produced from native elements by such means as derivation, semantic extension and compounding or from foreign elements by such means as borrowing or translating foreign words.

Exercises

2.1 Write what you consider to be the best definition of the term *word*. Justify the choice of the elements that you incorporate in your definition.

2.2 Suggest alternatives to the word *towel* to denote a towel. Account for your suggestions.

2.3 A certain object is generally denoted in the other Germanic languages either by a word that literally means *cowfoot* or *cowleg*, these alluding to its form, or by a word that literally means *breakiron*, this alluding to its function. What do we call this object?

3

Semantics

or
Why Don't Spaniards Watch Blue Movies?

3.1 The Function of Lexemes

Chapter 2 dealt with the word, with its origins. But it said nothing of the function of the word, of the lexeme. Without a function a word is a mere sequence of sounds, just as a red light would be little more than decoration if it did not indicate to drivers that they should stop (or indicate whatever a red light in a 'red light district' indicates!).

So what is the function of a word, of a lexeme? In the sentence *The daughter of the terrorist has been caught* we can identify two distinct types of word. While we can tell somebody what a daughter or a terrorist is, we cannot tell them what a 'the' or an 'of' is, for while the words *daughter* and *terrorist* denote something in the real world, the words *the* and *of* do not. What these latter words do is serve the others in some way, *the* by specifying, *of* by indicating a relationship. *Daughter* and *terrorist* are **content words**; *the* and *of* are **function words**. One can draw a parallel with an algebraic expression like $3y + 2z$; the $<y>$ and the $<z>$ can be likened to content words in that they are symbols that represent something substantial, while the symbol $<+>$ can be likened to a function word – it represents the function of addition in much the same way as the function word *and* indicates summation. The use of content words changes as society changes but the use of function words is much more stable; nouns and verbs may come and go for various reasons but we rarely have reason to change articles and prepositions.

In this chapter our attention will be focused on content words. Function words belong rather to the field of syntax.

3.2   The Meaning of Meaning

Semantics might be described as the study of meaning. But what do we mean by *meaning*? What is the nature of the relationship between our utterances and the world around us?

Clearly words often specify something in the world. The word *daughter* denotes a younger female relative as opposed to a younger male relative, an older male relative or, indeed, a lighthouse. To use terms employed by the Swiss linguist **Ferdinand de Saussure**, the word *daughter* is a *signifiant*, the thing that signifies, and the category of relative concerned is a *signifié*, the thing that is signified.

In their work entitled *The Meaning of Meaning* **C. K. Ogden** and **I. A. Richards** maintained that the word, what they called the **symbol**, and the actual object, the **referent**, are linked only indirectly, by way of our mental perception of that object, the **thought** or **reference** (Ogden and Richards, 1985, pp. 10–12). More recently **Stephen Ullmann** suggested that we might use more common terms: **name** to denote the sequence of sounds that is the physical form of the utterance, **thing** to denote the object or event that is being referred to, and **sense** to denote the information that the name conveys to the hearer (Ullmann, 1962, p. 57).

Other linguists have been loathe to accept an intermediate conceptual stage in the process of communication. **John Lyons**, for example, maintains that there is no evidence to suggest that concepts are relevant to the construction of a theory of semantics (Lyons, 1992, p. 137). Indeed, seemingly in contravention of their belief in the intermediary of mental perception, Ogden and Richards (1985, p. 60) went on to question the role of mental images:

> There are good reasons why attempts to build a theory of interpretation upon images must be hazardous. One of these is the grave doubt whether in some minds they ever occur or ever have occurred.

3.3   Semantic Range

In order to be able to deal with the world around us we have to put labels on things. This has required us to divide the world up into categories and to force an infinitely varied world into these categories. We have a category labelled *dog* into which we put poodles and spaniels but not foxes and wolves. We have to reach a compromise between having on the one hand an unmanageable array of categories and on the other insufficient precision.

The trade-off between manageability and precision clearly depends on how precise one has to be. Arabs may need to be able to make finer distinctions between different types of camels and different types of horses than we do. It has often been claimed that Eskimos have many more words than we do to identify different types of snow, although it is now widely accepted that this claim has been greatly exaggerated. I am in no position to judge as I do not speak an Eskimo language. I do, however, speak Danish fairly well and in the Danish novel *Frøken Smillas fornemmelse for sne* by Peter Høeg (1992) the eponymous narrator, an expert on ice who was born in Greenland, refers, for example, to *qanik*, defining it as fine-grained powdery snow, and to *pirhuk*, defining it as light snow. Similarly, those who specialise in a particular sphere of activity need to make finer distinctions in that sphere than others do. For most of us the word *horse* and a few others like *mare* and *foal* are all that we need to be able to talk about horses, but those involved in horse racing need such terms as *filly*, *yearling* and *gelding*. We could, of course, refer to anything, if only by using what seems more like a dictionary definition than a lexeme; we could denote a filly using the phrase *young mare*. But the more significant an object or concept is to a community, the greater the tendency to lexicalise the label used to denote it, to have a more succinct term.

The divisions that we draw in order to define our categories are very haphazard. In English we use the same verb, *play*, to denote the very different activities of a child amusing himself with his toys and a pianist performing at a concert. And yet the person who supervises a cricket match is given a different name to that given to the supervisor of a football match, the one being an umpire and the other a referee. When we eat lambs we call the meat *lamb* but when we eat calves we use a different word for the meat: *veal*. We distinguish between roofs and ceilings but Spaniards do not; they use *techo* for both. On the other hand Spaniards distinguish between an internal corner (*rincón*) and an external corner (*esquina*) while we do not.

The arbitrariness is clearly likely to be all the greater where there is little natural distinctiveness in the subject area concerned. It is fairly clear cut what is and what is not an egg. But how big does a hill have to be before it is a mountain? How big does a village have to be before it is a town? How big does a stream have to be before it is a river? The more arbitrary the division, the less reason there is for different languages to make divisions at the same points; thus, for example, the Spanish word *pueblo* equates to a large village or a small town. What we call a *river* can be denoted by either *fleuve* or *rivière* in French, the general view being that the former flows into the sea while the latter flows into another river. Sweden also has two types of river, an *älv* and an *å*, the former being larger than the latter. Moreover, Swedes use a third word, *flod*, to denote a river outside of Scandinavia.

The colour spectrum would appear to be a prime example of arbitrary division. Russian has two equivalents of *blue*: голубой and синий. The Welsh word *glas* equates to *blue* but also overlaps with *green*, as it also denotes the colour of grass. According to Berlin and Kay, however, colour terminology is not random for a study by them suggested a fairly universal hierarchy of terminology. If a language only has two colour terms they will, they claimed, be based on black and white; if it has three they will be based on black, white and red. The next distinction will be green or yellow, and so on (Berlin and Kay, 1969).

The set of items that we identify by means of a word or lexeme is the **semantic range** of that word or lexeme. Such sets may be grouped with others with which they share a common feature to form a **semantic field**. Thus the semantic range of the English word *red* is that part of the colour spectrum that we denote with this word, a range considerably more restricted than that of the corresponding term in a language that distinguishes only three colours. The range of *red* together with that of the other colour terms can be referred to as the semantic field of colour.

3.4 The Definition of Semantic Range

Presented with a colour chart or a box of paints we can, barring colour blindness, select a colour that most people would accept as being red. But there may be disagreement about whether something is red or orange. Similarly, few of us would deny that a crow is a bird for it is and does what we expect a bird to be and do: it has two legs and feathers, it flies, it builds a nest and it lays eggs. But there are birds that do not fly and there are creatures such as bats that do fly

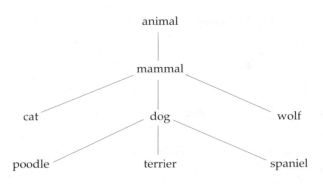

Figure 3.1

but are not birds, creatures such as snakes that lay eggs but are not birds. Thus we need a way of determining the boundaries of the semantic range of the words *red*, *bird* or any other word if we are to be able to judge when it is appropriate to use it.

We can define the English county of East Sussex either by saying which other counties surround it (West Sussex, Kent, and so on) or by saying which second-tier authorities it encompasses (Eastbourne, Wealden, and so on). Similarly, we can define a word in terms of what it is not or in terms of what it subsumes. Thus we can define the range of the word *dog* either by saying that it is any animal that is not a wolf, a cat, a goat, and so on or by saying that it is any animal that is either a poodle, a terrier, a spaniel, and so on. We can be assisted in this by a hierarchical diagram like Figure 3.1. Such a relationship between words whereby more specific terms are arranged under their more general superordinate terms is known as **hyponymy**. The word *poodle* is a hyponym of the word *dog*, which in turn is a hyponym of the word *mammal*, and so on. One can compare this arrangement to the natural history classifications by class, order, family, genus and species; the dog and the wolf both belong to the genus Canis, the dog being the *Canis familiaris* and the wolf the *Canis lupus*. The hyponyms of a word define its semantic range. A superordinate like *mammal* or *animal* can serve to designate a semantic field.

Complications can, however, arise. Firstly, as Figure 3.2 shows, we may ascribe different meanings to a word with the result that that word appears at different points on the diagram; we use the word

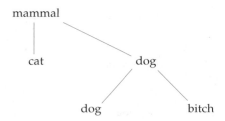

Figure 3.2

dog to indicate gender as well as to denote the species in general. Secondly, we cannot put *dog* and *bitch* alongside *poodle, terrier* and *spaniel* as hyponyms of *dog*, for while being a poodle precludes being a spaniel it does not preclude being a bitch; we are dealing with another dimension. *Love* can be presented as a hyponym of *emotion*. But is it an immediate hyponym or is there something else in between? *Roget's Thesaurus*, which adopts a hierarchical arrangement like hyponymy, has *love* as a hyponym of *sympathetic affections*, which in turn is a hyponym of *affections*. How does *love* relate to *loyalty* or *desire*? Are they related? If so, are they all on the same level or is one a hyponym of another?

Clearly some fields lend themselves to arrangement by hyponymy more than others do. Similarly, **componential analysis**, which defines the range of a word in terms of the presence or absence of particular components, is more easily applied to some fields than to others. Words denoting family relationship lend themselves to such a binary approach; words like *daughter, son* and *mother* denote either a male person or a female person, either an earlier generation or a later generation, and so on. In Figure 3.3 the ranges of the words *aunt, mother, son* and *daughter* are defined by giving each one a positive sign or a negative sign in respect of maleness, previous generation and relationship by birth. This is enough to give each word a unique range.

What components would one identify to define the range of the word *terrorist*? There is no predetermined system of categories; one keeps identifying distinguishing components until one has a set unique to each word unless one believes that one is dealing with true synonyms or that the difference is one of style, formality, attitude, and so on rather than denotation. Terrorists are people who

	Male	Previous generation	Related by birth
Aunt	–	+	–
Mother	–	+	+
Son	+	–	+
Daughter	–	–	+

Figure 3.3

use force to achieve a certain aim. But then the same could be said of soldiers and bank robbers. So what other components can we adduce to distinguish between them? Perhaps +authorized for soldiers and –authorized for terrorists in so far as soldiers operate within a framework established by their government whereas terrorists do not. Perhaps +political for terrorists and –political for bank robbers, thereby reflecting the aims of their actions.

The semantic range of a word can be defined with the assistance of another word that means the same thing, a **synonym**, or a word that means the opposite, an **antonym**. Thus it can help us to use the word *large* if we know that it means much the same as the word *big* or that it means the opposite of the word *small*.

Due in large part to the overlay of Norman French onto Old English, the English language has an extensive vocabulary. From Old English, for example, we have the word *hide* and from Old French we have the word *conceal*. We can say *He was determined to hide the truth* and *He was determined to conceal the truth*. Thus, as we can use either in this sentence, we might call the words *hide* and *conceal* synonyms. But if we try to replace *hide* by *conceal* in the sentence *He was determined to hide* we find that we do not get a satisfactory sentence, the reason being that, unlike *hide*, *conceal* cannot serve as an intransitive verb, cannot, that is, be used without an accompanying object. Thus the two words are not complete synonyms as they cannot substitute for each other in all circumstances. In this case the difference was one of syntax. In the case of the words *high* and *tall* there is a difference of reference; both may be used to qualify buildings but only *tall* can be used to refer to the height (!) of people.

In the case of antonyms we have to consider different types of relationship. The words *tall* and *short* are opposites, antonyms, as are the words *alive* and *dead*. There is, however, a fundamental difference between these two pairs, for while one person can be shorter than another, one person cannot be more dead than another; thus *tall* and *short* are termed gradable antonyms and *alive* and *dead* are termed complementary antonyms.

Different again are pairs like *buy* and *sell* which denote, for example, two facets of an action; these are converse terms.

When looking at antonyms we should note that a word can have different antonyms in different contexts; while the opposite of *a short person* is *a tall person*, the opposite of *a short walk* is not **a tall walk*. Context, indeed, plays a very important part in the definition of the meaning of words. If somebody tells us that a chair is yellow we think of a particular colour; if they tell us that a man is yellow we may think of cowardice. If they tell us that the chair is comfortable we understand that we would feel relaxed if we sat on it, but if we are told that a man is comfortable we are unlikely to conclude that it would be relaxing to sit on him. The meaning of the word *bank* becomes clear when it is preceded by either *savings* or *gravel*. The context, then, can do much to determine the meaning of a word. It can, indeed, result in a different word being used; is there any substantial difference between what a referee and an umpire do or is the choice of word solely dependent on the sport that he or she supervises?

Some linguists have concluded that one knows a word by the company that it keeps (J. R. Firth) or that the meaning of a word is its use in the language (Ludwig Wittgenstein).

3.5 Collocation and Idiom

When a word becomes closely associated with a particular context to the exclusion of other words with a similar meaning such that they form what is almost a set phrase, we have what linguists call **collocation**. From a logical point of view we could perhaps refer to a **complete moon* but we don't, we refer to a *full moon*. White coffee is not white and black coffee is not black; it would seem that *white* and *black* are being used to indicate polarity rather than to give an accurate indication of colour. In this way Catalans refer to white wine (*vi blanc*) and black wine (*vi negre* – not to be confused with *vinagre!*). If something is not far away a Catalan might refer to the distance as four steps (*quatre passes*); an Italian would tell you that it is only two steps (*due passi*) away. We can refer to a flock of sheep but not a flock of cows. In some cases the association is so close that we may well be able to anticipate it; most of us would, for example, expect *She has blond . . .* to be followed by *hair*.

One might ask whether collocation should be dealt with within the context of the semantic range of a word. As *blond* can describe little more than hair, should we include reference to hair in the definition of the semantic range of the word (+colour, –dark, +hair, etc.) or should the denotation of a word and the environment in which it occurs be kept separate? Geoffrey Leech (1974, p. 20) refers to collocation as simply an idiosyncratic property of individual words.

White coffee and white wine are only relatively white. In the case of white lies and blue jokes the logical link with a colour is less apparent still. With *white coffee* we are dealing with a set phrase where the meaning can at least be guessed at on the basis of the two constituent words. Conceivably the *white* in *white lie* suggests purity of intention. In the case of *blue joke* knowing what part of the colour spectrum is indicated by the word *blue* gives us no help in understanding what a *blue joke* is. When the phrase can only be understood as an entity it is an **idiom**.

This independence of the meaning of their constituent words gives idioms great freedom. As there is no reason for smutty jokes to be blue, Spaniards are equally justified in calling them green (*chistes verdes*). In China it is the colour yellow (*huángsè*) that is associated with such things. This freedom allows idioms to be more pleasing to the ear by such means as rhyme; the Norwegian equivalent of *One man's meat is another man's poison* is *Den enes død den andres brød*, literally *The one's death the other's bread*. It allows them to reflect some aspect of the society's history or culture; the Portuguese equivalent of *for the sake of appearances* is *para inglês ver*, literally *for the English to see*, arising from the fact that in the first half of the nineteenth century the Brazilians agreed to British demands that they should stop importing slaves from Africa but for a couple of decades only pretended to comply. Foreigners often feature in idioms, usually unfavourably. Thus while we take French leave, the French *filent à l'anglaise*. If a person does not speak French well the French may say that he speaks it like a Spanish cow (*parle français comme une vache espagnole*). If a Spaniard thinks that a person is acting dumb he may say that he is making himself the Swede (*se hace el sueco*).

3.6 Homonymy and Polysemy

As we have seen, for convenience we force a uniformity on the world around us. The word *dog* can denote quite different animals. The word *lamb* can denote an animal or a dish. A person's body can similarly be alive or dead. The word *play* can denote the activity of a pianist and that of a child. Thus the question arises of how extensive the semantic range of a word or lexeme has to be before we feel that we are dealing with two separate words that have the same form rather than with one word that denotes a variety of things. In the case of *lamb* we can consider the animal and the dish to be different referents of the one lexeme. In the case of *sound* in the sense of something that one hears and *sound* in the sense of a narrow stretch of water, on the other hand, we are likely to consider that we are dealing with two distinct lexemes that happen to have the same form. In the case of one lexeme with a variety of referents we have an example of **polysemy**. Two or more lexemes with the same form are **homonyms**. Lexemes may be alike to the ear but not to the eye, as with *meet* and *meat*, in which case they may be referred to as **homophones**. Conversely they may look alike but sound different in which case they may be referred to as **homographs**; examples are *wind* denoting a current of air and *wind* denoting tortuous movement. Unlike polysemic items, lexicographers will treat homonyms as different items, giving each one the status of a separate headword.

As so often, however, the real world does not fall neatly into our categories. Introducing language in the medium of language, the linguist encounters the problem of defining semantic range when talking of semantics! There can be little doubt that in the case of the two referents of the word *sound* that we referred to we are dealing with different lexemes; one is of Latin origin and the other is of Germanic origin. So, too, the word *bill* denoting an account or invoice and that denoting the beak of a bird must be deemed to be different lexemes, the former, a cognate of the French word *billet*, being of Latin origin and the latter being of Germanic origin. But we also have a word *bill* denoting a kind of axe, which may be related to that denoting a beak; should we treat these as homonyms or as different meanings of a single lexeme? What about *grow* used intransitively, as in *Your tomatoes won't grow well there*, and *grow* used transitively, as in *He grows tomatoes*? The Italian equivalents, for example, are distinct in this case: *crescere* and *coltivare* respectively. Such cases leave the lexicographer with the problem of deciding whether to arrange words under one or several headwords. Etymology is not always a good guide; as Mott points out, the word *bank* denoting a financial institution and that denoting the shore of a river, two items that are semantically very distinct, are etymologically related (Mott, 1993, p. 119).

3.7 The Human Element of Meaning

So far we have been dealing with meaning as though there were a natural association between word and thing. But, as we saw in section 3.2, it is widely held that the link between word and thing, between symbol and referent, is routed by way of our minds. Certainly life has given each of us a different set of experiences, a different set of attitudes, and these colour our perception of the world around us, affect the impression left by an utterance. To a child the lexeme *guinea-pig* is likely to suggest the animal, while to a scientist it might suggest somebody who is subjected to an experiment. To an anthropologist interested in life in the Andes it may suggest either. If the anthropologist thinks of the animal he is likely to have thoughts different to those that come to the child; while the child is likely to think of a small furry pet, the anthropologist may well think of the animal as a foodstuff. Similarly, due to their cultural backgrounds, Britons may think of Christmas when they hear the word *turkey*, Americans may think of Thanksgiving. Here we are dealing with **connotation**, more subjective links, links of the kind that result from word association exercises in which you are asked to say the first thing that comes into your mind when you hear a particular word. While once again we are not dealing with absolute categories, it is useful to think of the word *turkey* as denoting a particular kind of bird and connoting a particular festival.

We can, as we have seen, distinguish in a relatively dispassionate way between a terrorist and a soldier by reference to componential differences such as −authorized and +authorized. When, however, we come to distinguish between a terrorist and a freedom fighter our distinctions are likely to be founded to a much greater extent on our attitudes towards the cause for which the people concerned are fighting; the same person may well be called a *terrorist* by an opponent and a *freedom fighter* by a sympathizer.

Somebody's tenacious behaviour might be called *stubborn* or *obstinate* by those who are obstructed by this behaviour, while sympathizers might call it *determined* or *resolute*. As we considered with the word *blond*, do we attempt to account for the difference as a componential feature, in this case perhaps –good and +good, or does it constitute a different dimension?

Our attitudes towards some things may be so strong that we are reluctant to refer to them directly. A word that we are loathe to use may be called a **taboo** word and its more acceptable substitute may be called a **euphemism**. In this way Americans are reluctant to refer to a farmyard bird as a *cock* because of its association with the male genitals (note the inoffensive phrase used by the author!) and they use the word *rooster* instead.

We can differentiate between *kill*, *murder* and *assassinate* by reference to such components as +intentional and +political, but what components can we adduce to differentiate between *kill* and *do in*? Here again the difference might be seen to lie in another dimension, in this case on an axis of formality. When in the play *Pygmalion* by George Bernard Shaw the flowergirl Liza Doolittle, her speech not yet perfected by the phonetician Henry Higgins, says 'it's my belief they done the old woman in' it is not only what she says that arouses some consternation but also how she says it, the register that she uses.

Words, then, do more than identify things in the world around us. Ogden and Richards gave what they referred to as a representative list of the main definitions of *meaning*, that list ranging from 'An Intrinsic property' to 'That to which the Interpreter of a symbol (a) Refers (b) Believes himself to be referring (c) Believes the User to be referring' (Ogden and Richards, 1985, pp. 186–7).

Geoffrey Leech presents a simpler breakdown of meaning into seven aspects (Leech, 1974, pp. 10–23). The first is the fundamental denotative – or, as Leech refers to it, the **conceptual** – meaning, that which defines the meaning of a lexeme in terms of its constituent features. Thus, to use the componential analysis introduced in section 3.4, the conceptual meaning of the lexeme *woman* can be defined in terms of such properties as +human, −male and +adult. Here, then, we are dealing with a direct link between word and thing. But, as we observed in section 3.2, the intermediary of the human mind often affects the nature of the semantic range of a lexeme. Different people, having been subjected to different experiences in life, have different mental images when they hear a lexeme. When different people hear the lexeme *woman* such qualities as beauty, compassion, practicality and emotion will feature with differing relative significance. Moreover, the relative significance of features will change as society changes; the association of housewife is much less prevalent in our society than it was fifty years ago. Such association is called **connotative** meaning by Leech. A lexeme may be more appropriate in a particular style. To draw from Leech's examples again, *cast* is associated with literary style while *chuck* is colloquial. This is **stylistic** meaning. *Shut up* in the sense of being quiet similarly has stylistic meaning, being colloquial, but in so far as it is indicative of a disrespectful attitude on the part of the speaker it also has **affective** meaning. Our response to one sense of a lexeme may be affected by another sense of that lexeme. We can, for example, scarcely use the word *gay* in its older sense of merry as it now invokes homosexuality. This is **reflected** meaning. Lexemes may have a **collocative** meaning, requiring that they are used together with certain other lexemes but not with others. As we saw in section 3.5, collocation may be so restrictive that we can guess which word will follow a given word, an example being *blond*. Finally Leech refers to **thematic** meaning, to the emphasis that attaches to a lexeme as the result of the speaker's choice of grammatical structure or his use of stress; if in saying the sentence *John broke the vase* the speaker stresses the name *John* we understand that the question to be resolved was who broke the vase, whereas if he stresses the word *vase* we understand that the question was what it was that John broke.

3.8 Pragmatics

In section 2.1 we saw that a unit of meaning can be as small as a morpheme and as large as an idiom. Here we extend the range to include whole sentences. The speaker of the sentence *The daughter of the terrorist has been caught* might, for example, be simply conveying information, but he might also be suggesting that there is now an opportunity to exert some pressure on the terrorist. Like an idiom, then, a sentence may have a meaning that is only conveyed by the whole. *What did you say?* may simply mean that the speaker did not hear, but it could also be a challenge to repeat something that will not find favour. *Do you have a spare biro?* could constitute an offer of a biro, a request for a biro or simply a request for information. Here, too, context clearly provides support, as may intonation. We have now entered the field of linguistic study that is called **pragmatics**.

We communicate more than we say explicitly. This disparity between what we intend to communicate and what we actually say is central to pragmatics. It is bridged by what the speaker implies and what the listener infers on the basis of shared knowledge, shared assumptions and the context of the utterance.

If a man at a party has no easy means of getting home and a woman says that she has got a car, she may be offering him a lift. If so, making the offer entails a number of what may be called implicatures or presuppositions. She is implying that she is able and willing to drive the man home, that the car is nearby, that it is not broken down, that she has time to go by way of his place, and so on.

The woman might, of course, be letting others know that she does not need a lift or even gloating about the fact that she is in a better situation than the man. But we tend to assume that other people are being helpful. As Paul Grice puts it, a co-operative principle tends to apply. He developed four maxims to take account of how we facilitate communication by being co-operative. A maxim of quality is based on the tendency for an utterance to be true; the man would assume that the woman does indeed have a car. A maxim of quantity reflects the tendency for the amount of information given to be appropriate; the offer of a lift would not be clear if the woman said that she has a ten-year-old red Volvo. A maxim of relevance reflects the inclination for the man to assume that what the woman said was relevant to his situation. And in accordance with a maxim of manner, information is usually presented in an orderly fashion. By allowing us to take certain things for granted, then, the assumption of co-operation allows us to say less than would otherwise be necessary.

Context is a major source of supplementary information. Hearing

What did you say? from a frail old man, we are likely to infer that he has not heard what we said. Hearing it from a young man holding an iron bar we might infer that we are in a potentially violent situation.

So, too, proximity between speaker and listener minimises what has to be explicitly said. An utterance like *That shop over there is where I bought the pork yesterday* only works if the speaker and listener are together. Without the common reference points of time and space more information would have to be given: something like *The butcher's shop in Richmond Street is where I bought the pork on Tuesday 25 April*. Even this might leave one wondering which town and which year was being referred to. Proximity in this sense is generally a matter of shared knowledge. If the speaker and the listener have common acquaintances the speaker might be able to say *I met Anne in the butcher's*; if not, he might need to use an expanded utterance like *I met a friend of mine, Anne Richards, in the butcher's*. If a communication is between people with different cultural backgrounds, then much more might have to be explicitly stated if the communication is to succeed. We are likely to interpret in two very different ways notices on the door of a butcher's shop which say *Sorry, no rabbits* and *Sorry, no dogs*. As we do not eat dogs we assume that the second of these two notices is telling us that, for reasons of hygiene, we are not allowed to take a dog into the shop. Somebody from a very different cultural background might, however, assume that the butcher was apologising for having run out of dog meat.

Knowledge might, then, be shared by virtue of the immediate situation or common experience. Alternatively, it might have been introduced earlier in the discourse; just as you can refer to somebody by *she* if you can point to her, so, too, you can refer to somebody by *she* if that person has just been referred to more explicitly earlier in the conversation. The extent of the knowledge shared by speaker and listener determines the amount of explicit information required. If the listener does not know Anne Richards we might need to refer to her dog by saying *the dog of my friend Anne Richards*. If the listener does know her, if he knows that she has a dog and if that dog has just been mentioned, the speaker can refer to her dog by saying nothing more than *it*. On a scale in between we have such forms as *Anne Richards' dog*, *Anne's dog* and *her dog*.

At the end of the scale where we find *it* we are dealing with items that are referentially so vague that they are useless without substantial contextual information. Here we are in the field of **deixis**, a deictic item being an item which has very little referential force without the support of context. As we have seen, the amount of contextual support required by the items on the above scale varies; as a result, it is arguable what is to be considered deictic and what is not. Possessive adjectives like the *her* in *her dog* are considered to be deictic. But then there are many Annes in the world. And presumably there is more than one Anne Richards.

Pronouns like *it* and *she* are, then, highly deictic. Having similar reference to pronouns, possessive adjectives are, as we have just seen, also deictic. So, too, are demonstrative adjectives like *this*. The definite article is also considered to be deictic for we need the context to know which dog the phrase *the dog* refers to. Also highly deictic are adverbs or adverbial phrases like *there* and *last week*; in a sentence like *She went there last week* we do not know where *there* is or when *last week* is without reference points, spatial and temporal respectively.

If we are to investigate the intention and the context of utterances it is useful to attempt a categorisation of utterances by function, by **speech act**.

One basic distinction is that between statements, often called declarative utterances, questions (interrogative utterances), and requests or commands (imperative or directive utterances). We may be able to distinguish these by their syntax. A statement typically has the word order subject–verb–object, as in *He shuts the door*, a question typically has the word order verb–subject–object, as in *Can you shut the door?*, and a command typically has no explicit subject: *Shut the door*. Form may, however, be misleading; social considerations, considerations of politeness may result, for example, in a command being expressed in the form of a question: *Can you shut the door?* Thus we need context as well as form to draw the correct inference from such utterances as *Do you have a spare biro?*

He apologized could be classed as a declarative utterance. So could *I apologize*. But there is a significant difference between the two; whereas the former describes an action, the latter not only describes an action, declares it to others, but in fact *is* the action. By saying we are doing. Such utterances are called **performative utterances**. It follows from their nature that performative utterances are, like *I apologize*, typically in the first person and the present tense. The use or the potential use of the word *hereby* is also indicative of a performative utterance: *I hereby sentence you to three years in prison.* An utterance is, however, only a performative utterance if the conditions necessary to make it an act prevail. *I apologize* only constitutes an apology if the speaker has done something wrong and if he acknowledges that he has done so. Nobody would end up behind bars if I said *I hereby sentence you to three years in prison*; to constitute an act this utterance requires such conditions as the listener having been found guilty of a crime and the speaker having the authority of a judge. As we saw in the case of the man and the woman at the party, an offer is only an offer if the speaker is able and willing to do what is said. Such conditions are called **felicity conditions**.

Some linguists would claim that most utterances are performative utterances. By arguing that they can be preceded by performative verbs, with or without *hereby*, such linguists claim, for example, that commands and questions are performative utterances; *Shut the door*, they argue, is an abbreviated form of *I (hereby) order you to shut the door*, *Do you know where the key is?* is an abbreviated form of *I (hereby) ask you where the key is.*

3.9 Discourse Analysis

Closely allied to pragmatics, perhaps part of it, is **discourse analysis** or **conversation analysis**, this being the study of the organisation and the dynamics of conversation.

We are more at ease when a conversation flows smoothly. We are less at ease if there are pauses in the conversation or if, conversely, two people are speaking at the same time (overlap). We dislike people interrupting, beginning to speak at an inappropriate point. Discourse analysis investigates the mechanisms that facilitate smooth flow in conversations.

One topic of study, for example, has been turn-taking, how the 'floor' passes from one person to another with a minimum of disruption. One technique for handing over the floor is the use of tag questions: *It's going to be very difficult, isn't it?* Another is the use of a falling intonation contour. If the handover does not go smoothly, if for example there is overlap, the problem may be resolved by a struggle for domination whereby there is an increase in loudness and a slowing of the pace of speech.

Another example of the topics investigated within discourse analysis is why some responses to a proposition reflect more unease than others. Reflecting Grice's co-operative principle, we are happier going along with a proposition than going against it. Because going along with a proposition, such as an invitation to go to the cinema, is a preferred option, the related utterance exhibits no unease: *Yeah, fine*. Going against the proposal, on the other hand, exhibits unease, the speaker perhaps hesitating, softening the refusal, feeling obliged to justify the refusal: *Uum, I don't think so. I've got an essay to finish*.

Summary

Words may be divided into content words, those which identify something in the world around us, and function words, those which serve to specify, link, and so on the content words. Semantics is principally concerned with content words. The set of objects, actions, and so on that such a word denotes is known as the semantic range of that word.

The semantic range of a word can be defined by such techniques as hyponymy and componential analysis, by reference to synonyms and antonyms. Context contributes to the defining of the range of a word. In some contexts the meaning of a word cannot be fully determined without reference to a wider phrase; in such a phrase where there is a conventional association between the constituent words we are dealing with collocation or, if the constitutent words give little, if any, indication of the meaning of the phrase, idiom.

It is not always clear whether two words represent two different meanings of the one lexeme or are two different lexemes; in the case of the former we are dealing with polysemy, in the case of the latter with homonymy.

We communicate more than we say explicitly. This can be so because we are generally co-operative, generally want to help the listener to understand. What we need to say is minimised by the support provided by the context in which the utterance takes place and by shared knowledge. Such factors fall within the study of pragmatics. Related to pragmatics is discourse analysis, the study of the organisation and dynamics of conversations.

Exercises

3.1 The titles of the books referred to in the bibliography of this work contain some words which begin with a capital initial and some which do not. How might one account for when one uses a capital initial and when one does not in the title of a book?

3.2 Complete the following diagram by (a) devising a category that distinguishes the word *bus* from the word *car*, and (b) giving the appropriate symbol against each component for the word *motorcycle*.

	Powered	Carries people	Four-wheeled
Bus	+	+	+
Car	+	+	+
Van	+	−	+
Bicycle	−	+	−
Motorcycle			

3.3 Arrange the vehicles in the above exercise, together with some appropriate superordinates and hyponyms, in a hyponymy diagram.

3.4 How valid do you consider the concept of synonym to be?

3.5 For each of the following pairs of words, state the principal reason why they may not be considered to be synonyms:

man boy   toilet loo   determined stubborn
pavement sidewalk   walk run

3.6 Discuss the problem of distinguishing between homonyms and polysemic lexemes. Give an example of the practical relevance of this distinction.

3.7 What might somebody intend to convey by saying *He's got a gun*?

3.8 Somebody might say to a soldier *Fire!* What felicity conditions are likely to apply before the soldier responds by firing a gun? Account for the fact that a firefighter would react very differently to this utterance.

3.9 Rewrite the following sentence, using information of your choice, so that it is less dependent on deixis:

She will try to sell it here tomorrow.

4

Phonetics

or
Can Enough Rational Women Explain *Ghoti*?

4.1 The Organs of Speech

Semantics is concerned with the association in the mind of the speaker and in that of the listener between the real world and utterances that represent it. For communication to take place the utterances have to pass from speaker to listener so that, by the principles of Ogden and Richards, they can be decoded to produce in the mind of the listener an image similar to the image that was in the mind of the speaker or so that, by the principles of the behaviourist Leonard Bloomfield (1933, pp. 22–7), they directly cause a reaction.

We can communicate certain things by clapping our hands, by clicking our fingers, by frowning, and so on. But by far the greatest part of the transmission of utterances from one person to another is done by means of speech sounds. The study of these speech sounds is **phonetics**. Speech sounds may be referred to as phonetic **segments** or **phones**.

The power source of our speech sounds is the flow of air from our lungs. The distinctiveness of each sound results from the way in which the flow of air is manipulated as it passes through the throat and head. One can draw an analogy with bagpipes, the bag producing a stream of air that is formed into a distinctive sequence of sounds by its manipulation in the chanter. When we say *dog* we start with the tip of our tongue held against the roof of our mouth just behind the teeth. In this way we dam the flow of air. We then remove the obstacle, thereby completing the sound /d/. The vowel sound /ɔ/ is distinguished by a low tongue position and rounded

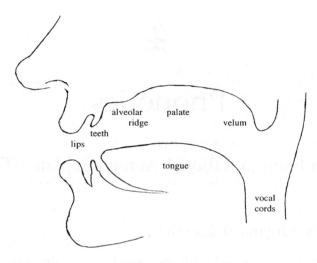

Figure 4.1

lips. The sound /g/, like /d/, is produced by closing and then releasing the flow of air, but in this case the obstruction takes place further back in the mouth, at the soft palate or velum. For each sound the vocal cords have vibrated.

When we say the word *dog*, then, our air flow is manipulated by our lips, by the tongue being held against different parts of the roof of the mouth, by our vocal cords, and so on. When we say *fog* the use of our teeth is required, for we start off with our top teeth pressed against our lower lip. Some sounds require that part of the flow of air is diverted through the nose. Figure 4.1 shows the location of the various parts of our anatomy that shape our speech sounds.

Of these speech organs the very flexible tongue is of particular importance. So much so that the word for it is often used as a synonym for language: English *mother tongue*, French *langue*, Russian язык, and so on.

The vocal cords are located in the larynx, in what we perceive as the 'Adam's apple'. They are like curtains of muscular tissue that can be drawn across the windpipe. When certain consonant sounds are produced the vocal cords are open and the flow of air passes unimpeded; such sounds are **voiceless**. When other consonants and vowels are produced the vocal cords are closed with the result that they vibrate as the flow of air forces its way between them; such sounds are **voiced**. The sound [f], for example, is voiceless; the voiced equivalent is [v]. One way of telling the difference is to make each sound with a finger in each ear; when you do this you hear a buzzing with the voiced sound that you do not hear with the voiceless sound. You may also be able to tell the difference by resting your fingers on your larynx as you make each sound.

It should perhaps be noted that what linguists call organs of speech have other functions even more crucial for the survival of the species such as breathing and eating. Speech has developed as a secondary use of organs already in place for other functions.

4.2 Consonants

We have seen that the sound /d/ in the word *dog* is produced by vibrating the vocal cords, by pressing the tip of the tongue against the roof of the mouth behind the teeth, by damming and releasing the flow of air. We saw that the production of the sound /g/ differs in that the tongue touches the roof of the mouth further back, at the velum. If we draw the vocal cords back to allow the air to flow past for the final sound so that there is no vibration we produce, instead, the word *dock*. If instead of damming the flow of air we allow a restricted but continuous passage we produce the German word *doch*.

Consonants, then, are determined by whether the vocal cords vibrate, where the air is impeded and how it is impeded; to use the linguist's terminology, they are determined by **voicing**, by **place of articulation** and by **manner of articulation**. The sound [g], for example, being the product of the vibration of the vocal cords and of the tongue being held against the roof of the mouth at the velum to allow a build-up and sudden release of air, is described as a voiced velar plosive. As the tongue engages the velum, rather than vice versa, the tongue may be referred to as the active articulator and the velum as the passive articulator.

Figure 4.2 arranges the principal consonant sounds by their place of articulation and manner of articulation. The further to the right a sound is on the diagram, the further back in the mouth is its place of articulation. Where two sounds occur side by side in a box, the first is voiceless and the second is voiced.

At the top left-hand corner of Figure 4.2 we find [p] and its voiced equivalent [b]. They are **plosives** because, as with the two

Place of articulation

	Bilabial	Labiodental	Dental	Alveolar	Palatal	Velar	Glottal
Plosive	p b			t d		k g	ʔ
Fricative	β	f v	θ ð	s z ʃ ʒ	ç	x ɣ	h ɦ
Nasal	m			n	ɲ	ŋ	
Liquid				ɬ l r	ʎ	R	
Semi-vowel	w				j	w	

Manner of articulation

Figure 4.2

consonants in the word *dog*, their manner of articulation is the pressurization and sudden release of the air stream. In this case the air is dammed by the two lips; thus they are **bilabial** sounds. The sounds [t] and [d] are called **alveolar** sounds, their place of articulation being the upper teeth ridge, otherwise known as the alveolar ridge. The sounds [k] and [g], as we have seen, are articulated further back at the velum. Plosives are also called **stops**. Down in the throat, at the larynx, is produced the glottal stop, the damming being done by closure of the vocal cords. This occurs, for example, in place of the /t/ when some Londoners say *better*. It is akin to a gentle cough.

A major alternative to plosion is friction, allowing a continuous flow of air but constricting it so that there is an audible friction as in the consonants in the words *face* and *vase*. As Figure 4.2 shows, such **fricative** sounds can be articulated at a variety of places. The initial consonants of *face* and *vase* are **labiodental**, being produced with the top teeth against the lower lip, while the final consonants are alveolar. With the tongue either against the upper teeth or between the upper and lower teeth we produce [θ] and [ð], these being the sounds represented in English by <th> in the words *thick* and *this* respectively. If one removes all articulation, if, for example, one starts by saying [f] and then removes the teeth from the lip, one gets the [h] that is often described as a voiceless glottal fricative. But being devoid of articulation [h] may also be viewed as a voiceless prelude to the following vowel.

Amongst the fricatives we find the first of a number of sounds included in Figure 4.2 that are not normally encountered in English. The bilabial fricative [β], for example, is a feature of the sound system of Spanish rather than that of English. It employs both lips like [b] but, like [v], it restricts rather than stops the passage of air; it is the sound represented by the <b> in *saber*, meaning *to know*, and by the <v> in *lavar*, meaning *to wash*.

The sounds [m], [n] and [ŋ], the three consonants in the word *meaning*, have the same place of articulation as [b], [d] and [g] respectively. What distinguishes them is that in the case of the latter the velum touches the back wall of the pharynx, thereby directing the whole airstream through the mouth, the oral cavity, while in the case of the former the velum falls, allowing the airstream to pass through the nasal cavity. Thus [m], [n] and [ŋ] are called **nasal** sounds.

As one goes down the rows in Figure 4.2 the sounds are articulated with less constriction of the air stream. One can also say that the sounds become more sonorous. Thus the sounds [l], [r], [w] and [j], as in the words *leer*, *rear*, *weir* and *year*, are less distinct from vowels in that the flow of air is less disrupted; these sounds are called **continuants** or **approximants**. As the diagram shows, the sounds [l] and [r] can be distinguished as **liquids** and [w] and [j] as **semi-vowels**. The somewhat vocalic nature of the liquids allows them to stand in a syllable without a vowel. The word *funnel* has two syllables but only one vowel; it is pronounced /fʌnl/. There may be no contact with the alveolar ridge in which case a vowel sound results; a Brazilian will refer to his country as /braziu/, the Dutch equivalents of *old* and *gold* are *oud* and *goud*. The Serbo-Croat for *Serbian* is *srpski*. Many sources will put [l] and [r] into two distinct categories. The sound [l] may be called a **lateral** sound. The word *lateral*, derived from the Latin word *latus* meaning *side*, describes a sound where the tongue is pressed against the alveolar ridge but without causing a stop, the air being allowed to pass the closure on either side. When the closure is further back, at the palate, the lateral sound is [ʎ], a sound common in some Romance languages, for example Italian *figlio*, meaning *son*. The character <r> may represent a single **tap** of the tongue against the alveolar ridge or a **trill** whereby the tip of the tongue vibrates rapidly against the alveolar ridge; the difference between these two sounds is reflected in the Spanish words *pero* meaning *but* and *perro* meaning *dog*. Articulated back at the velum or the uvula is the sound [R], a sound that can be likened to a dry gargle. As their label suggests, the semi-vowels [w] and [j], also called **glides**, have properties of both consonant and vowel; like most consonants they need to be accompanied by a vowel and unlike vowels they cannot be maintained, but like vowels they are articulated without audible friction.

The diagram of consonants presented in Figure 4.2 aims to give an introduction to the principal features of consonants. Inevitably this requires simplification of a complex situation. The roof of the mouth and the tongue positions each form a continuum and so the diagram introduces arbitrary divisions. You will encounter additional categories. The sounds [ʃ] and [ʒ], as represented by <s> in *sure* and *treasure*, are articulated further back than [s] and [z] and are often called **palato-alveolar** sounds. These four fricative sounds have greater acoustic energy and may be distinguished as **sibilants**. The initial sounds of the words *chair* and *jump*, as the phonetic symbols used in Britain, [tʃ] and [dʒ], suggest, are a combination of plosive and fricative sounds; if they are considered to be single segments as opposed to combinations of two segments – opinion varies – they are called **affricates**. Some sounds articulated particularly far back in the mouth may be classified as **uvular** sounds rather than velar sounds. Some sounds have dual articulation; [w], shown in the diagram as being both bilabial and velar, is a case in point.

The sound represented by a symbol may differ between dialects or languages. The sound [l] has been presented as an alveolar sound but many speakers produce a dental [l], their tongue being against the upper teeth. The sounds [t] and [d] have also been presented as alveolar sounds, as they are in English, but in many other languages, such as French, Spanish and Russian, they are dental. It is in this position, with the tongue against the upper teeth, that most Britons articulate the sound /θ/ as in *think*, but many Americans do so with the tip of the tongue between the upper and lower teeth. It is in this latter way that a Spaniard articulates the sound /θ/ in, for example, the word *cinco* meaning *five*. Even within the same variety of speech a sound may vary depending on its environment. In the word *top* the first stop is released before the voicing of the vowel starts, with the result that there is a moment when voiceless air is expelled; in such cases the /t/ is said to be **aspirated**. In the word *stop*, however, the /t/ is not aspirated. In the word *month* the /n/ is dental under the influence of the dental /θ/ that follows it. The sound [k] is articulated further forward when followed by a vowel that is articulated at the front of the mouth; the first /k/ of *King Kong* is articulated further forward than the second. The difference between the position of the tip of the tongue between alveolar [n] and dental [n] is easily felt; it is more difficult to feel the place of articulation further back in the mouth, as in the case of [k].

4.3 Phonemic Notation

In the previous section we have seen sounds represented by familiar characters such as [d] and [g]. But we have also seen characters that do not form part of the English alphabet such as [ð] and [ŋ]. These characters, familiar or otherwise, form part of the **International Phonetic Alphabet** (IPA) published in 1888 in an attempt to produce a one-to-one correspondence between sound and character.

It takes little thought to realise that the alphabet that we use to write English is not sufficiently precise to represent speech sounds. Some characters represent more than one sound and some sounds are represented by more than one character. Thus the character <c> represents both [s] and [k] in the word *cycle*, while the words *cycle*, *sick* and *psychology* all represent each of these sounds differently. Indeed the character <c> is superfluous in English and many other languages; the Norwegian word for a bicycle is written *sykkel*. Vowels are particularly erratic. In standard English the vowel in the words *term*, *firm* and *worm* are the same. In the previous section we saw *leer*, *rear*, *weir* and *year*, four words in which the same vowel sound is spelt in three different ways. The poor correlation between sound and spelling in English results in large part from the fact that the spelling has not kept pace with changes in the sounds. The words *write* and *right* have developed from Old English *writan* and *riht*. At that time the <w> of *writan* and the <h> of *riht* were both sounded, the latter being the palatal fricative that may still be heard in Scotland. The sounds have coincided but this has not been reflected in the spelling.

Clearly the variation is all the greater if one compares a number of languages. Before a front vowel the character <c> represents /k/ in the Celtic languages; that is why we usually pronounce the word Celtic as /keltik/, one exception being when we are referring to the Glasgow football club. In Spanish <c> before a front vowel represents /θ/ or /s/ depending on the dialect, and in Italian it represents /ʃ/ or /tʃ/. The character <j> represents a different sound in each of English, German, French and Spanish, these sounds being [dʒ], [j], [ʒ] and [x] respectively.

George Bernard Shaw highlighted the lack of precision in English orthography by spelling the word *fish* as *ghoti*; the sound /f/, he argued, could be represented by <gh>, the sound /i/ by <o> and the sound /ʃ/ by <ti>, his reasoning being based on analogy with such words as *enough, women* and *rational*. We might add that the spelling of English is so idiosyncratic that the digraph <gh> can represent the sound [f] at the end of a word but not, as in Shaw's concoction, at the beginning of a word. This idiosyncracy was something that he felt strongly about, to the extent that he made provision in his will for the development of a phonemic alphabet for English. In his play *Pygmalion* he begins by trying to represent the lower-class London accent of the flowergirl Liza Doolittle but then apologetically states that 'this desperate attempt to represent her dialect without a phonetic alphabet must be abandoned as unintelligible outside London' (Shaw, you will note, talks of a *phonetic* alphabet – this usage is still common but linguists tend to prefer to use the phrase *phonemic alphabet* as the characters represent phonemes).

The symbols are clearly based for the most part on the Roman alphabet or variants of it such as the <ð> that was used in Old English and is still used in Icelandic. The voiceless equivalent of [ð], [θ], is one of a few sounds represented by Greek characters. International though it claims to be, the IPA is not without its variation. The palato-alveolar sounds that British linguists generally represent by [ʃ], [tʃ], [ʒ] and [dʒ] are, for example, represented in the United States by [š], [č], [ž] and [j].

A phonemic character may represent a range of sounds. Just as the semantic range of a lexeme is a compromise between precision and a manageable vocabulary, so, too, a phonemic character is an arbitrary compromise. We have seen that the character [t] is used to represent a sound articulated at the alveolar ridge and a sound articulated at the upper teeth; it is also used whether the sound is aspirated as in the word *top* or not aspirated as in the word *stop*. But just as we can use specialist terminology if the range of general terminology is too wide, so the phonemic alphabet can be made more precise by supplementing the character with a diacritic; the dental [t] can be represented by [t̪] and the aspirated [t] can be represented by [tʰ]. More precise transcription like this is called **narrow transcription**.

Before leaving the subject of phonemic notation it should perhaps be noted that Shaw's dream of a phonemic alphabet would be achieved at the expense of a weakening of cohesion in other aspects of language. The plural morpheme of the word *cakes* is realised as /s/ while that of *buns* is realised as /z/; phonemic representation of the plural marker would be at the expense of its visual uniformity. In the phrase *ten cakes* the character <n> represents the sound /ŋ/, while in the phrase *ten buns* the <n> in *ten* represents the sound /m/; writing the word *ten* as *teng* in some cases and as *tem* in others would clearly upset a lexical cohesion.

4.4 Vowels

The core of a syllable is usually a **vowel**. A vowel provides the force that is shaped by any consonants that there may be in the syllable. It is in the nature of vowels that they are voiced. What differentiates them is the way the **tongue** and the **lips** shape the channel through which the air passes after leaving the larynx. When we say *least* our tongue is raised at the front and our lips are **spread**. When we say *loosed* our tongue is raised at the back and our lips are **rounded**. When we say *last* our tongue is low and our lips are somewhat rounded.

As the phrase *somewhat rounded* suggests, *spread* and *rounded* are not absolute terms for the lips can adopt any shape between the two extremes. The same applies to the position of the tongue for it is very flexible; the operative high point of the tongue can be more or less high and more or less forward. Vowels produced when the tongue is high are called **close** vowels and vowels produced when the tongue is low are called **open** vowels. Vowels produced when the tongue is pushed forward are called **front** vowels and vowels produced when the tongue is drawn back are called **back** vowels. The high point of the tongue can, then, lie anywhere within a large part of the oral cavity, with the result that vowels have a stepless variability. It is the vowels particularly that give rise to regional and social variations in accent. Mastering the vowels of French is likely to be more difficult for us than mastering the consonants of that language.

There is a tendency for front vowels to be accompanied by lips that are spread rather than rounded and for back vowels to be accompanied by lips that are rounded rather than spread. This is the case in English. This applies more to close vowels; the lower the jaw, the more difficult it is to adopt the extreme lip shapes. There are, however, languages with rounded front vowels and, more rarely, languages with spread back vowels. The pronunciation of French vowels is made all the more difficult for us by the fact that French has a series of rounded front vowels as well as a series of spread front vowels; if, for example, you hold the sound [i:] and gradually round your lips you get the rounded equivalent [y], the sound in the informal form of address *tu*.

Because of the variability of vowels linguists find it useful to have a set of reference points to which they can relate the vowels of a language. Such a set of reference points, proposed by the British phonetician Daniel Jones, is known as the **cardinal vowels**. There are eight primary cardinal vowels. One of them, represented by the symbol [i], is the sound produced when the tongue is as high and as far forward as possible. Another, represented by [ɑ], is the sound produced when the tongue is as low as possible at the back. That is why a doctor tells us to say 'aah' when he wants to look at our throat. The vowel in the word *least* approximates to [i], that in the word *last* as pronounced in standard British English approximates to [ɑ]. The other six vowels have been plotted between these two extremes, the front vowels being plotted at equal acoustic intervals, as are the back vowels. Vowels are usually represented by a point on a trapezium that is a stylised representation of the vowel space in the mouth, the front of the mouth being understood to be to the left. In fact, the tongue can rise higher at the front than at the back. The cardinal vowels are represented as shown in Figure 4.3.

As in English, the front vowels are spread and the back vowels rounded. These vowels are complemented by a set of secondary cardinal vowels in which the front vowels are rounded and the back vowels are spread. Thus, in French, the close front vowel [i] is accompanied by a close front vowel [y], and so on.

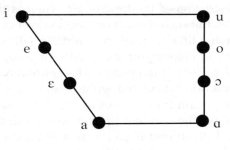

Figure 4.3

Above I said that the vowel in the word *least* approximates to [i], not that it is [i]. The cardinal vowels are an abstraction, a yardstick to be used by the linguist. If they represent an actual vowel in some speech variant, that is accidental. If an actual vowel is close to a cardinal vowel it may be acceptable to use the symbol for that cardinal vowel. Thus the vowel in the word *dog* can be represented by [ɔ] or, in the case of many Americans, by the more open [ɑ]. Where the actual vowel is not close to a cardinal vowel or where greater precision is required another symbol may be used; the vowel in the word *dug* as pronounced in standard British English is represented by the symbol [ʌ].

The vowel in the English word *less* may be represented as /e/. The word *lace* is pronounced in the same way as *less* except that there is a glide from /e/ towards a more close front sound, the tongue rising and the lips spreading. In *louse* the tongue rises to a close back sound, the lips rounding, while in *lice* it rises from a similar starting point to the close front position with spread lips that was reached in *lace*. Such gliding vowel sounds are **diphthongs**. The diphthongs in the words *lace*, *louse* and *lice* are /ei/, /au/ and /ai/ respectively. The exact nature of a diphthong is a matter of debate among linguists. Some consider it to be a single segment, regarding it as a sequence initiated by one stress pulse; others consider it to be a sequence of two segments. This latter position allows further debate: are the two segments always vowels or may one be a semi-vowel? Some words may even have a **triphthong**, such as the /auə/ of *hour*.

Consonants and vowels have been dealt with in two separate sections. But, as we saw in section 4.2, the approximants, the sounds [l], [r], [w] and [j], share some of the qualities that we associate with vowels. It is said that the articulation of a consonant involves the interruption or restriction of the flow of air, whereas the air flows freely with a vowel. But such distinctions are a matter of degree, and approximants, having little disruption of airflow, fall into a middle ground. So do nasal consonants as, barring a cold, the airflow through the nasal cavity is unimpeded. The approximants [w] and [j], the semi-vowels, are articulated without audible friction; these are the sounds that result if one closes further the close vowels [u] and [i]. After a vowel the segment [l] may be close to being a back vowel; this is well illustrated if you hear a Brazilian naming his native country. The approximants [l] and [r], the liquids, and the nasals [m] and [n] can be maintained like vowels; [r] and [m] may, for example, be used to imitate motor vehicles and we maintain [m] when we hum. As we saw, the liquids can stand in a syllable without a vowel; the same applies to the nasals [m] and [n]. In addition, [h], involving no restriction of the airflow, may, as we have seen, be regarded as a voiceless prelude to a following vowel.

4.5 Sounds in Sequence

This chapter has outlined how different speech sounds are produced. Having done that we must now correct any idea that an utterance consists of a sequence of discrete sounds. Rather than engage, disengage or change position sharply between segments, our articulators flow from one to another. We have just seen that diphthongs can be regarded as one segment that glides or two separate segments, this uncertainty reflecting the fact that segments merge into each other. The profile of a sound varies under the influence of its neighbours. We saw in section 4.2 that before a front vowel the sound [k] is articulated further forward, towards the palate; it is **palatalised**. The vowel in the word *month*, being surrounded by nasal consonants, becomes **nasalised** as the velum lowers to allow air into the nasal cavity for these consonants. We saw that the /n/ in *month* is dental rather than alveolar under the influence of the dental /θ/. Some people pronounce the word *exit* as /eksit/, some as /egzit/; either way the first two consonants share the same position of the vocal cords. Sharing the same feature in this way, being **homorganic**, minimises the movement that the articulators have to undergo, makes speech easier. Thus there is a tendency for sounds to adopt a feature of neighbouring sounds, a process known as **assimilation**. We saw examples in section 4.3; the plural morpheme of English is realized as /s/ after a voiceless consonant and as /z/ after a voiced consonant. This is an example of what we might call voice assimilation. In the word *unkind* the prefix *un-* is pronounced /ʌŋ/, the nasal sound being velar in anticipation of the velar /k/. In the word *unbelievable* it is pronounced /ʌm/ to share with the /b/ the bilabial articulation. These are examples of assimilation of the place of articulation. Such assimilation may have been reflected in the spelling of a word; if we put somebody into prison we *incarcerate* or *imprison* them. Assimilation to a preceding segment as with the plural morpheme is called progressive assimilation; assimilation to a following segment, as with the negating morpheme in *unkind*, is called regressive assimilation. Assimilation takes place irrespective of word boundaries; as we saw in section 4.3, in the phrases *ten cakes* and *ten buns* the word *ten* is pronounced with /ŋ/ and /m/ respectively.

Summary

Consonant sounds are defined in terms of where they are articulated, how they are articulated and whether or not the vocal cords are engaged. Vowels are defined in terms of the position of the tongue and the shape of the lips. A diphthong is a glide from one vowel position to another within a syllable. The distinction between consonant and vowel is not absolute; consonants vary in the degree to which the air flow is constricted, in their degree of sonority, and some can stand in a syllable without a vowel.

Sound segments are not articulated in isolation from each other and one may influence a neighbouring segment to minimise the movement of the articulators in the course of speech.

The International Phonetic Alphabet allows a more precise representation of sounds than conventional alphabets do. Phonetic transcription may be broad or narrow.

Exercises

4.1 Account for the difference in articulation in each of the following pairs of words:
coast ghost   ghost boast   boast most   most mist

4.2 Which sound may be described as
a voiced bilabial plosive
a voiced labiodental fricative
a voiceless velar plosive.

4.3 What is the manner of articulation of the initial sound of each
of the following words?
plosive   fricative   nasal   liquid

4.4 Explain why somebody giving a lecture on semantics might
seem to pronounce the word *meaning* as /biːdɪg/ if he had a
cold.

4.5 Why is it supposed to be difficult for a ventriloquist to say
bottle of beer?

4.6 Why might a photographer ask the person she is photo-
graphing to say *cheese*?

4.7 Describe the changes that take place in the course of the
pronunciation of the diphthong in the word *boy*.

4.8 How absolute is the distinction between consonants and
vowels?

4.9 Transcribe the following into phonetic script:
Our son was drunk twice last month.

4.10 How do the words *surface* and *service* differ phonetically?

4.11 Pitman's Shorthand is based on the principles of phonetics.
How is this reflected in the following examples:
phonetic symbol   t p s f v d
shorthand symbol   I \ ) ⌣ ⌣ I

5

Phonology

or
Why Should Ephraimites and Spaniards Keep Away from the Passages of Jordan?

5.1 Sound Systems of Languages

In chapter 4 symbols representing speech sounds appeared either between squared brackets or between slashes. It is the usual practice to use the former when referring to the speech sound produced by a particular articulatory combination and the latter when referring to the actual sound realized in a given context. We might, for example, read that the sound [k] is a voiceless velar plosive and that the /k/ in the English word *kill* is articulated further forward than the /k/ in the English word *cull*.

This leads us into the distinction between phonetics and **phonology**. As we saw in chapter 4, phonetics is concerned with the production of sounds which can serve as speech sounds in a language. Phonology studies sounds in the context of languages and other speech varieties. It is concerned with which sounds a language uses and how it arranges them. It is concerned with the contribution of sounds to the task of communication. Viewed from the point of view of phonetics the words *foal* and *vole* differ only in that the initial sound is voiceless in the former and voiced in the latter. We do not need to know what these words denote or even that they belong to the vocabulary of English. A phonologist, on the other hand, needs to know that these are English words for his work is by its nature within the context of a particular language system. His concern when confronted with a pair of words that only differs in that one begins with /f/ and the other begins with /v/ is that the difference is semantically significant, that the choice of initial segment alters

55

the sense. He wants to know whether these segments can stand in other positions in a word and which segments they can stand next to. He wants to know whether a segment is phonetically affected by a neighbouring segment. He would want to determine, for example, whether *froaf* would be admissible as an English word. In short, he wants to understand how the sound system of a language functions. We might describe phonology as applied phonetics.

5.2 The Phoneme

Speech sounds may vary from region to region and between social contexts. Some people have a speech impediment. We may have a cold. Indeed we all have a different voice quality. And yet the speakers of a language generally manage to communicate with each other, for some variation is possible without seriously impeding comprehension. How much variation is possible clearly depends on how far you can go before one word is in danger of being confused for another. In English the /s/ of *sue* cannot be articulated very far back in the mouth before you hear the word *shoe*. Voicing the /s/ gives the word *zoo*. A Spaniard has much more leeway in this area for in Spanish substituting /ʃ/ or /z/ for /s/ cannot produce a different word; thus where one Spaniard produces the sound /s/ another may produce a sound closer to /ʃ/.

The phonologist, we have seen, is concerned with functional contrast, with identifying amongst the mass of sound variation those contrasts which are semantically significant. His aim is to group those sounds that have no functional contrast in one set and place that set in opposition to another set. In the case of Spanish /s/, /z/ and, in so far as it exists, /ʃ/ would be in one set for, as we have just seen, they cannot be substituted for each other; /z/ only exists as a variant of /s/ before voiced consonants, as in the word *mismo*, meaning *same*, which is pronounced /mizmo/. In the case of English the occurrence of /s/ and /z/ may also be determined by neighbouring sounds, the plural morpheme being /s/ after voiceless consonants and /z/ after voiced consonants; the phrase *cats and dogs* is pronounced /kæts ænd dɔgz/, or in America /dɑ:gz/. But in English these two sounds can also be substituted for each other as we have seen with the words *sue* and *zoo*.

This substitutability is of such significance to the phonologist that he gives substitutable segments a special status, that of **phoneme**. A phoneme is a sound or group of sounds that is functionally distinctive in a language system. The proof of phoneme status is the **substitution test** which is nothing more than seeing, as we have done with the words *sue* and *zoo*, whether substituting one segment for another can produce a different word. A pair of words that are distinguished by just one segment is called a **minimal pair**.

The sound variants which are within the one set and so are not mutually contrastive are regarded as **allophones** of the same phoneme. The occurrence of an allophone is often determined by phonetic environment. As we have just seen, in Spanish /z/ is an allophone of /s/, it being the form that takes the place of /s/ before another voiced consonant. In Spanish /ŋ/ is an allophone of /n/, the form that occurs before another velar consonant, as in, for example, *cinco*, meaning *five*, this being pronounced /θiŋko/. These are examples of the assimilation that was referred to in section 4.5 and as such are fairly universal; the English word *think* has /ŋ/ before the /k/. In English /n/ and /ŋ/ can, however, also be contrastive, as in the minimal pair *thin* and *thing*, and so are separate phonemes. To us /n/ and /ŋ/ are clearly two distinct sounds. It is much less apparent to us that the two lateral sounds in the word *lateral*, are different; our awareness of the difference is obscured by the following factors: (i) in English they are allophones; (ii) the difference is of no functional significance to us; (iii) we use the same symbol to represent both. That they are in fact different is illustrated by the fact that in Polish these two sounds are contrastive phonemes. When the occurrence of one sound as opposed to another is determined by their phonetic environment the sounds concerned are said to be in complementary distribution.

5.3 Phonological Rules

Certain sequences of sounds are acceptable in a word, others are not. We know that Lewis Carroll's nonsense words like **slithy* **toves* could be put into service as English words; this has, in fact, happened to a couple: *chortle* and *galumph*. We know that **stape* could be an English word and that **zdape* could not. A phonologist needs to know why we would accept one and not the other, why one is in accord with the phonological system of English and the other is not. He needs to know why, even if we have never seen a word

before, we would agree that the plural morpheme of *toves* is
realised as /z/ and why that of *stapes* is realised as /s/.

We have seen in the English words *unkind* and *think* and in the
Spanish word *cinco* that the symbol <n> may represent the segment
/ŋ/. The English plural morpheme may be realized as /s/, /z/ or
/iz/. Clearly a phonologist wants to know the situations in which
different allophones occur. We could say that the plural morpheme
is /s/ after such consonants as <f, k, p>, and /z/ after such consonants as <b, d, g, l, m, n>. But it is more efficient and leads to greater
understanding if one identifies the underlying forces. The force in
this case is the common one of assimilation, and the phonologist will
very quickly observe that voiceless consonants are accompanied by
the voiceless /s/ and that voiced consonants are accompanied
by the voiced /z/. So efficiency and understanding result from
identifying the operative **distinctive feature**, in this case voicing.

Where more than one rule affects a word one has to consider rule
ordering, for the final form that the word takes may depend on the
order in which the rules affected it. To take the example used by
Francis Katamba (1992, pp. 122–3), the French word *an*, meaning
year, pronounced /ɑ̃/, must have been subjected to nasalisation of
the vowel by the /n/ before the loss of this final consonant took
place; if the two rules had affected the word in the reverse order
there would have been no consonant to nasalize the vowel. The
Latin word *focus* meaning *hearth* gave Italian *fuoco* and the Latin
word *paucus* meaning *little* gave Italian *poco*. The diphthongisation
of the /ɔ/ in the former development must have taken place before
the monophthongisation of the /au/ in the latter development; if
not, the Italian reflex of *paucus* would have been *puoco*. For a third
example we can consider such mutated plural forms as *teeth*, the
root vowel having been fronted under the influence of a front vowel
in a plural suffix that was subsequently lost; clearly the mutation
must have taken place before the suffix that caused it was lost.

5.4   The Phonology of English

We have seen that /n/ and /ŋ/ belong to the same phoneme in
Spanish but to different phonemes in English. We saw a similar
thing in respect of /s/ and /z/. English has, indeed, a phonological

system with relatively fine distinctions, a relatively large number of phonemes: some forty-four. Of these, twenty-four are consonants:

/p/ as in pan	/f/ as in fan	/ʃ/ as in shatter	/m/ as in man
/b/ as in ban	/v/ as in van	/ʒ/ as in seizure	/n/ as in thin
/t/ as in tan	/θ/ as in thank	/tʃ/ as in chatter	/ŋ/ as in thing
/d/ as in done	/ð/ as in than	/dʒ/ as in junk	/l/ as in lung
/k/ as in can	/s/ as in sank	/w/ as in won	/r/ as in rung
/g/ as in gun	/z/ as in zinc	/j/ as in young	/h/ as in hung

As they are phonemes, we can for each sound find a word that would be changed to another word by the substitution of that segment; /n/ and /ŋ/ are separate phonemes because substituting the latter for the former changes the word *thin* into a different word, *thing*. We cannot, however, substitute /ŋ/ for /n/ in the word *not* for not only is there no word pronounced /ŋot/ but, more importantly to the phonologist, there could not be such a word. Nor can we any longer add /k/ to produce /knot/. There are, then, restrictions on how we use our phonemes and the phonologist has to understand what these restrictions are, in order to identify the phonological rules affecting the phonetic environments in which phonemes can and cannot occur. It may be that a phoneme cannot occur in a certain position; in English /ŋ/ cannot occur in initial position. There will be restrictions on which other phonemes a phoneme may accompany; /kn/ is not possible in initial position because initial clusters of consonants must either begin with /s/ or end with a liquid or a semi-vowel. Thus the words *snot* and *clot* can be pronounced /snɔt/ and /klɔt/ but the word *knot* cannot be pronounced /knɔt/. The king that the Danes call Knud is called Canute by us, the insertion of a vowel allowing us to pronounce both the /k/ and the /n/. An English syllable can have up to three consonant segments before the vowel, e.g. /str/ as in *strong*, /skw/ as in *square*, and up to four after the vowel, e.g. /ksts/ as in *texts*.

We may identify some twelve vowels and some eight diphthongs in English.

Some vowels are longer than others; the vowel of the word *least*, for example, is longer than that of *list*. Some linguists use this feature to distinguish between the close vowels, showing length by means of a colon; thus *least* would be transcribed as /li:st/ and *list* as /list/. But these two sounds are also articulated somewhat differently, the former being more close and more front than the latter, and some linguists choose to use different symbols, /i/ for the vowel in *least* and /ɪ/ for that in *list*. I am using the symbols used by Daniel Jones, which include /iː/ and /i/. Using these symbols, the twelve simple vowels of Standard British English are as follows:

/iː/ as in least	/əː/ as in learn	/uː/ as in Luke
/i/ as in list	/ə/ as in the (unstressed)	/u/ as in look
/e/ as in less	/ʌ/ as in luck	/ɔː/ as in lord
/æ/ as in lass	/ɑː/ as in last	/ɔ/ as in lost

The vowel represented by /ə/, known as schwa, is widespread in English, unstressed vowels being commonly realised as this vowel. The first vowel of the word *balloon*, for example, is represented by /ə/ as opposed to the /ɔː/ of *ball*. The words *phonetics* and *fanatics* are only distinguished by the stressed second syllable, the first syllable having the vowel /ə/ in both cases. The two vowels of the word *hazard* are /æ/ and /ə/. Figure 5.1 shows the approximate position of these vowels relative to the eight cardinal vowels introduced in section 4.4, the cardinal vowels being represented by the dots.

The eight diphthongs are as follows:

/iə/ as in tear (in the eye)	/uə/ as in tour
/ei/ as in tray	/ou/ as in throw
/ɛə/ as in tear (=rip)	/ɔi/ as in toy
	/ai/ as in tie
	/au/ as in town

We have been looking at the sounds of Standard British English, the variant of English that is said to be spoken with **received pronunciation** (RP). But there is also Standard American English, English spoken in Australia and elsewhere, and in each country there are regional and social variants. Given the variety of accents and the relatively large number of phonemes in English, variations may overlap different phonemes with the result that context may be required to identify a word. Without the aid of context a speaker of Standard British English might misunderstand a Londoner and an Irishman who tell him that they thought something, believing that the one fought something and that the other taught something.

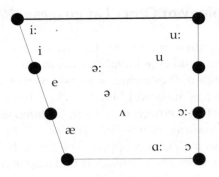

Figure 5.1

Americans generally voice /t/ after a stressed vowel and before an unstressed vowel with the result that one might be left wondering whether somebody spent the morning writing or riding. Indeed letters and ladders may be confused in the United States for many Americans make little distinction between the first vowel in these words. For these Americans there will be no audible distinction at all between *phonetics* and *fanatics*. As we know, due to the flexibility of the lips and the tongue, vowels are particularly variable. We saw in section 2.2 that the American linguist Leonard Bloomfield, talking of sound symbolism, gave the word *clump* as an example of the association between clumsiness and the sequence – *omp*, something that seems a little strange to British readers. Many Americans would pronounce the vowel in *lost* with a lower tongue position, producing /ɑ:/ rather than /ɔ/. The direction of the glide of diphthongs varies greatly. This is shown by J. D. O'Connor's diagrams for diphthongs. That for Standard British English /au/ shows a rearward glide in the case of the London 'Cockneys' and a forward glide in the case of the people of Northern Ireland (O'Connor, 1991, pp. 168–9). In Northern Ireland this diphthong often starts at the cardinal vowel [ɑ] and finishes as a rounded front vowel, a glide similar to the 'Cockney' production of the diphthong /ai/; if a person from Northern Ireland told you that he found the child's mouse one might be excused for thinking that he is using the present tense and that he finds more than one mouse. O'Connor says that in London the surname *Poole* may be pronounced in such a way as to sound like *Paul* (1991, p. 13). As a Poole who grew up in London I can confirm that I have been thought to have given my name as *Paul*.

5.5   The Phonology of Other Languages

When Spaniards address me by my Christian name a number of problems arise. The first is the initial consonant cluster /stj/ – even though, like Americans, they reduce it to /st/ as they are not in the habit of inserting a semi-vowel before a close back vowel. They require the support of a vowel; thus Latin *studium*, which gave us the word *study*, became *estudio* in Spanish. A final cluster is unacceptable and so the /t/ is dropped. And Spanish does not have weak unstressed vowels. The net result is that a Spaniard is likely to say /ɛs'tuar/ rather than /'stju:ə:t/. Different languages, then, have different phonological rules and it may require some effort for a speaker of one language to adapt to the phonological rules of another language. Remember that, just as Spaniards seek the aid of a vowel to articulate /st/, we have inserted a vowel between the /k/ and the /n/ to produce *Canute*. Not having the glottal fricative [h], Spaniards often use the velar equivalent [x], their *jota*, when speaking English.

And having for the most part lost the segment /ʃ/, Spaniards might be well advised to avoid the passages of Jordan in the light of what we read in the Bible, Judges 12:

> 5 And the Gileadites took the passages of Jordan before the Ephraimites: and it was so, that when those Ephraimites which were escaped said, Let me go over; that the men of Gilead said unto him, Art thou an Ephraimite? If he said, Nay;
> 6 Then said they unto him, Say now Shibboleth: and he said Sibboleth: for he could not frame to pronounce it right. Then they took him, and slew him at the passages of Jordan: and there fell at that time of the Ephraimites forty and two thousand.

From this source the word *shibboleth* has come into English from Hebrew to refer to a test word or speech peculiarity.

Different languages, then, use different phonemes. French and German have fewer phonemes than English: some thirty-five. While the French and the Germans both have initial /ʃ/ they might be in trouble by the end of the word *shibboleth* as they do not have the dental fricatives /θ/ and /ð/; hence the popular perception that

Frenchmen and Germans pronounce *the* as /zə/. French does not have a phoneme that corresponds to our velar nasal /ŋ/. On the other hand it has a palatal nasal /ɲ/ that we do not have, this being the final segment of *Bretagne*. Nor do we have the velar or uvular liquid /R/ that French has, the sound that is so striking when one hears a recording of Edith Piaf singing *Non, je ne regrette rien*. This sound is, in fact, found throughout a large part of Europe, as far north as southern Sweden where, for example, the equivalent of *red*, *röd*, is pronounced /Rød/.

German has the velar fricative [x] as in the word *Loch* meaning *hole*, a sound that is found in Scotland but rarely in England; an Englishman talking about a trip on the Caledonian Canal in Scotland may well not distinguish between locks and lochs. Other sounds that are strange to us include the voiceless alveolar lateral [ɬ] found in Welsh in, for example, the word *llawn* meaning *full* and the palatal lateral [ʎ] found in the Spanish equivalent of *full*, *lleno*.

Comparison at the level of narrow transcription reveals many more differences. The English word *time* begins with an aspirated alveolar plosive, /tʰ/, whereas the Spanish word *tiempo* begins with a dental plosive, /t̪/. The English word *think* begins with a /θ/ articulated with the tongue against the upper teeth, while the Spanish word *cinco* begins with a /θ/ articulated with the tongue between the teeth.

As we have seen, the /ŋ/ that we hear in the word *cinco* only occurs as an allophone of /n/ in Spanish; it cannot be substituted for /n/ as in English.

The second /b/ in *bib*, not being followed by a vowel, is less voiced than the first /b/ is. In some languages plosives become completely voiceless in final position. Thus the Russian word for bread, хлеб, ends with the segment /p/ although the final character normally represents /b/. The German and Dutch words for a dog, *Hund* and *hond* respectively, end with the segment /t/. The Catalan word for a female friend is *amiga* and that for a male friend is *amic*. In these languages, then, plosives are generally voiceless in final position. Certain sounds, then, may never or rarely occur in certain environments. In Finnish few words begin with a voiced plosive consonant; the Finnish words for a bank, a doctor and gas are *pankki*, *tohtori* and *kaasu* respectively.

Different languages compound consonants in different combinations. English accepts the initial cluster /sk/ as in *school* but not the voiced equivalent /zg/. Italian has both as in *scuola* meaning *school* and *sgonfiare* meaning *to deflate*. Similarly, Italian has /z/ before the voiced plosives /b/ and /d/ as in, for example, *sdrucciolare*, meaning *to slip* or *to slide*. The German word for a horse, *Pferd*, begins with the cluster /pf/ – if one accepts it as a cluster, this being debated in the same way as the status of the affricates /tʃ/ and /dʒ/ in English is. There is certainly a cluster in the German word *pflegen*, meaning *to look after*. Russian has such initial clusters as /vdr/ as in вдруг meaning *suddenly*.

Many other languages are much less ready to accept consonant clusters. While English and Italian have happily accepted the initial consonant cluster of the Latin *schola*, French and Spanish required the support of a vowel; the French word, having subsequently lost the /s/, is *école* and the Spanish word is *escuela*. The Finnish equivalent is *koulu*. Thus a cluster of consonants may be avoided either by inserting vowels or by discarding consonants. Such developments contribute to the argument that there is a natural tendency towards open syllables consisting of a consonant and a vowel, a syllable structure of CV. This is the usual structure in Japanese. Thus when Japanese adopts foreign words with clusters, vowels are inserted; in this way the equivalent of *milk* is, when transcribed into Roman script, *miruku*, and *girlfriend* has become *garufurendo*.

The number of vowels in a language varies, but however many there are there is a tendency for them to be evenly spaced throughout the vowel space, the part of the oral cavity in which the tongue can shape a vowel, to form a symmetrical arrangement with maximum spacing. This ensures maximum perceptual differentiation. Spanish has a close front vowel, a close back vowel, an open vowel and two intermediate vowels:

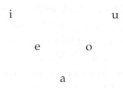

As the Spanish vowel system is much simpler than that of English, Spanish speakers often fail to make appropriate distinctions when speaking English; thus in the Hispanic English of the United States *dip* and *deep* may both be pronounced as /di:p/. Spanish also has /ɛ/ and /ɔ/ but only as allophones occurring in closed syllables, syllables ending with a consonant. In Italian these vowels are phonemes and so Italian has a seven-vowel system:

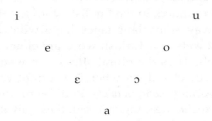

The vowel system of French is much more complex. Firstly, in addition to counterparts to the Italian vowels it also has /ɑ/, albeit tenuously. These eight vowels are similar to the set of primary cardinal vowels. Secondly, as we saw in section 4.4, it also has unstressed /ə/. Thirdly, it has a set of rounded front vowels: /y/ as in *tu*, meaning *you*, /ø/ as in *bleu*, meaning *blue*, and /œ/ as in *jeune*, meaning *young*. Thus the oral vowels are as folllows:

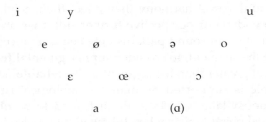

Fourthly, four of these vowels have a nasalized counterpart: /œ̃, ɔ̃, ɛ̃, ɑ̃/ as in *un bon vin blanc*, meaning *a good white wine*. Apart from in the case of the indefinite article *un*, the first of these is, however, in decline, /ɛ̃/ being used in its place.

Like the uvular [R], the rounded front vowel is a feature that is widespread in north-west Europe. Similar to the /ø/ in the French word *bleu* is that in German *schön*, meaning *beautiful*, that in Dutch *deur*, meaning *door*, and that in Swedish *röd*, meaning *red*.

In the Germanic languages back vowels may be fronted by the process of **i-mutation**, also known by the German word **umlaut**. Under the influence of a front vowel in a suffix a back vowel may front. The suffix may be a plural morpheme, a verb morpheme or a morpheme indicating comparison; thus Swedish has such pairs as *fot* (*foot*) and *fötter* (*feet*), *val* (*choice*) and *välja* (*to choose*) and *ung* (*young*) and *yngre* (*younger*). Such mutation also accounts for the English pair *foot* and *feet*, but whereas in the Swedish word *fötter* the vowel remained rounded, in the English word *feet* the lips spread.

In a similar way some languages have what is called **vowel harmony**. The vowels of a Turkish word are either all front vowels or all back vowels. Thus the plural affix is *-lar* when the preceding vowel is a back vowel and *-ler* when it is a front vowel, so that the plural of *oda*, meaning *room*, is *odalar* and the plural of *ev*, meaning *house*, is *evler*. In *tuzlu*, meaning *with salt*, the equivalent of *with* is *-lu* with a back vowel and in *sekerli*, meaning *with sugar*, it is *-li* with a front vowel.

5.6　Suprasegmental Features

We now have a good acquaintance with the speech sounds, the segments, of language. We have seen that by such processes as assimilation and vowel harmony they affect their neighbours. We now need to widen our perspective further still if we are to understand the variation in sound patterns between utterances. We need to rise above the segment, to consider **suprasegmental features**.

A major unit greater than the segment is the **syllable**. The concept of the syllable is supported by many phonological rules. As an example, monosyllabic words in English tend to be of the same length, a vowel being longer when followed by a voiced consonant than when followed by a voiceless consonant, the voiced consonants being shorter than the voiceless consonants, and longer still when no consonant follows; thus in the words *seat*, *seed* and *see* the vowels are progressively longer. In Spanish the syllable serves as the basis of the rhythm of speech. When we talk of permissible consonant clusters or the aspiration of voiceless plosives in initial position, of unvoicing in final position, and so on, we generally mean syllable-initial and syllable-final rather than word-initial and word-final; the sequence /ðdr/ in the word *withdraw* can only be reconciled with our rules for consonant clusters because we regard /ð/ and /dr/ as belonging to different syllables, a split which in this case, as in many others, coincides with a morphological split, the two syllables coinciding with semantic units.

Every syllable has a nucleus, its power source. This is usually a vowel but it can also be a liquid or nasal consonant as in the second syllable of the word *people*: /piːpl/. A syllable may consist of nothing but the nucleus, as in the word *owe*, but the nucleus is usually accompanied by at least one consonant. A preceding consonant or consonant cluster is called an onset and a following consonant or consonant cluster is called a coda. The nucleus and the coda may be viewed as a unit, the rhyme. In the previous section we saw the suggestion that there may be a natural tendency towards open syllables with a single consonant in the onset, towards a consonant–vowel (CV) structure. In support of this hypothesis we can cite the fact that pidgins, varieties of speech system at an early stage of development, tend to have open syllables and to avoid consonant clusters. This tendency might help to explain why in French an unstressed vowel may be elided when another vowel follows, as in *l'homme*, why a final consonant may be silent, as in *les*, /le/, and why such a consonant is heard when a vowel follows in the same phrase, as in *les hommes*, /lezɔm/. In Italian the equivalent of *and*, usually *e*, may be *ed* before a vowel (*parla italiano ed inglese*). We similarly say *a pear* but *an apple* and some of us insert /r/ between, for example, *saw* and *it*.

The force with which a syllable is produced in speech varies. When we say the word *syllable* we put more emphasis on the first syllable than on the other two. As we have seen, the word *hazard* has the vowels /æ/ and /ə/, the latter being the weak schwa because it is unstressed. The quality of vowels, then, is affected by **stress**, by increases in the pressure of air expelled by the lungs and by increases in the tension of the vocal cords. We commonly talk of stressed and unstressed syllables, but stress may be relative, and in words with several syllables this binary distinction may be too simplistic; in the word *opportunity*, for example, there is a primary stress on the third syllable, a secondary stress on the first syllable, and so on.

The difference that stress makes to the quality of a vowel varies between languages. As in English, it makes a relatively big difference in Russian; in the word дорога, meaning *road*, the stress is on the second syllable with the result that the first vowel is like the final vowel rather than the second one. In Spanish there is much less difference in the quality of stressed and unstressed vowels; the two vowels in *casa*, meaning *house*, are much more similar than are those in the English word *hazard*. When learning Spanish at school from a native speaker I was told to open my vowels more. Incidentally, the teacher unwittingly also impressed on me the lack of differentiation between the sounds represented by <b> and <v> in Spanish, for what struck me most as an adolescent boy was that it sounded as though he was telling us to open our bowels more. There is, however, diphthongisation of what had been short /ɛ/ and /ɔ/ when they receive the stress. Thus the Latin word *focus* became *fuego*, meaning *fire*, in Spanish, while the diphthongisation did not occur in the reflexes *hogar*, meaning *home*, and *hoguera*, meaning *bonfire*, the stress not falling on the first vowel. As we have seen, a similar development produced *fuoco* in Italian.

In some languages the position of the stress in a word is more predictable than in others. In Russian it is relatively unpredictable; while, as we have just seen, it is the second syllable in the word дорога, in the word молоко, meaning *milk*, the stress is on the final syllable. In Polish, on the other hand, the stress nearly always falls on the penultimate syllable. This is the usual position for stress in Italian, examples of such *parole piane* being *animale* /aniˈmaːle/, meaning *animal*, and *ancora* /aŋˈkoːra/, meaning *again* or *still*. In many words, however, *parole sdrucciole* (remember that *sdrucciolare* means *to slide*), the stressed syllable is followed by two unstressed syllables, as in for example *povero* /ˈpɔːvero/, meaning *poor*, and *ancora* /ˈaŋkora/, meaning *anchor*. As these examples show, Italian is one language in which there is a correlation between stress and the length of the vowel.

As we see from *ancora*, which can mean *again* or *anchor* depending on the position of the stress, stress can be semantically contrastive. In English we see this in *invalid* and *entrance* which have different meanings depending on whether one stresses the first or the second syllable. There are many pairs in English where stress distinguishes between verb and noun, an example being /kənˈtrɑst/ and /ˈkɔntrɑst/. Talking of contrast, stress is also functional in that it can indicate emphasis or contrast, as in *I wanted the white one, not the green one*.

In some languages the stressed syllable is the basis of the rhythm of the language. This applies to both Italian and English. In such languages the rhythm requires stressed syllables to occur at fairly regular intervals. As the number of intervening unstressed syllables may vary, the speed of delivery has to vary if they are to fill the same period of time; the phrase *that huge dog* can be delivered at a more leisurely pace than *that enormous alsatian* can. Hence the correlation between stress and vowel length. In the phrase *limes and lemons* the *and* may well be pronounced /ænd/ but in the phrase *oranges and lemons*, in which two more unstressed syllables have to be accommodated between the stressed syllables, the *and* is more likely to be weakened to /ənd/ or /ən/. The position of the stress may occasionally change to make things a little easier; the word *unknown* said in isolation is stressed on the final syllable but when it is followed by a word with initial stress, as in *unknown soldier*, the stress moves to the first syllable thereby avoiding two stressed syllables in immediate succession. In French, which is not greatly stressed, or in Spanish, on the other hand, the rhythm of the language is based on the syllable, whether stressed or not, hence is syllable-timed rather than stress-timed. It is for this reason that there is no need to subdue unstressed vowels in Spanish.

As we have just seen, when we say *I wanted the white one* we put greater stress on the word *white* if we want to emphasise that we did not want one of another colour. This alters the pitch variation of the utterance, produces a different **intonation** contour, a different 'melody'. If we emphasised *I* instead of *white* we are drawing attention to the person as opposed to the object. Intonation, then, is functional in that it can alter the message conveyed by an utterance. You might tell somebody that you met John the postman and old Charlie. In the written language the lack of a comma suggests that John is the postman whereas the insertion of a comma suggests that John and the postman are two different people. In speech, intonation fulfils a similar function. The person you are speaking to might reply *Did you?* and from their intonation you can guess whether they are surprised, whether they disapprove or whether they could not care less. Intonation also plays a part in the dynamics of discourse, of conversation; a falling contour may, for example, indicate that the speaker has finished saying what he wanted to say.

Differences in pitch within a word may be the equivalent of phonemes in that they can serve to distinguish between different meanings of a word. An example that is often quoted to illustrate this is the group of Mandarin Chinese words that we transcribe as *ma*. When said with a level high pitch it means *mother*, when said with a high rising pitch it means *hemp*, when said with a falling–rising pitch it means *horse* and when said with a falling pitch it means *scold*. For variety we can also consider the pair *ba* with a level high pitch and *ba* with a falling–rising pitch, the former meaning *eight* and the latter meaning *to take, to grasp*. It is interesting – perhaps, indeed, important if you are planning to go to a Chinese market – to note that the pitch distinguishes between buying and selling; *to buy* is *mai* with a falling–rising pitch and *to sell* is *mai* with a falling pitch. Languages in which pitch is semantically contrastive in this way are called **tone languages**.

We conclude by pointing out that stress and pitch are relative. A child has a higher pitch than a man but both have meaningful intonation as it is the relative levels that are significant, not absolute levels. Only by pitch ranges being variable can tone languages also have intonation, as they do.

Summary

Phonology is the study of the sound systems of languages. Phonologists are particularly concerned with the functional significance of speech sounds. As a result the phoneme is an important concept, this being a sound that can distinguish between different words. A variant of a phoneme that cannot be contrastive is called an allophone.

The sound system of each language is governed by phonological rules that determine the permissible clusters of consonants, whether a sound affects a neighbouring sound, and so on. Vowel systems tend to be symmetrical and to maintain maximum differentiation.

Segments are grouped in syllables. In words with more than one syllable one is likely to be stressed more than the others. In some languages the rhythm of speech tends to be based on all syllables, in others it tends to be based on only the stressed syllables. Variations in pitch give utterances an intonation. These suprasegmental features of stress and pitch can be functionally significant.

Exercises

5.1 Identify seven pairs of contrasting phonemes amongst the following Italian words:

/'tanto/ *so much*   /'kanto/ *singing*   /'tʃiŋkwe/ *five*
/'tɔrto/ *twisted*   /'kolto/ *cultured*   /'tʃɛnto/ *hundred*
/'kwando/ *when*   /'torta/ *cake*   /'kolpo/ *blow*
/'tɔrta/ *twisted*   /'tʃɛrto/ *certain*   /'kwanto/ *how much*
/'konto/ *account*   /'tʃjɛːko/ *blind*

5.2   Devise a phonological rule that accounts for the variations in the articulation of the phonemes represented by the characters <b>, <d> and <g> in the following German words:

    lieben /liːbən/   *lieb* /liːp/   *baden* /baːdən/
    Liebling /liːpliŋ/   *Sieg* /ziːk/   *Bad* /baːt/

5.3   Transcribe the realization of the past tense morpheme for each of the following words: *waited, waved, wiped, waded*. Account for the differences.

5.4   The following Swedish verb stems add either *-de* or *-te* in the past tense. What would you expect the past tense form of the verb to be in each case?

    köp- *to buy*   bygg- *to build*   lev- *to live*   lek- *to play*

5.5   Propose a rule for the realization of <s> in Portuguese on the basis of the following sentence:

    Sei que estes estudantes portugueses falam inglês
    /s/   /ʃ//z//ʃ/   /ʃ/   /z//ʃ/   /ʃ/

5.6   Which of the following would be phonologically acceptable as English words?

    *thlite, *grawl, *dlesher, *shlink, *tritch, *sruck, *stwondle

5.7   Make a list of ten English words which begin with a cluster of three consonant sounds. Make your examples as varied as possible. Define as closely as possible the sound(s) that may occur in the first position of the cluster; then do the same for the second and third positions. Are all combinations of these sounds possible?

5.8   Why can we not use the sequence /ŋkl/ in *twinkle* as an example of a consonant cluster?

5.9   Give one example of how Finnish differs phonologically from English.

5.10 The Danish equivalents of *big* and *bigger* are *stor* and *større*. Account for the /ø/ in the comparative form.

5.11 Give three English words where stress distinguishes between verb and noun.

5.12 For each of the following pairs compare the position of the stress. Comment.

economy/economic   *wonder/wonderful*
beauty/beautiful   *acid/acidic*

5.13 Explain why somebody might choose to stress the following utterances as indicated by the bold type:

*John **wanted** to do this today.*
*John wanted to do **this** today.*
*John wanted to do this **today**.*

6
Morphology

or
Why Are the Finns People of Few Words?

6.1 The Composition of Words

The words *manly* and *virile* are both stressed on the first syllable. The noun *manliness* retains the stress on the first syllable but in the noun *virility*, a Latinate as opposed to Germanic word, the stress moves to the second syllable. The possessive form of the lexeme *wife* is pronounced /waifs/ while the plural form is pronounced /waivz/. Here we have just two examples of the relationship between phonology on the one hand and the composition of words on the other. Just as there may be arbitrary boundaries between semantic ranges, so, too, ordering knowledge may require us to impose divisions across linkages. Having said that, I shall in this chapter study the composition of words under the usual heading of **morphology**.

The word *black* is a minimal unit in so far as it cannot be broken down into smaller semantic or functional units. The words *blackbirds* and *blackened*, on the other hand, can be broken down into significant elements, three in each case. In the case of *blackbirds* two of the elements, *black* and *bird*, stand together to denote a particular kind of bird and the third, *-s*, serves to indicate plurality. In the case of *blackened* the adjective *black* is accompanied by the element *-en* which changes the adjective into a verb and the element *-ed* which specifies the past tense or past participle.

A word must contain an element that can stand by itself, such as *black*; such an element is called a **root**. It may contain more than one root, in which case it is a **compound** word (for example *blackbird*). It may contain one or more elements that cannot stand by themselves, such as the *-en* and the *-ed* in *blackened*; such elements that can only

73

exist when joined to a 'host' are called **affixes** and the 'host' may be called a **base**. Affixes may be joined to the beginning of the base, in which case they are called **prefixes**, or to the end of the base, in which case they are called **suffixes**. There are other alternatives such as infixes that are significant in some languages. Some affixes like the -*en* of *blacken* create a new lexeme, while others like the -*ed* of *blackened* restrict the word grammatically.

The number of such semantic and grammatic elements that are typically combined in a single word varies from language to language. In section 2.1 we saw that the Finnish equivalent of *in my house* is *talossani*: Finnish incorporates in one word the concepts that we express in three separate words. Finnish is often described as an **agglutinating** or **agglutinative** language, it being a language in which such concepts as are realised as prepositions and possessive adjectives in English are realised as affixes. In the case of *talossani* the element *talo-* denotes a house, the element -*ssa* indicates position within the house and the element -*ni* indicates that the house belongs to the speaker. *In my house* is indicative of an **analytic** or **isolating** language, each concept being expressed by a separate word. On a scale reflecting the average number of concepts incorporated in a word, then, agglutinating languages lie at one end and analytic languages lie at the other. In between linguists usually recognise another type, **inflecting** languages. Such languages, like French, make greater use of affixes than analytic languages do; as we have seen, the French equivalent of *I shall give* is *je donnerai*. Compared to elements in agglutinating languages, inflections may be said to have less of the semantic substance that we associate with words – to use Sapir's phrase, the affixes in agglutinating languages tend to have a greater 'psychological independence'.

In my house and *I shall give* would suggest that English is very much an analytic language. But in the phrase *in my houses* the concept of plurality is added without an increase in the number of words; it is added instead by inflecting the word *house*. We might, then, rather say that English is a fairly analytic language. As an alternative to *je donnerai* a Frenchman might use the more analytic utterance *je vais donner*. Here too, then, we are imposing on languages categories that are not clear-cut in the real world.

6.2 Morphemes

The Finnish word *talossani*, then, is composed of three significant elements. The French *je donnerai* is also composed of three significant elements: *je* indicates who is doing the action, *donner-* indicates what the action is and *-ai* indicates that it will be done in the future. Elements like this that have a semantic or grammatical function are known as **morphemes**; a morpheme may be defined as a minimal functional element of a word.

As we have seen, some elements can stand by themselves and some cannot. The former we call roots, the latter we call affixes. They can also be referred to as **free morphemes** and **bound morphemes** respectively. Of the three morphemes in *talossani*, the first is a free morpheme but the other two are bound morphemes. As a marker of future tense the *-ai* of *je donnerai* is a bound morpheme although its origins are those of the free-standing element *ai* meaning *have*.

While the Finnish equivalent of *in the house* is *talossa*, the equivalent of *in the forest* is *metsässä*. Thus the idea of location inside something is expressed by either *-ssa* with a vowel closer to cardinal [ɑ] or *-ssä* with a vowel closer to cardinal [a], the choice depending on the root vowels. In the previous section we saw that the possessive form *wife's* has a root that is pronounced /waif/ while the plural form *wives* has a root that is pronounced /waiv/. This plural form ends with the segment /z/ but the plural form *aunts* ends with the segment /s/. Thus a morpheme may have different phonetic realisations. The variation is often determined by phonological environment; the final segments of the words *boat*, *train* and *bus* determine that the plural morpheme will be realised phonetically as /s/, /z/ and /iz/ respectively. To distinguish the phonetic realisations from the functional morpheme linguists often call the former a **morph**. Thus we might say that the plural morpheme is realised in English by the morphs /s/, /z/ and /iz/. As realisations of a morpheme that are in complementary distribution to each other we can call /s/, /z/ and /iz/ **allomorphs** of the plural morpheme, just as we call two or more phones allophones if they are in complementary distribution.

6.3 Derivation and Inflection

In section 6.1 we drew a distinction between the elements *-en* and *-ed* in the word *blackened*. The element *-en* created a new lexeme, a label for the action of making something black, while the element *-ed* restricted functionally the lexeme *blacken*. The first case is an example of **derivation**, the second an example of **inflection**. Derivation, being concerned with the creation of new labels, draws morphology towards lexis while inflection, being concerned with function, draws morphology towards syntax.

The affix *-er* in *teacher* is clearly derivational, it creating a new lexeme. The affix *-es* in *teaches* is clearly inflectional: it restricts the use of the lexeme *teach* to the present tense, third-person singular. In some cases, such as *teaching is rewarding*, the distinction is less obvious. *Painting* as in *she is painting the girl* is clearly inflectional: it is a syntactically restricted variant of the verb *to paint*. *Painting* as in *I don't like that small painting* is clearly derivational: it is a lexeme that, like *photograph*, denotes an object. *Painting* as in *she has taken up painting* is perhaps more debatable, although the fact that she could alternatively have taken up *photography* suggests that it is derivational. The following are some useful guidelines.

Derived words are syntactically unmarked, whereas inflected words are marked in some way; inflected nouns may be marked for the plural, inflected verbs may be marked for person or tense. A derivational affix may produce a related lexeme of a different word class (as with the adjective *weak* and the noun *weakness*); an inflectional affix does not alter the word class (as with the verb *wish* and the verb *wished*). Derivational suffixes are less predictable in occurence; while *weak* acquired the noun form *weakness*, *strong* acquired the noun form *strength*. Derivational affixes are also less predictable semantically; while *fatherhood* denotes the state of being a father, *brotherhood* denotes an association of men as well as the state of being a brother. Inflectional affixes are more productive, that is they can be used with new words, this being facilitated by their greater predictability; as has been illustrated by introducing the nonsense word **wug* to children, there is generally agreement about what the plural form of the word should be even if we have never encountered the word before.

Inflectional affixes often form paradigms, predictable sets. The Portuguese verb *falar*, meaning *to speak*, for example, has the regular set of affixes associated with the *-ar* conjugation:

	Singular	Plural
First person	*falo*	*falamos*
Second person	*falas*	*falais*
Third person	*fala*	*falam*

This is clearly a much more complex system of affixes than the one that we have in English; our equivalent paradigm has *speaks* in the third-person singular and *speak* everywhere else. The Portuguese verb paradigms, like those of Spanish, Catalan and Italian, are so differentiated that it is not necessary to use a pronoun to specify the subject, just as we might be able to get away with saying *Am English*.

Romance languages like Portuguese have extensive **agreement** or **concord** within noun phrases, articles and adjectives adopting the form required to reflect the gender and number of the noun that they accompany. Thus in Portuguese we have the following:

o homem gordo	*the fat man*
a mulher gorda	*the fat woman*
os homens gordos	*the fat men*
as mulheres gordas	*the fat women*

Inflection is much more dependent on the environment surrounding the word concerned, on the context of the occasion, than derivation is. It therefore follows that in a word with both a derivational affix and an inflectional affix, as with, for example, *teachers* and *subsidises*, the former will be placed closer to the root of the word, the latter will be more peripheral.

6.4 Productivity and Word Formation

We have seen that inflectional affixes are more productive than derivational affixes. Even if we had never seen the word *subsidise* before, we are likely to correctly form the third-person singular of the present tense: *subsidises*. But even if we were asked to produce a new lexeme, a noun to denote the giving of subsidies, we are likely to come up with *subsidisation*. So some derivational affixes are also very productive.

A new adjective might well be transformed into a noun after the fashion of *shallowness*; it is unlikely that it would be derived in the same way as *depth*. As Francis Katamba (1993, p. 67) says, productivity is a matter of degree and it varies over time. Similarly, Laurie Bauer (1988, p. 57) highlights the facts 'that productivity is not all or nothing, but a matter of more or less' and that 'it is a synchronic notion'.

Over time the full value of morphemes may be lost. *Recount* and *recover* can easily be split into two morphemes in the senses of to count (votes) again and to put a new cover on, but this is hardly the case with the senses of to tell and to get better. The word *recoil* derived from an ancestor that literally meant to fall back on one's behind (Latin *culus*) but now the only free morpheme is the whole word.

To a greater or lesser extent there may be restrictions on which roots an affix may be joined to. The affix *-ant*, for example, can only be joined to a Latinate root; we have *assistants* but we do not have **helpants*. We have *unhelpful* but *inconsiderate*, the negating prefix *in-* generally being used with Latinate roots. The Germanic suffix *-dom* accompanies such Germanic roots as *king* and *free*. Often, of course, such pairings pre-date alternative possibilities; the morphs of the word *kingdom* were linked in Old English as *cynedōm* before there was extensive use of Latinate elements in English.

As further examples of the factors that constrain the composition of words we can refer to the use of the negating prefix *un-* and the comparative suffix *-er*. The former is only used with positive roots; we can be *unhappy* but not **unsad*, *unkind* but not **uncruel*. The latter is only used with words of one syllable, such as *sad*, or words of two syllables in which the stress is on the first syllable, such as *happy*; we cannot be **dejecteder* or **deliriouser*.

Affixation may result in a phonological change; while *divine* has the stressed vowel /ai/, *divinity* has the stressed vowel /i/. As we saw with *virility* at the beginning of the chapter, the stress may change position; as another example, the noun *productivity* is stressed on the third syllable, whereas the adjective *productive* is stressed on the second. Some loss may occur, as in *negotiate* and *negotiable*.

6.5 Problems of Morphological Analysis

The word *unhelpful* clearly consists of three morphemes which are realised by three morphs: the semantic root *-help-*, *-ful* which derives the adjective and the negating prefix *un-*. These are easily identified because each has an obvious function and because one follows another, because they are concatenated. But there are many cases where the morphological analysis of a word is less straightforward.

We have seen that there is no problem with *recover* in the sense of put a new cover on but that there is less obvious justification for treating as two morphemes *recover* in the sense of getting better. Many words have an ancestor that consisted of two or more morphemes but are now morphologically indivisible, there now being no part of the word that has a distinct function. The word *reject* derives from the Latin elements *re-* and *iactare* giving the sense of throwing back, but nevertheless we cannot sensibly divide the modern English word; as we cannot **ject* something, we cannot **ject* something back or **ject* something again. Our analysis must leave us with a root that can exist by itself.

Several linguists have referred to the problem of analysis presented by the word *cranberry*. If one is not content to regard the whole word as a single morpheme one is left with the problem of accounting for the element *cran-*. In fact, the name of this slender plant might relate to that of the bird that we call a *crane*; in Swedish the bird is called *trana* and the cranberry is called *tranbär*.

The words *gums* and *lambs* are easily analysed as the composition of a semantic root and a plural morpheme realised as /z/. But how do we analyse the words *teeth* and *sheep*? Similarly the word *walked* is easily analysed as a semantic root plus a past tense morpheme but the word *ran* is not. How do we analyse the structure of a word where the morphs are internalised rather than concatenated?

In the case of *sheep* we can argue that the plural morpheme is realised by a zero morph. But what about the words *teeth* and *ran* which undergo a change to the vowel of the root? Indeed, what about the word *went* which phonologically is totally unrelated to the word *go*?

One morph may realise more than one morpheme. The Italian word for a chain, *catena* (concatenation is joining in a row like the links of a chain), has the plural form *catene*. Thus the morph *-e* indicates plurality. If one also considers that it is morphologically significant that it indicates feminine gender as well, then it is fulfilling a dual function. If so, this morph might be referred to as a **portmanteau morph**.

To address such problems many linguists, such as Stephen Anderson (1995), have concentrated on the word form rather than segments of the word. Such an approach is known as **word-and-**

paradigm morphology. One or more morphemes are associated with the word as a whole; thus the semantic root *tooth* and the plural morpheme are realised as the morph *teeth*, the semantic root *run* and the past tense morpheme are realised as the morph *ran*. But in the opinion of many this approach is superficial, revealing little about the process of word formation; to quote Laurie Bauer, word-and-paradigm morphology has the major disadvantage 'that the mechanisms it employs appear to allow almost anything as a morphological operation' (Bauer, 1988, pp. 161–2).

Where the realisation of a morpheme results in a form that is phonologically quite distinct, that form is usually derived from a different lexeme. The form that realises the past tense of the verb *go* belongs to the lexeme *wend* as in *to wend one's way*. This situation is called **suppletion**. In the Romance languages the equivalent of *go* may use derivations of three Latin verbs: *ire*, *vadere* and *ambulare* or *ambitare*. Thus the infinitives in Spanish and Italian are *ir* and *andare* and the first-person singular of the present tense are *voy* and *vado*.

The scope for discussion is extensive and I shall finish this chapter with a couple of the debatable issues that we have not dealt with.

The Swedish equivalent of *two days ago* is *för två dagar sedan*, *för . . . sedan* corresponding to *ago*. Similarly French has the two part negative *ne . . . pas* as in *elle ne le mange pas*, meaning *she is not eating it*. Are *för . . . sedan* and *ne . . . pas* single morphs? They do not have to be single morphs just because the English *ago* and *not* are. The concept may be expressed by a more complex construction; the French equivalent of *ago*, *il y a*, translates literally as *it has there*. But if we do accept that they are single morphs we then have to accept that one morph may surround one or more others.

If a Frenchman has eaten meat he may say *j'ai mangé de la viande*; if he has eaten cheese he may say *j'ai mangé du fromage*, the masculine equivalent of *de la* being fused into one word. *J'ai mangé* and the English equivalent *I've eaten* each exhibit partial fusion as indicated by the use of an apostrophe. Clearly the *-'ve* in *I've* and the *j'-* in *j'ai* are essentially equivalent to the words *have* and *je* but in the elided form – lacking a vowel, they are dependent on a host root. Are they still separate words or are they affixes? Perhaps to avoid this question, they have a term of their own: **clitics**.

In this grey area between the status of affix and that of word we are ready to progress to the topic of the next chapter: syntax.

Summary

Morphology is the study of the semantic and grammatical structure of words. A semantic or grammatical element constitutes a morpheme. A morpheme that can be expressed as a word is a free morpheme, a morpheme that can only be expressed in conjunction with another is a bound morpheme. In agglutinating languages like Finnish a relatively large number of morphemes is expressed by affixation, while English makes relatively little use of affixation.

The form in which a morpheme is expressed may be called a morph and any variation in a form may be called an allomorph. Some morphs may to a greater or lesser extent have ceased to be productive and the use of morphs may be restricted in various ways.

A major distinction is between morphemes which create new lexemes (derivational morphemes) and those which restrict a lexeme grammatically (inflectional morphemes).

Morphological analysis is complicated by such factors as morphs losing their significance over time, morphemes not being realised as identifiable morphs and words developing a variant that is so elided that it needs a host word.

Exercises

6.1 (a) Identify in the following sentence four bound morphemes. State the function of each and say whether each is derivational or inflectional:

The teacher's brother considered the project impossible.

(b) Do you consider the word *project* to contain one morpheme or two? Account for your opinion.

6.2 For each of the following words transcribe phonetically and account for the allomorphs of the past tense morpheme:
waited   waved   waded   wiped

6.3 (a) Which one of the following Swedish words could be said to have a zero morph?
(b) What are the functions of the two morphemes that are realised as *-en*?

bil	car	barn	child
bilen	the car	barnet	the child
bilar	cars	barn	children
bilarna	the cars	barnen	the children

6.4 The Swedish for *a small car* is *en liten bil*. The Swedish for *two small cars* is *två små bilar*. Which linguistic phenomenon is repres- ented by the use of *små* as opposed to *liten* in the plural?

6.5 List as many factors as you can to support the word *height* being classified as a derivational form rather than an inflected form.

6.6 Which morphological issues are illustrated by the following sentence:
I haven't inspected the mice.

7
Syntax

or
How Does my Wife and her Beauty Like You?

7.1 Syntax as Opposed to Morphology

In chapter 6 we considered morphology, the structure of words. Clearly, if we are to make a sensible utterance we need to know how to put the words together. *The teachers fear the strength of the blackbirds* does not mean the same as *The blackbirds fear the strength of the teachers*, despite the fact that we are using the same words in each case. *Strength fear the the of teachers blackbirds the* means nothing. An utterance requires a certain structure. The study of that structure is **syntax**, a word derived from two Greek elements that equated to *together* and *arrangement*.

A principal distinction between morphology and syntax, then, is that the former is concerned with the internal composition of a word, whereas the latter is concerned with combinations of words. The distinction hinges on the word being a substantial concept. But in section 2.1 I suggested that this may not be the case and if that view is accepted it undermines this distinction.

In any event there are problems. A function that is fulfilled by a single word in one case may be fulfilled elsewhere by a succession of words. As you no doubt know by now, where we use the three words *in the house* Finnish-speaking Finns use only one: *talossa*. Swedish-speaking Finns use two: *i huset*. As we saw in section 6.3, the Romance languages of southern Europe do not usually use a subject pronoun. The Italian equivalent of *I give* is *do*. When referring to an action in the future we speakers of English need an additional word to indicate future tense, whereas speakers of these Romance languages do not; the Italian equivalent of our three-word phrase *I will give* is the single word *darò*. Even within the same language there may be elements that can be expressed either as words in a phrase or as morphemes in a word. There is little semantic or functional difference between *more expensive* and *dearer*. Similarly, the idea of something being very expensive can be expressed in Italian by either *molto caro* or *carissimo*. The Italian equivalent of *They give it to me* is *Me lo danno*; the equivalent of *They want to give it to me* is *Vogliono darmelo*, the pronouns being suffixed to the infinitive. Then there are the clitics that I referred to at the end of the last chapter; we can say *They have given me it* or *They've given me it*.

If one regards the word as an inconsequential distinction it may be logical to dispense with it and to analyse sentences in terms of morphemes. One would thereby fuse the study of morphology and the study of syntax; many linguists do, indeed, consider morphology to be part of syntax. In any event, both may be grouped together as grammar.

As an aside, we can remind ourselves of the awe in which the common folk held those with a command of the skill of writing; this is reflected in the fact that the word *grammar* is related to the word *glamour*. We can similarly refer to the different senses of the word *spell*, one denoting the representation of a word by letters, the other denoting control by means of magic.

7.2 Word Classes

*Strength fear the the of teachers blackbirds the is, as we have seen and as we all knew anyway, not acceptable as an English sentence. *The teachers fear the strength of the blackbirds* is acceptable, even though its meaning might strike us as a little strange. What we are concerned with is grammatical structure. Whether a word can occupy a certain position in a sentence depends on its grammatical category rather than its meaning. We can replace *fear* and *strength* by *admire* and *speed* and the sentence is still grammatical, each word having been replaced by a word of the same category.

The categories concerned, traditionally known as parts of speech, are now generally referred to as **word classes**. The words *teachers*, *strength* and *blackbirds* are classed as **nouns**. Nouns are words which denote something in the world around us, something inanimate, something animate like teachers and blackbirds, an attribute like strength, and so on. Nouns are generally accompanied by a deter-miner, something which helps to identify what is being referred to. In the above sentence each noun is accompanied by the definite article *the*; other determiners are indefinite articles (*a*, *an*), possessive adjectives (e.g. *my*), numerals (e.g. *three*), and so on. The word *fear*, as used above, is a **verb**, a class that has such functions as indicating an action or a state of being. *Of* is a **preposition**, a class that indicates a relationship between other elements of the utterance.

Now that we can put the words of our sentence *The teachers fear the strength of the blackbirds* into classes we can represent the sentence, S, as follows:

S > art., N, V, art., N, prep., art., N.

Other classes are the **pronoun**, the **adjective**, the **adverb** and the **conjunction**. A pronoun replaces a noun and anything that may accompany it; thus the pronoun *they* could be substituted for *the teachers* and the pronoun *them* could be substituted for *the blackbirds*. An adjective provides more information about the thing or person indicated by the noun; the adjective *old* may be inserted between *the* and *teachers*. In *The very old teachers greatly fear the blackbirds* we have two adverbs: *very* which is qualifying an adjective and *greatly* which is qualifying a verb. If we add to *the blackbirds* the sequence *and the crows* we are using a conjunction, a word which links elements of the utterance.

Lexemes in two or more word classes may share the same word form; *fear*, for example, may, as in our sample sentence, be a verb or it may be a noun. To help us to identify which class a word belongs to we can enlist the aid of either morphology or syntax. Morphology shows us that in this case *fear* is a verb; if the sentence were set in the past tense it would be *fear* that acquired the past tense morpheme, realised in this case by the segment /d/. Here syntax shows us very simply that *fear* is a verb; a sentence must have a verb and there is nothing else in our sentence that could fulfil that function. That the word *blackbirds* is a noun is suggested by the morphological fact that the final segment /z/ may represent the plural morpheme and the syntactic fact that this word can stand alone after the determiner *the*.

As we have seen, we could replace the verb *fear* by the verb *admire* and say *The teachers admire the strength of the blackbirds*. We could not, however, substitute the verb *sleep* because, quite apart from the fact that it is semantically nonsensical, the verb *sleep* cannot be followed by a grammatical object. *The teachers* could be replaced by the pronoun *they*, as could *the blackbirds* if that sequence were being used to represent the grammatical subject, but if we only had one teacher and one blackbird they would be represented by a different pronoun in each case: *he* or *she* in the case of the former and *it* in the case of the latter. Thus if we are to use word classes as a guide to what is a well-formed utterance, finer distinctions are required. When a verb requires an object, as in *The teachers admire the blackbirds*, it is classed as a transitive verb; when it does not, as in *The teachers sleep here*, it is classed as an intransitive verb. *He* and *she* are personal pronouns: they are used to represent people.

The sequence *the very old teachers* is acceptable. The sequence **old the very teachers* is not. Using the word classes, we can devise rules to define what is a grammatically acceptable utterance and what is not. In English the order art., adv., adj., N is acceptable, the order adj., art., adv., N is not. The rules which govern the structure of utterances are known as **phrase structure rules**. Such rules allow for the generation of grammatical sentences in a language; they constitute a **generative grammar** for that language.

7.3   Constituent Structure

We can, then, describe the structure of *The very old teachers greatly fear the blackbirds* as S > art., adv., adj., N, adv., V, art., N. This description fails, however, to reveal the fact that the sentence is not just linear, that it has a more complex, hierarchical structure. The four words *the very old teachers* have a coherent reference, the four words *very old teachers greatly* do not. The coherence of the sequence *the very old teachers* can be illustrated by the fact that it can be represented by a single word, the pronoun *they*. It can be illustrated, too, by the fact that when translated into a language with agreement, the article and the adjective may exhibit the gender and number of the noun. In the Portuguese equivalent of *the very old teachers*, for example, the article, the adjective and the noun are all masculine plural: *os professores muito velhos*. Unless, that is, the teachers were all female in which case the article, the adjective and the noun would be feminine plural: *as professoras muito velhas*.

The coherence of the sequence *the very old teachers* is such that it constitutes a **phrase**. In this case we have a **noun phrase**, the **head**, the key word, being a noun. The reason for the coherence of this part of our sentence is that it constitutes a fundamental part of that sentence: the subject. An utterance typically identifies something and then supplies some new information about that thing; the 'thing' identified in our case is *the very old teachers*, the new information is *greatly fear the blackbirds*. The first element is the **subject** of the sentence, the second element is its **predicate**. Similarly one can use the terms **topic** and **comment** and the terms **theme** and **rheme**.

A sequence with a subject and a predicate constitutes a **clause**. This may be a whole sentence, as in *The very old teachers greatly fear the blackbirds*. Alternatively, a sentence may consist of more than one clause, as in *Many people think that the teachers greatly fear the blackbirds*. In this latter example the second clause, *that the teachers greatly fear the blackbirds*, is known as a dependent or subordinate clause.

A linguist analysing the **constituent structure** of our sentence will refer to the subject and predicate as a noun phrase and a verb phrase. In linguistic notation, S > NP, VP. This represents a deeper level of analysis than S > art., adv., adj., N, adv., V, art., N. Analysis at this deeper level allows us to define more general principles of sentence structure. Thus we can say that a noun phrase precedes a verb phrase in a declarative sentence whether that noun phrase is *the very old teachers* or simply *they*.

These two levels of analysis can be related to each other by constructing a tree diagram as shown in Figure 7.1. If we wanted to

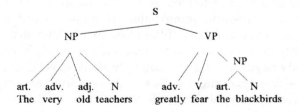

Figure 7.1

add *in the park* to specify the blackbirds concerned we would be adding a **prepositional phrase** to the second noun phrase, thereby producing the structure shown in Figure 7.2.

Figure 7.2

The elements on one level are **constituents** of those on a higher level, **immediate constituents** of those on the level immediately above. Words are immediate constituents of a phrase. In a simple sentence like *The teachers died* that phrase may be an immediate constituent of the sentence, a clause. In more complex sentences there may be more than one phrase and more than one clause between word and sentence.

To understand the grammar of a language we need to know what can serve as constituents of an element. We need to know that a noun phrase must contain a noun or a pronoun. We need to know that a noun other than a proper noun like *Fred* needs a **determiner** which may be the definite article (*the*), an indefinite article (*a* or *an*), a demonstrative adjective (such as *this*), and so on. We need to know that a noun may be qualified by an adjective. We need to know that these all precede the noun.

Our awareness of what is and what is not a well-formed utterance helps us to understand almost immediately, and to discard as soon as possible false interpretations. As soon as we hear *the* we expect a noun, but not necessarily immediately. If the next word is *very* we expect an adjective to follow. If the word that follows that is *old* we are probably expecting a noun to complete the noun phrase, but we may already have the complete noun phrase if *old* is being used as a noun. If we then encounter *fear* that might be a noun to complete the noun phrase or it might be a verb. We need to see if there is still a verb to come before we can select the correct interpretation. And so the process of decoding goes on.

Within the clause *The very old teachers greatly fear the blackbirds* we can insert another in order, for example, to further determine the teachers; we might say *The very old teachers you met yesterday greatly fear the blackbirds*. The structure of this sentence would be repres-

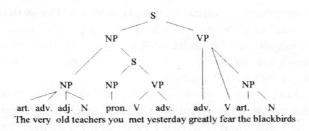

Figure 7.3

ented as shown in Figure 7.3. Incorporating a clause within another clause in this way is **embedding**.

A constituent structure representation may clarify an ambiguity in a sentence. If we were told that old teachers and priests fear blackbirds, we might wonder whether all priests or only old priests fear blackbirds. If the adjective *old* was meant to qualify *priests* as well as *teachers*, the sentence would be represented by the diagram shown in Figure 7.4. If the adjective *old* was meant to qualify *teachers*

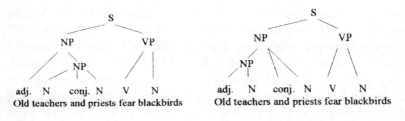

Figure 7.4   **Figure 7.5**

alone, the diagram would be as shown in Figure 7.5. What one is doing in the case of the former is like the bracketing that a mathematician uses to distinguish $3(y + z)$ from $3y + z$. Indeed linguists may also use bracketing; this latest sentence might alternatively be represented as follows:

[[[Old teachers] and priests][fear blackbirds]]

7.4 Noam Chomsky

The phrase *the teachers* is composed of an article and a noun. The

Swedish equivalent, *lärarna*, is simply a noun, the article being suffixed to it. But in both cases we are dealing with a noun phrase. Thus the further one delves below the forms that the realisation of utterances takes in individual languages, the more one finds commonality between languages.

Incidentally, given my use of the expression *delves below*, you might like to consider whether it might be more appropriate to present the constituent structure tree diagram the other way up. If nothing else, it would then look more like a tree!

Anyway, back to commonality. Constituent structure analysis facilitates the quest for the universals of human language. Understanding and representing the nature of these universals was a major goal for **Noam Chomsky**, a linguist at the Massachusetts Institute of Technology who introduced fresh approaches from the second half of the 1950s onwards. He recognised that **surface structure** is fairly arbitrary. The sentences *John is eager to please* and *John is easy to please* have a superficially similar structure but they convey a substantially different message; in the former John is doing the pleasing and in the latter he is on the receiving end. Conversely, a similar message may be conveyed by means of quite different structures. Where we would say *Do you like my wife?* an Italian would say *Ti piace mia moglie?*, literally *Does my wife please you?* In Middle English we used a construction like that used in Italian; in *The Canterbury Tales* Chaucer wrote *How lyketh thee my wyf and hir beautee?*, the phrase *my wyf and hir beautee* being the subject with the consequence that the verb is in the third person and the pronoun is in the object form, *thee* as opposed to *thou*. For Chomsky it was essential to get below the surface realisations to the underlying principles, to the **deep structure**.

The earlier linguist Ferdinand de Saussure, published posthumously in 1916, had distinguished between the fundamental *langue*, the language system within which a person produces his utterances, and the superficial *parole*, the actual utterances produced. Chomsky made a similar distinction, using the term **competence** to denote a person's underlying awareness of the rules of his language and **performance** to denote the actual use of the language.

The generation of the surface forms was accounted for by **transformational rules**. Converting the active construction *My wife pleases you* into the passive construction *You are pleased by my wife*, for example, conforms to the transformational rule

$$NP1 + V + NP2 > NP2 + aux + VPP + by + NP1$$

where *aux* refers to an auxiliary verb and VPP to the past participle of a verb. Putting *My wife pleases you* into the negative requires the use of the dummy auxiliary verb *do*: *My wife does not please you*. This transformation might be described as

$$NP1 + V + NP2 > NP1 + aux + not + V + NP2$$

The proposed techniques have been adjusted over the years to meet concerns. As an example of the imperfections encountered, applying a similar transformational rule to *Many women do not please you* produces something with a somewhat different meaning as it implies a lower rate of pleasing: *You are not pleased by many women*. The quest for the universal grammar and ultimately for the nature of man's innate disposition towards speech goes on.

7.5 Syntactic Forms

In the meantime, let us rise to the surface again and consider different ways in which the structure of a sentence manifests itself in utterances.

The sentences *The child saw the teacher* and *The teacher saw the child* are composed of the same words but they convey different messages. In the first of these two sentences we understand that it is the child that saw and the teacher who was seen, that it is *the child* that is the subject and *the teacher* that is the object. We understand this because English refers to the subject before it refers to the object. **Word order**, then, is of extreme importance in indicating the relationship between the elements of a sentence. The customary word order may differ in different languages. Whereas English has the order subject–verb–object (SVO), the Celtic languages put the verb first (VSO); the Welsh sentence *Gwelodd y plentyn yr athro* translates literally as *Saw the child the teacher*. Japanese puts the verb at the end (SOV). There is a natural tendency to refer to the subject before the object, to establish first what it is that one is talking about, but the actual word order is of little significance as long as the speakers of the language concerned can associate a particular message with a particular arrangement.

So, too, it is the word order – supported by our experience of the world in which we live – which tells us that in *The child gives the teacher the letter* it is the letter that the child is handing over and that the teacher is the recipient. Confronted with *The child gives the letter the teacher* we would be confused, it being difficult to reconcile what our grammatical understanding suggests with the fact that we do not usually give teachers to letters.

Word order, then, is very important for the understanding of an utterance. This is particularly true in the case of a language such as English that is largely analytic. But there are other devices available for indicating syntactic function.

Japanese marks the function of a word by placing a free-standing **particle** after it. Thus, for example, the particle that, using Roman script, is written *ga* indicates the subject of a sentence, the particle *ni* indicates an indirect object and the particle *o* indicates a direct object. Thus the Japanese equivalent of *The child gives the teacher the letter* is *Kodomo ga sensei ni tegami o ageru*, literally *Child (subject) teacher (indirect object) letter (direct object) gives*.

The German equivalent of this sentence is *Das Kind gibt dem Lehrer den Brief*. In this case the form of the definite article helps to indicate the relationship between the elements of the sentence. The *das* of *das Kind* indicates either a subject or a direct object, the *den* of *den Brief* indicates a direct object and the *dem* of *dem Lehrer* indicates an indirect object. Where there is a relationship of this kind between form and function we may talk of a **case** system. Traditionally the subject form is referred to as the nominative case, the direct object form as the accusative case and the indirect object form as the dative case. In our German example only the articles reflect the case. In other languages with a case system there is usually greater variation in the form of the nouns; in Russian, for example, the equivalent of *teacher* is учитель in the nominative case, учителя in the accusative case and учителю in the dative case.

These languages also have a genitive case which indicates possession; the German equivalent of *the teacher's child* is *das Kind des Lehrers*. A comparison of *the teacher's* and *des Lehrers* shows a common feature, the suffix indicating possession. English has not always been as analytic as it now is; Old English had a well-developed case system and we have a vestige of it in the possessive form of the noun. The Old English ancestor of *father* was *fæder*, this having a genitive form *fæderes*. We have retained the case system, too, in the personal pronouns. While *The child saw the dogs* relies on word order for its meaning, *The dogs saw the child* meaning something quite different, we cannot change the meaning of *He saw them* by a simple rearrangement because *he* and *them* are marked for the functions of subject and object respectively.

As an alternative to *The child gives the teacher the letter* we could say *The child gives the letter to the teacher*. As an alternative to *the teacher's child* we could say *the child of the teacher*. In each case we would be using a **preposition** to indicate the relationship between the elements concerned, the preposition *to* to indicate direction towards an indirect object and the preposition *of* to indicate possession. As English became more analytic, as it relinquished the case system, it had to rely more heavily on prepositions. Similarly, the Romance languages came to rely more heavily on prepositions than their ancestor Latin had, because for the most part they abandoned the case system; the equivalent of *the father's* was *patris* in Latin, the genitive form of *pater*, this becoming *del padre* in Spanish.

Summary

Syntax is the study of the structure of utterances. It is commonly distinguished from morphology on the basis that syntax deals with combinations of words whereas morphology deals with the internal structure of words, but this distinction is not clear-cut.

To understand how words may be combined to construct utterances we need to distinguish between word classes. Using word classes we can devise phrase structure rules. We must recognize that a sentence is composed of groupings of words rather than just being a linear concatenation; by means of tree diagrams constituent structure analysis illustrates the grouping of words into phrases and clauses. Noam Chomsky built on such an arrangement to argue that mankind has a universal grammar and to illustrate how that is transformed into a language's surface structures.

The means employed by a language to indicate the relationship between the elements of a sentence include word order, a case system, prepositions and particles.

Exercises

7.1   Do you think that morphology and syntax should be treated as
separate areas of study? Give your views and support them
with reasons.

7.2   In the following sentence there is one example of each of the
following word classes: noun, pronoun, verb, adverb, preposition and possessive adjective.
  Her dog always sleeps under it.
Rearrange the list of word classes to reflect the order in which
they are represented in the sentence.

7.3   Write five noun phrases in English. Use a different
combination of word classes in each case and incorporate a
clause in one of your examples.

7.4   (a) Construct a sentence in English that has the following
structure:
  S > art., adj., N, V, prep., art., N.
(b) Represent the structure of your sentence in the form of a
tree diagram.

7.5   Prepare a tree diagram for the following sentence:
  The dog he bought likes young children.

7.6   The dog bit the man in the car.
The phrase *in the car* could be being used (a) to indicate where
the biting took place or (b) to specify that it was the man in the
car that was bitten. How would the tree diagram for each
differ?

7.7   Explain the difference between the situations represented by
the sentence in (a) and the sentence in (b):

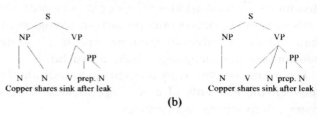

     (a)   (b)

7.8   The very old fear . . .
Write two sentences that begin with the above, one in which *fear* is a noun and one in which it is a verb. Incorporate a prepositional phrase in each sentence.

7.9   *Us visit she on Sundays.
(a) Explain why the above is ungrammatical.
(b) Which personal pronoun in English would have the same form whether it occupied the position of *us* or *she* in the above?

7.10   If English still had a case system, which phrase in the following sentence would you expect to be (a) in the nominative case, (b) in the accusative case, (c) in the dative case?
My youngest son threw the ball to the white dog.

8

Regional Variation

or
Div ye Ken Fit he's Spikkin Aboot?

8.1 Variations of Variations

'Hello, it's me.' That may be all that we need to hear to recognise
somebody who rings us up if we know them fairly well, for no two
people speak exactly alike. His or her speech profile has been
shaped by such factors as where he or she grew up, by the kind of
education that he or she received, by his or her occupation and by
the same range of factors in respect of his or her parents. His or her
speech profile is, of course, affected by whether it is *his* or *her* that is
appropriate. It is affected by age. It is affected by many other physical differences that influence the individual's acoustics, that make
up the individual's voice quality. The unique nature of a person's
speech is his **idiolect**. If, then, we played a recording of a bus driver
in Bolton, Lancashire and a bus driver in Brighton, East Sussex it is
likely that most people would be able to identify which driver was
from which town if presented with the two alternatives. Similarly,
most people could distinguish between a bus driver from Bolton
and a judge from Bolton. In principle, then, a person's idiolect can be
plotted on a matrix with a regional axis and a social axis. A postman
from Preston might be plotted as A on the matrix shown in Figure
8.1 while a doctor from Dover might be plotted as B.

In this chapter I shall be dealing with variation in speech between
regions. Social variations are the subject of the next chapter.

If you do not recognise a caller you may at least be able to guess
which part of the country he comes from. The extent of our ability to
do so clearly depends on how well acquainted we are with the
speech variety concerned; if the caller is from Aberdeen in Scotland

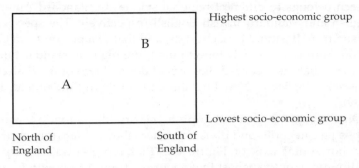

Figure 8.1

an American might correctly recognise that he is Scottish, while a Scot is more likely to know that he is from the Aberdeen region and not from, say, Glasgow. The fact that we can at least to some extent tell where a person grew up on the basis of his speech suggests that the characteristics of an individual's speech, while ultimately unique, are in large part common to those who grew up in the same region. Where there is a systematic set of features, phonological, lexical, and so on, that is shared by a subgroup of those who speak a language but not by others we can refer to the speech of that group as a **dialect**. If some features are shared by several but not all the dialects of a language, we can perhaps distinguish a **regional standard** (see Figure 8.2).

Any given individual who grew up at C, some point on the spatial continuum AB, has a unique variety of speech which in principle belongs to a particular dialect, which in turn belongs to a particular regional standard, which in turn belongs to a particular language. Thus, for example, a person from Boston, Massachusetts, speaks the same language as a person from Boston, Lincolnshire. But their

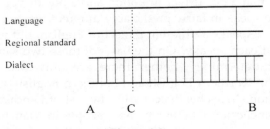

Figure 8.2

speech belongs to different regional standards: Standard American English and Standard British English respectively. The speech of a person from Boston, Massachusetts, and that of a person from Charleston, South Carolina, belong to the same regional standard but to different dialects; Leonard Bloomfield defined two of the dialects of American English as New England and Southern (Bloomfield, 1933, p. 49).

Once again, in our attempt to clarify the situation, we are imposing categories and divisions where they are far from clear-cut. The horizontal axis of Figure 8.2, that representing the spatial continuum, would suggest that a journey from A to B with frequent stops would reveal a succession of discrete dialects. In fact, it would generally be difficult to identify a boundary between dialects. Indeed the situation is likely to be so complex that it would be debatable how many dialects there are on the route. Similarly, the vertical axis is likely to be an oversimplification of reality; the grouping of idiolects into languages may occur with no obvious thresholds with the result that the decision of what is a dialect and what is a regional standard may be fairly arbitrary. Even one individual's idiolect is not as uniform as the dot on the diagram would suggest, as one's speech varies between situations. The question of defining dialects horizontally, of determining where spatially one dialect ends and another begins, is dealt with in the next section. The question of defining dialects vertically, of determining the status of speech varieties, will be dealt with in section 8.3. Variation in the speech of an individual is largely determined by social context and will be dealt with in chapter 9.

8.2   Horizontal Definition of Dialect

I have said that a bus driver in Bolton and a bus driver in Brighton are likely to speak in fairly predictably different ways. Thus we can say that each speaks a different dialect of English. But what are the dialects that each speaks? On the basis of these two samples alone we cannot determine whether there are only two dialects in England, say Northern English and Southern English, whether our man in Bolton shares his dialect with the rest of Lancashire or with Greater Manchester, whether he and people in Manchester speak different dialects, and so on. We might try to throw some light on the

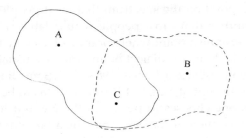

Figure 8.3

question by walking from Bolton to Brighton and visiting a bus garage every day. If we found no change at all for the first three days, then on the fourth day encountered several new sounds, several new words and one or two new syntactic features, this new set of features persisting for three days, and so on, we might have little difficulty in identifying several discrete dialects. But it is very unlikely that we would find such a neat arrangement. Figure 8.3 represents what might be the spatial distribution of two features which distinguish between the speech of town A and the speech of town B. In such a situation do the people of town C speak the same dialect as the people of town A, do they speak the same dialect as the people of town B or do they have a dialect of their own which shares features with the dialects of A and B? If these are the only two features that vary in the region, can we justify any dialect split at all? As one progresses on one's journey between two points, different features will wax and wane, each doing so at different places and with greater or lesser abruptness. Thus we do not even have the precision that the lines on the diagram suggest; they merely represent the point where one form loses its majority to another, where one form ceases to be spoken by as much as 51 per cent of the people concerned. We generally experience a **dialect continuum** rather than distinct threshholds. One could travel from Lille to Lisbon, that is from a city in which French is spoken to a city in which Portuguese is spoken, and find little abrupt change in local speech as one passed through the areas of such varieties as Occitan, Catalan, Castilian and Galician. Recognising the elusive nature of dialect boundaries, dialectologists often identify **focal areas** and refer to the areas in which features change their form as **transitional areas**. An analogy has been made to the colours of the rainbow;

there will be a point on the spectrum that most people would label *orange* and another that most people would label *yellow* but it is difficult to determine a point where orange gives way to yellow.

To quote W. N. Francis, 'dialect boundaries are usually elusive to the point of non-existence' (Francis, 1983, p. 1). Some linguists would argue that the concept of a dialect is so elusive as to be useless.

If, however, one chooses to persist in the attempt to distinguish dialects, one has, then, to be prepared for a bewildering array of boundaries, of **isoglosses** (lines which delimit the area in which a particular feature dominates). One can only look for fronts with a relatively great coincidence of boundaries, fronts where there are what one might consider to be isogloss bundles. On our walk from Bolton to Brighton we would be likely to find more changes on the section between Birmingham and Oxford than on the longer sections between Bolton and Birmingham and between Oxford and Brighton. In Birmingham as in Bolton a driver is likely to refer to his vehicle as a /bus/; in Oxford as in Brighton he would say /bʌs/. When talking of a long bus or the last bus those on our route who say /bus/ are also likely to say /lɔŋg/ and /læst/ while those who say /bʌs/ are likely to qualify it with /lɔŋ/ and /laːst/. If there were only two dialects in England, we might feel, the boundary between them must pass between Birmingham and Oxford. And indeed the most substantial dialect boundary in England does pass to the south of the West Midlands (see Figure 8.4).

In France the *Atlas linguistique de la France* published by Jules Gilliéron at the beginning of the twentieth century showed a major division between the speech of the north of France and that of the south, this division running from the region of Bordeaux north to that of Limoges and east to Lyons (see Figure 8.5). Like developments elsewhere, the speech of the south has increasingly approximated to Standard French but it still retains such distinctive features as the retention of nasal consonants as opposed to the nasalisation of the preceding vowel; thus *bon*, meaning *good*, is pronounced /boŋ/ as opposed to /bɔ̃/.

In Germany a major isogloss bundle was identified as running from west to east to the south of Berlin, its significance being that it marked the northern limit of the consonant shift that distinguished High German. In the region of the Rhine, however, as Figure 8.6 shows, the isoglosses fan out, the areas in which the voiceless stops

Figure 8.4

Figure 8.5

became fricatives being different for each sound; the development /k/ > /x/ spread beyond Cologne whereas the development /p/ > /f/ stopped short of Cologne and the development /t/ > /s/ stopped further south still.

Dialect areas generally surround a centre of cultural and/or political influence. The boundaries between them may be sharpened by obstacles to communication such as a range of mountains or a political boundary. It has been suggested that the boundary that

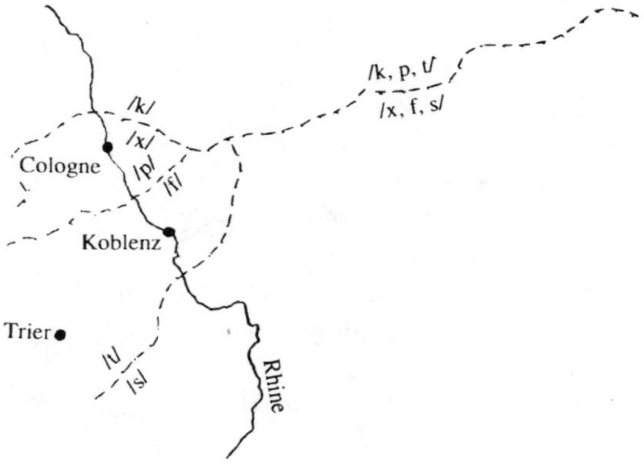

Figure 8.6

meets the east coast of England at the Wash has settled where it is because there the pull between the population mass of the north and the population mass of the south are equalised, a state of equilibrium having been attained. One can add that inlets like the Wash and obstacles like the Fens minimised the interface between the two varieties. In the case of the Rhenish fan the isoglosses for /p/ vs. /f/ and for /t/ vs. /s/ have been equated with the northern and southern boundaries respectively of the diocese of Trier. As it flows through the Netherlands the Rhine itself constitutes a major dialect boundary; reference is often made to speech 'north of the rivers' and 'south of the rivers', the rivers concerned being the Lek and the Waal, branches of the Rhine.

As a change spreads the front is often drawn by urban centres. In so far as the people of the towns are more mobile and exert greater influence, changes tend to establish themselves in the towns and then spread to the surrounding areas. Thus the speech of the more dominant region – the south of England, the north of France and the south of Germany – will to a greater or lesser extent also be found in the towns of the less dominant region.

8.3 Vertical Definition of Dialect

We have seen, then, that it may be difficult to define the dialect that is spoken by a person in Bolton or a person in Brighton but that we can safely say that they speak different dialects. At a higher tier we can say that they both speak a dialect of Standard British English. One might arguably propose that one should recognize an intermediate tier and say that a person from Bolton and a person from Brighton speak a dialect of a northern England regional standard and a dialect of a southern England regional standard respectively. In any event the speech of the person from Bolton belongs to a different regional standard to that which encompasses the speech of a person from Boston, Massachusetts. An Englishman and an American, then, speak varieties that belong to different regional standards. But they do speak the same language; an Englishman and a Dutchman do not.

As we said, we are imposing categories on a state of affairs that is in actual fact less clearly differentiated and there is scope for debate about any categorisation. Arguably the distinctions between dialects, regional standards and languages are as arbitrary as those between hills and mountains, between streams and rivers. Perhaps it is only because we have these labels that we seek a differentiation between concepts. When discussing the relationship between language and thought Hudson

> suggested that the reason why we assume that dialects and languages are distinct may be because modern English has different names for them; if we had been brought up speaking English before the Greek word *dialect* was introduced we might well not have made this assumption, and there would have been no need to question the reality of the distinction. (Hudson, 1996, p. 95)

Let us nevertheless assume that there is a substantial difference between a dialect and a language, and consider how one might determine whether two speech varieties are dialects of the one language or whether they belong to separate languages.

Almost everybody would agree that most Englishmen and most Americans speak the same language, English, and that Englishmen and Dutchmen speak different languages. It is generally considered that Flemish, spoken in Belgium, is a dialect of Dutch but that Afrikaans, a language of South Africa derived from Dutch, has attained the status of a separate language. On what basis do we make such distinctions? One might reasonably reply that most Englishmen can understand most Americans but they cannot understand the Dutch. This distinction has a number of flaws but it is about the best that linguists have come up with; to use the linguists' terminology, the distinction is based on **mutual intelligibility**. A language may be considered to be a speech variety that is spoken by everyone who understands it, while a dialect is a speech variety that is spoken by only some of those who understand it. To quote W. N. Francis's definition of a dialect, dialects are 'varieties of a language used by groups smaller than the total community of speakers of the language' (Francis, 1983, p. 1). If people use varieties that are not mutually intelligible they would be deemed to speak different languages.

A major deficiency of this yardstick is that intelligibility is a matter of degree, not all or nothing. An American might on occasion have difficulty understanding an Englishman. On the other hand an Englishman might on occasion understand something of what a Dutchman says; a Dutchman who wants you to know that his book is under the clock might well be understood by an Englishman when he says /mən buk iz ɔndər də klɔk/. Swedes and Norwegians generally understand each other without much difficulty; Swedes and Danes find it more difficult to understand each other. One or both speakers may accommodate their speech to that of the other person or to a more standard variety by avoiding certain features that they feel would be unfamiliar to the other person. Mutual intelligibility is greater when people are using a standard variety of speech than when they are using a local variety. The communication might be assisted by context; a person from Aberdeen who pronounces the word *speak* with a short vowel, as /spik/, is less likely to be understood if he says *They cannot speak* than he is if he says *They cannot speak English*, an extra clue having been given by reference to a language.

The situation is further complicated by dialect continua. People living near the edge of a language area may understand people in the neighbouring language area better than they understand people living on the other side of their own language area. People in the north of Germany, for example, may well find it easier to understand a Dutchman than to understand an Austrian despite the fact that the Germans and the Austrians nominally speak German while the Dutch do not.

The mutuality may not be in balance; one participant in a conversation may understand more than the other does. People from a cultural centre may be understood better than people from a peripheral area, it being likely that the speech of the former approximates more closely to a regional standard, to the speech heard on radio and television, and so on.

Linguists will not generally accept political boundaries as a relevant factor. Given their high level of mutual intelligibility it might be appropriate to consider Norwegian and Swedish to be dialects or regional standards of one language. The fact that they are spoken in two separate countries does not make them two separate languages any more than the American War of Independence resulted in an American language. The break-up of Yugoslavia did not of itself create separate Serbian and Croatian languages. What may happen in the long term is that differences may develop, either naturally or forced by desires for a national identity, and that their adoption is stimulated by such means as national media. But in over two hundred years this has not driven a wedge of incomprehension between Britons and Americans.

One can turn to the standard variety that people encounter, for example, in the speech of the local court, the language of their tax-forms, and so on. That, however, may also be shaped by nationalistic considerations. Sweden and Norway have different albeit similar standards; indeed Norway has two.

Perhaps one is as well to turn to the witticism that a language is simply a dialect with an army and a navy!

8.4 The Nature of Variation

Like the varieties that we consider to be languages, the varieties that we consider to be dialects may differ with regard to pronunciation, syntax, lexis, and so on.

We saw examples of differences in the pronunciation of English in section 5.4. In this chapter we have seen that in the West Midlands the word *long* is pronounced with /g/; a native of Birmingham pronounces the name of his city as /bə:miŋgm/. But it is principally the more variable vowels that give regional pronunciations their distinctiveness. We have seen that the pronunciation of the vowels in *last bus* can indicate that the speaker is from the West Midlands or somewhere further north. A person from Northern Ireland referring to the last bus might sound as though he were referring to his previous employer, saying /læst bɔs/. As a London schoolboy I once confused a German acquaintance when I said *today* for he took it to be *to die*. This same feature of London speech is seen in Shaw's play *Pygmalion* when Liza Doolittle talks of running away without paying; she does so before embarking on her course of training in pronunciation and Shaw transcribes what she says as 'ran awy athaht pyin'. I believe that I make no distinction between the vowels of the words *term*, *firm* and *worm*. It would appear that the Revd. W. A. Spooner, famous for transposing sounds, similarly made no distinction for he is attributed with telling a student that he had tasted two whole worms rather than wasted two whole terms. Those of my students who are native to Edinburgh are likely to disagree that these sounds are alike. Scottish English retains /uː/ in, for example, *about the house* where in England the sound developed to the diphthong /au/. A Glaswegian telling you that he has washed his hands may invert the vowels to produce /wæʃ/ and /hɔndz/, using vowels more akin to those that a Dane would use when telling you the same thing. Such varieties of pronunciation constitute **accents**.

The English of America has had less time to develop variations, the history of English in America being only about a quarter as long as the history of English in England. To some extent, of course, America could have inherited variations in so far as settlers from a particular region of England tended to go to a particular colony in America. In any event, the United States also has differences. In *Travels with Charley* John Steinbeck gave an example of how the speech of Texas can be misunderstood in New York, the word *pen* sounding like the word *pin*, and he refers to the doubling of syllables such that, for example, the word *guess* sounds, to use his transcription, like 'gayus'. One might add that in the Midwest *guess* and *gas* often sound the same, the sound [æ] rarely being heard there.

To turn briefly to morphological and syntactic variations, various dialects, for example, omit the third-person markers /s/, /z/ and /iz/ in the present tense of the verb; these include the speech of East Anglia and Black English in the United States. Black English omits the verb *to be* in certain circumstances, e.g. *She tired*. Irish English, modelling itself on the Gaelic equivalent, has such forms as *She is after washing the windows* as opposed to *She has washed the windows*.

Vocabulary, of course, also varies between regions. In Britain the direction followed by a train is determined by *points*, in the United

States by a *switch*. In Britain a motorist puts his luggage in the *boot*, in the United States he puts it in the *trunk*. Incidentally, the large number of differences in the terminology relating to railways (or railroads!) and the motor car is due, it has been suggested, to the fact that these technologies have been developed since Britain and the United States became separate countries. What is called a *stream* in the south of England is called a *beck* in that part of northern England once settled by the Danes, the word *beck* being of Norse origin. In Scotland it is called a *burn*. Where a person from the south of England might say *The girl knows the stream* a Scot might say *The lass kens the burn*.

There is a general tendency for dialects to become tempered, for them to drift towards the regional standard. Part of this is the loss of some of their characteristic vocabulary; lexis, being modular rather than systematic, is relatively easily substituted. This standardising of varieties is stimulated by social factors such as mobility and education, these being more significant among some sectors of the population than among others; we are now ready to deal with social variation, the subject of the next chapter.

Summary

Each person has a unique speech variety, his idiolect. Yet many millions of such people speak sufficiently similarly that they are considered to speak the same language. Between these extremes we may propose more or less local dialects and regional standards. It must, however, be appreciated that any attempt to impose such categories is to a greater or lesser extent an arbitrary representation of the actual situation. It is difficult to define dialects as different features will change more or less abruptly and in different areas; there is generally a dialect continuum rather than a distinct succession of dialects. One can more easily identify a focal area and a transition area, the former generally being based on a centre of cultural or political influence. It may also be difficult to determine whether two speech varieties are dialects of the same language or belong to different languages. The distinction is usually based on mutual intelligibility but this can only be a guide.

Exercises

8.1 How significant do you consider the concept of a regional dialect to be?

8.2 Explain the significance of the concept of dialect continuum.

8.3 How useful is the concept of mutual intelligibility to dialectologists?

8.4 What factors would you consider in arguing whether or not Scots is a language?

8.5 How relevant is independent statehood to a consideration of the status of a speech variety?

8.6 Where did you spend the greatest part of your childhood? State some of the ways in which the speech of that region differed from what you would consider to be Standard English.

9

Social Variation

or
Fit Wye Div ye Ken I'm Nae a Judge?

9.1 The Social Dimension

'Hello, it's me again.' It would be quite natural for a friend who is phoning you for a second time to say that. It would be less natural for him to say 'Good morning, this is me once more.' A judge talking to the Home Secretary, on the other hand, might consider it more appropriate to use the latter sentence. In these examples there is a difference of vocabulary (*again* is less formal than *once more*) and morphology (elision as in *it's* is more likely in informal speech). The informal style is more likely to be spoken with a regional pronunciation. What people say and how they say it varies in accordance with who they are, who they are speaking to and the context of the conversation. In *Pygmalion* Henry Higgins says that it would take him three months to pass off Liza Doolittle with her 'kerbstone English' 'as a duchess at an ambassador's garden party'. Such variation forms part of the field of study of **sociolinguistics**.

I suggested in section 8.1 that an individual's speech can be plotted on a matrix with one axis representing the spatial dimension and the other axis the social dimension. In practice, of course, one is then faced by the problem of establishing a social scale. Are wealth, occupation and education all relevant factors? Are there others? What is their relative significance? Where do you rank a successful 'self-made' entrepreneur relative to a doctor or the son of a rich landowner? One available scale is the socio-economic groupings used by planners.

By observing the speech of people who live near a line drawn from the north of England to the south of England and recording

109

u	ʌ	ʌ	ʌ	ʌ	ʌ
u	u	ʌ	ʌ	ʌ	ʌ
u	u	u	ʌ	ʌ	ʌ
u	u	u	u	ʌ	ʌ

Highest socio-economic group

Lowest socio-economic group

North   South

Figure 9.1

their socio-economic group one could produce a matrix for a feature of the language such as the pronunciation of the vowel in the word *bus*. In simplified form, such a matrix might resemble Figure 9.1. This would show that the higher a person is on the social scale, the more likely they are to use the southern /ʌ/, this also being the vowel of the more prestigious standard. It shows that there is less regional variation at the highest social level; to reflect this, the situation is often represented by means of a truncated triangle (see Figure 9.2). This latter representation removes the relationship between upper-class individuals and the spatial dimension, but it serves to emphasise the relatively short linguistic distance between individuals of the upper classes.

Generally, then, people in higher socio-economic groups – and perhaps some who aspire to be in such groups – have an idiolect that is less conditioned by the region in which they grew up, that approximates more closely to a standard variety. This is likely to be a variety that they were exposed to by parents and friends. In Britain it may have been consolidated by a public school education. Their profession may require the use of a standard form of speech. They

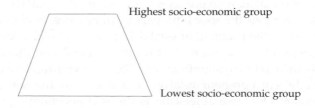

Highest socio-economic group

Lowest socio-economic group

Figure 9.2

are likely to be geographically mobile. Thus, as Figure 9.1 suggests, it is likely to be easier to identify a bus driver's region of origin than a judge's. And because the standard language is based on the speech of the south of England it is likely to be easier to distinguish between a judge and a bus driver in Bolton than between a judge and a bus driver in Brighton.

We saw in section 8.2 that dialects are not divided by the sharp boundaries suggested by isoglosses. A glance at Figure 9.1 makes it clear that the situation becomes much more complex still when one introduces the social dimension. The isogloss in Figure 8.4 is less valid for upper-class speech, for at the higher social levels the southern features will be widely used to the north of the line. Similarly, High German is widely spoken to the north of the isoglosses shown in Figure 8.6. These isoglosses, then, represent a distinction at grassroots level, at the level of the stable rural population, a state of affairs that is greatly influenced by social factors.

9.2 The Standard Language

The higher one's social standing, then, the less likely one is to use a regional dialect, and the more likely one is to use a more standardised variety. This is in part due to the greater mobility of those on the higher social levels; the wider one's social and geographical horizons, the more one's speech and that of one's children will lose regional features. Another major factor is the prestige that is associated with the more standardised varieties; a judge's authority is likely to be lessened if he speaks a regional dialect.

It is this prestige that sets a **standard language** apart. Linguistically a standard language is just another dialect; its origins are usually as humble as those of the other dialects. But socially it has been elevated, put on a pedestal as the supreme variety. R. A. Hudson (1996, p. 33) specifies four characteristics of a standard language: it has been selected from among the varieties of the language, it has been codified, it is suitable for use as an official, written medium, and it has been accepted by 'the relevant population'. As it is codified, as it serves as a literary language, as it is perpetuated by the education system, the standard language tends to be conservative, these factors acting as a brake on change. Being codified, it can be used as a yardstick for assessing a person's 'correctness'. A standard language can also serve as a symbol of nationhood.

As the nation states in Europe developed, the centralised govern-ments, assisted by the invention of printing, spread the use of a particular variety. As one might expect, the variety that rose to assume the role of the prestigious ideal was often that of the seat of power. As we have seen, Standard British English is more akin to the speech of southern England than that of northern England, the seat of power being in the south. For similar reasons the speech of the region centred on Paris, Francien, became the prestigious variety in France. Often, then, the standard form of a language is based on the speech of the educated inhabitants of the capital city; in the case of Danish, for example, 'the most prestigious pronunciation is that of an educated Copenhagener' (Haugen, 1976, p. 39). In Italy, however, it was Florence rather than Rome that provided the prestigious variety; Italy has only been a political entity since the second half of the nineteenth century and the status of the speech of Florence goes much further back, to the Renaissance. The prestige may, then, have its roots in cultural rather than political influence. A variety may become a standard language as the result of being adopted as a religious norm; standard German and standard Arabic are in large part the result of a particular variety being selected as the form for the Bible of Martin Luther and the form of the Koran respectively. Often, of course, the development of a standard will be influenced by a greater complexity of factors than the above suggests; the spread of Luther's East Central German, a variety of High German, was, for example, made easier by the decline of the Hanseatic League and with it the influence of Low German.

9.3   The Urban Vanguard

At the beginning of the last section I referred to mobility and the expectations of the professions as factors which tend to further the use of the standard language or varieties close to it. Such factors tend to affect urban areas rather than rural areas.

This complicates yet further the attempt to represent on a map boundaries between features, for rather than advancing by pushing forward a front, standardisation often establishes itself in urban centres and then spreads from them into the surrounding area. Thus isoglosses may show urban islands surrounded by unaffected rural areas. Trudgill (1995, p. 149) illustrates this state of affairs by comparing the speech of London, Manchester and Hyde. The city of Manchester exhibits the vowel /u/ where London has /ʌ/, the word *such* being pronounced /sutʃ/ in the former as opposed to /sʌtʃ/ in the latter, but the differences are systematic; in Hyde, which lies immediately to the south-east of Manchester, there was not the same influence from London, and the forms were less predictable. Keller (1978, p. 376) tells us that following the work of Martin Luther in the early sixteenth century High German was adopted as the official language by a succession of northern cities and that it was later adopted as the spoken media of the bourgeoisie.

9.4 Men and Women

A person's speech, then, tends to relate to his social class, to his education and occupation. City-dwellers may speak differently compared to those who live in the surrounding rural areas. Also of relevance to our speech is whether we are a man or a woman.

Many studies have shown that women generally use forms which approximate more closely to those of the standard language than do men of the same social background, age, and so on. In his study of the variable /iŋ/ vs. /in/ in the verbal ending *-ing* in the speech of his native Norwich, for example, **Peter Trudgill** found that women were more likely to use the standard form /iŋ/ than men were (Trudgill, 1995, p. 70).

Trudgill showed, moreover, that women were more likely to believe that they use forms closer to the standard language than those they actually use. This has been explained in terms of a greater consciousness of status on the part of women. The status of men, it has been argued, has been traditionally defined by their occupation and wealth, while women have had to find other ways of establishing their position and one of these has been their speech. Women are expected to behave better than men; traditionally, just as society has been harsher on women with regard to such vices as promiscuity and drunkenness, a better standard of language may have been required. Now that women are in employment much more, one can argue that they tend to work in service industries where a high standard of communication is particularly important.

On the other hand, the spread of sexual equality may be eroding many of these factors. Perhaps women are increasingly feeling that they do not have the same need to impress, to justify themselves. If so, they might move towards the less formal style of speech that has been more associated with men who, to quote Trudgill, 'are at a subconscious or perhaps simply private level very favourably disposed towards non-standard speech forms', a situation that has been ascribed to a greater concern with group solidarity than with the desire to rise on the social scale. Men may associate masculinity with the physical labour of the working class. It may be coarse language that helps you attain your social goal when that goal is to be 'one of the lads'.

According to Hudson, this correlation between sex and style of speech must be regarded as 'one of the most robust findings of socio- linguistics' (Hudson, 1996, p. 194).

9.5   Power and Solidarity

Women, then, tend to want to give an impression of high status more than men do. Women are more concerned than men are with a vertical social dimension, men setting greater store than women by a horizontal social dimension, by group identity. In connection with these two dimensions sociolinguists use respectively the terms **power** and **solidarity**.

Whether it is power or solidarity that is more significant in a particular social relationship depends not only on who is speaking but also on whom the speaker is speaking to. *Hello, Lizzie* is an appropriate way of greeting a sister or friend called Elizabeth; if you were talking to the Queen of the United Kingdom it would be more appropriate to say *Good morning, Your Highness*. Saying *Hello, Lizzie* to the Queen would be considered extremely disrespectful. If you said *Good morning, Elizabeth* to your sister she might wonder what she had done to upset you. In a conversation with the Queen it is the rules associated with power that are the most relevant, there being a substantial difference in social status. In a conversation with your sister it is the rules of solidarity that apply. The former require a more formal speech variety than the latter do. If we want to be accepted by those 'above' us or to distance ourselves from those 'below' us we use more formal speech. Using formal speech with our equals might give them the impression that we consider ourselves better than them or, as we have just seen, that they have done something to upset us.

As we saw at the beginning of this chapter, our speech may be marked as more or less formal by the choice of vocabulary or by whether or not segments are elided. We may make our speech more formal by such means as avoiding the imperative and using more complex formulae; *May I see the photograph* is more polite than *Show me the photograph*.

If we wish to use a person's name when talking to or about them we need to decide whether it is appropriate to use their given name (e.g. Elizabeth) or their surname (e.g. Miss Smith). Whatever our social relationship we can, however, always address that person with *you*. In most European languages, on the other hand, there are two equivalents of the singular *you*, a formal form and an informal form. In French these are *vous* and *tu* respectively and the linguist often refers to these two varieties as the V form and the T form. The Spanish equivalents are *usted* and *tú*, the German ones *Sie* and *du*, the Russian ones вы and ты.

Generally the informal form is gaining ground as society becomes more egalitarian and the criterion of solidarity becomes more significant at the expense of that of power. In France, for example, it was once common for children to address their father, a figure of power, with *vous*, but now most address their father with *tu*, the determining factor being that he is a close relative.

In some oriental languages such as Japanese and Korean the relationship between the speaker and the person to whom he is speaking has to be reflected more extensively in the form of the utterance. In Japanese verbs have a basic form and a polite form; *imasu*, an equivalent of *to be*, has a deferential form, *irasshaimasu*, that elevates the person being spoken to and a humble form, *orimasu*, that indicates the modesty of the speaker.

A noun may be prefixed by *o-* as a mark of respect for the addressee; if a person is asking somebody what his name is he may say *o-namae* rather than just *namae*.

Our relationship with somebody may affect not only how we address him but also what we say. If somebody rings you on the telephone you may feel an obligation to ask him/her how he/she is if that person is a friend. Here we are touching on the rules governing a conversation, the requirements that our social values impose on what we say and how we say it. This is an area of study called **discourse analysis**.

9.6   Registers and Diglossia

If we are talking to a judge we may be in court, perhaps as a lawyer, perhaps as a witness. If we are talking to a friend we may be playing golf or discussing a personal problem. Thus, related to the consideration of who we are talking to is the consideration of the social context in which we are talking. We interact with others in many different situations. I am an employee, a colleague and a teacher, a son, a husband and a father, a member of an archery club, a neighbour and a dental patient. While differences reduce as society becomes less formal, my speech will vary somewhat between roles. A speech variety that is appropriate to a limited social context is known as a **register**. Alternating between registers is known as **code-switching** or **style-switching**.

Such alternation means that once again we need to refine the diagrams presented in chapter 8. We have seen that there are no clear-cut guidelines for grouping the speech of individuals into dialects and languages. Now we are seeing that even the speech of the individual, the idiolect, is variable. The postman from Preston and the doctor from Dover represented in Figure 8.1 will use different registers when talking to members of their family and when talking to members of the public in the course of their work. We should, then, now refine that diagram as shown in Figure 9.3 to reflect the fact that their speech can vary over a range of formality, the <A> being at the centre of the range of the postman and the <B> being at the centre of the range of the doctor.

Trudgill's study of the variation between /iŋ/ and /in/ in Norwich showed that it correlated not only with the social class of the speaker but also with the formality of the situation. Middle-class people generally use the standard /iŋ/ in casual speech, whereas working-class people generally use the non-standard /in/. All groups increase their use of /iŋ/ in formal speech, particularly those in the middle class, those who had already preferred it in casual speech (Trudgill, 1995, pp. 93–4).

These findings reflect those of the pioneering studies of the American sociolinguist **William Labov** who examined the speech of the Lower East Side of New York in the 1960s, looking at the articulation of a number of phonemes that varied between individuals and, indeed, between the registers of the one individual. In New

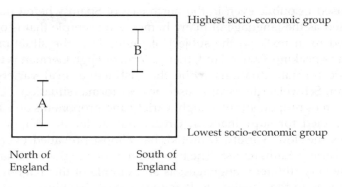

Figure 9.3

York the initial phoneme of the word *think* may be articulated as /t/. Labov found that the middle class – the highest class that is normally found in the district – produced /θ/ in over 80 per cent of cases when speaking in a formal register, and he found that the incidence of /t/ increased with people in a lower social position and at every level increased in less formal registers.

Clearly if a person uses an informal variant of a particular feature there is a greater chance that they will use informal variants of other features in the same utterance. If a New Yorker says *He's thinking* as opposed to *He is thinking* the likelihood that he will pronounce the word *thinking* with /t/ as opposed to /θ/ is increased. There tends, then, to be co-occurrence of features. When such co-occurrence is so systematic that there are two distinct varieties for formal contexts and informal contexts respectively, we can say that there is a state of **diglossia**. Where there is diglossia the social position of the speaker may not be a significant factor, the choice of variety being determined principally by the degree of formality of the context. One may argue that there is diglossia in the south of France, for example; Dennis Ager (1990, p. 45) tells us that Occitan, the long-established variety spoken to the south of the isogloss in Figure 8.5, is used in the home and in informal situations while French is used in formal situations and in administration, that Occitan is used to speak of basic human needs and during leisure activities while French is used to speak of intellectual matters. Further south, on the other side of the Pyrenees, the repressive centralist policies of Franco in the middle of the twentieth century resulted in Spanish being the language used in public even in the north-east of Spain where Catalan persisted as the language of many homes. An example that is often referred to in texts on the subject of diglossia is the situation in German-speaking Switzerland; there a form of High German is used in more formal situations while the distinctive local variety of German, Schweizerdeutsch, is used in less formal situations. Until recent times proponents of a 'high' variety and proponents of a 'low' variety vied for supremacy in Greece but under the democratic regimes the 'low' variety, Dimotiki, has almost prevailed over the 'high' variety, Katharevusa. The two varieties of a diglossic situation may be very different languages; as an example of this reference is often made to the situation in Paraguay where the 'high' variety is Spanish, the language of the former colonial power, and the 'low' variety is Guaraní, the indigenous language. In former colonial societies there may be a 'high' variety that is, or is close to, Standard English, Standard French, and so on, and a 'low' variety that is a creole (see section 10.7) that is lexically based on the standard. 'High' and 'low' varieties may also be referred to as **acrolects** and **basilects** respectively.

9.7   Taboo and Political Correctness

Some terms are rarely used in formal contexts because they are socially unacceptable in such contexts. You might use the word *crap* when talking to a friend but you would not do your employment prospects much good if you used it in a job interview. Such 'four-letter words' often denote sexual organs, sexual intercourse or, as in the case of *crap*, the expulsion of the body's waste material. The sensitive areas will vary from society to society depending on their values. They may involve death or religion. When Scandinavians swear they often refer to the Devil. As we saw in section 3.7, such socially sensitive terms are called **taboo** words.

   As alternatives to using taboo words we can either use medical terms (if respectable doctors use them they must be acceptable!) or evasive terms. Thus acceptable alternatives to *piss* are *urinate* and *pass water*. If, like me, one were particularly considerate, one might even use such constructions as *expel the body's waste material*! This is not a new phenomenon; what is *to relieve himself* in the New English Bible (the first book of Samuel, chapter 24) was *to cover his feet* in the

King James Version. We can avoid profanity by amending a word or phrase; thus *heck* can be used instead of *hell*, *jeepers creepers* can be used instead of *Jesus Christ*. Such alternatives to unacceptable terms are known as **euphemisms**. In *The Linguist* (no. 5, 1995), the journal of the Institute of Linguists, the translation specialist Peter Newmark suggested that a euphemism might be defined as 'an inoffensive or embellishing word or phrase substituted for one considered offensive, frightening or hurtful, especially one relating to religion, sex, crime, death, drunkenness, violence, excretion, mental health and serious diseases'.

The French verb *baiser*, once meaning *to kiss*, came to denote a more intimate activity, with the result that an alternative, *embrasser*, came to be used to denote kissing. A euphemism may be evasive, discreet, but if it is to be of use it must, like any other word, be unequivocably associated with the concept that it denotes. Most people understand that *sleeping with somebody* implies something more stimulating than getting a good night's rest beside somebody else. This being the case, the euphemism can through time become as tainted as the term that it replaced. Thus a concept may be denoted by a succession of terms. In a work published in 1974 Geoffrey Leech gave the word *nigger* as a denigratory equivalent of *negro* (Leech, 1974, p. 52); now, a quarter of a century later, many would be unhappy with *negro* and would prefer a term such as *black*, *coloured person*, or *Afro-Caribbean*.

We have now entered the field of **political correctness**. As society becomes more egalitarian, more liberal, we are less sensitive to terms related to sex and other bodily functions but more sensitive to the concerns of the disadvantaged; people with deficient eyesight, for example, are now often described by the phrase *visually impaired* rather than *blind*. *Crap* is on the way in, *cripple* is on the way out.

At the end of section 9.5 I wrote 'to ask him/her how he/she is' in the style of those concerned about the traditional practice of using the masculine term to refer to people of either gender. Elsewhere I have for the most part followed that traditional practice, partly because I do not like anticipating the changes in our language, partly because such pairs as *he/she* are cumbersome and partly because I do not like the alternatives suggested; *(s)he*, for example, cannot be used in the spoken language and it is alien to the English language to bracket part of a word. It is perhaps a pity that the third-person singular pronouns force us to choose one gender or the other. Finnish uses one pronoun, *hän*, to refer to both men and women, and indeed we make no distinction in the plural: *they* tells us nothing about the gender of the people referred to. Indeed a few paragraphs back I resorted to another way out that we use, substituting the plural pronoun *they* for the singular *a person*.

9.8 Slang

Taboo words are often avoided because they are unacceptable in many social situations. Other words may not be widely used because they are not even known to most people. A section of society may wish to reinforce its identity and exclude other people. The social élite may do so by such means as social etiquette. Linguistically it may do so by adherence to the standard language. Other sections of society may strive to achieve the same end by going to the other extreme, by using a variety that is so different from the standard language that it cannot be easily understood by the uninitiated. Such a variety is **slang**. When slang is used to conceal the activities of a group of people such as criminals it may be called **argot**.

One example of slang is the rhyming slang associated with the East End of London. This refers to an object, action, and so on by using a phrase which rhymes with the standard term; thus a telephone may be referred to as a *dog and bone*. The exclusivity may be increased by omitting the element that rhymes with the standard term; thus a Londoner may refer to his friend or mate as his *china*, the first element of the phrase *china plate*. Some examples, on the other hand, have been more widely adopted to the extent that people are often unaware that the word has its origins in rhyming slang; many people will not be aware, for example, that when they say the phrase *use your loaf* as an alternative to *use your head* they are using an abbreviated form of *loaf of bread*.

Another example is to be found in French which has a form of slang known as *verlan*. The basis of this form of slang is the inversion of syllables and the word *verlan* is itself an example, it being the slang equivalent of *l'envers* meaning *the reverse*. Other examples include *tromé* instead of *métro* and *renpats* instead of *parents*.

In a similar way certain ethnic groups may revert to a creole. In the 1950s and 1960s immigrants to Britain from the Caribbean brought with them varieties such as Jamaican creole. Over time this generally approximated towards standard English. Some, however, particularly the young, who feel themselves to be marginalised by society, may turn back towards the creole, in so far as it can be readopted, in order to have an alternative identity.

Some of today's slang words will eventually be elevated to the standard language. Some will disappear. Slang words are an aspect of language that is particularly prone to change. Language change is the topic of the next chapter.

Summary

A person's speech is influenced not only by where he grew up but also by his social background. At the higher social levels there are standardising factors which result in less regional variation. The most uniform and prestigious variety is the standard language, the variety that is used in official contexts, the variety that provides the written norm. The standard language has generally been elevated from amongst other dialects because it was the dialect of a centre of influence. People who live in cities and women tend to approximate more closely to the standard language than do people who live in rural areas and men.

A person's speech is also influenced by whom he is speaking to; if the two people concerned have a 'power' relationship the speech will be more formal than if they had a 'solidarity' relationship. The significance of this depends on the formality of the society concerned. Our speech varies between social situations. Where two distinct varieties exist for formal and informal situations we may say that there is a state of diglossia.

Some terms are avoided in formal situations because they may cause offence; such terms are taboo words. Instead, euphemisms or politically correct forms are used. Some terms are not widely used because they are exclusive to certain social groups; such terms are slang.

Exercises

9.1 Why is it likely to be easier in the north of England than in the south of England to determine from their speech whether people are hospital porters or surgeons?

9.2 Why might a person avoid using the standard language?

9.3 There are various suggestions why women tend to approximate more closely to the standard language than men do. What do you consider to be relevant factors? Why?

9.4 List five words or phrases which you would say to a friend but not to your doctor. Against each give an equivalent that you would say to the doctor.

9.5 If you wanted somebody to close a window, what might you say if (a) you wanted your brother to do it, (b) you wanted a lecturer to do it?

10

Historical Linguistics

or
How Wostow that I Was Nat an Astronaut?

10.1 The Diachronic Dimension

Instead of the standard *How do you know that . . . ?* a native of
Aberdeen in Scotland might say *Fit wye div ye ken that . . . ?* An
Aberdonian is more likely to use his local form if he is a bus driver
than if he is a judge. Both are more likely to use the local form with
friends than in a courtroom. As we have seen in the last two
chapters, language varies between regions, between social classes
and between social situations. Thus an item of language – a word, a
syntactic structure, and so on – may occur within a certain area of a
grid that has regional variation and social variation as its axes (see
Figure 10.1).

Such a grid represents a contemporary state of affairs. If we want
to understand how such a state of affairs has come about, if we want
to know whether it is fairly static or whether it is evolving, it is of
great help to look at a third dimension, that of time. It may be that
the situation is very much as it was, say, 500 years ago, in which case
it could be represented by Figure 10.2. An item may have changed
and expanded its regional and/or social domain (Figure 10.3). It
may not have existed 500 years ago (Figure 10.4). In addition, it may
well have changed its phonological form and its semantic range.

When we study language as it exists at any given point in time we
are looking at it from a **synchronic** point of view. When we consider
how it has changed over time we are looking at it from a **diachronic**
point of view. Those who study language from this latter point of
view are working in the field of **historical linguistics**. Section 10.2

123

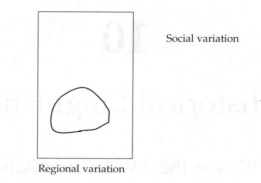

Social variation

Regional variation

Figure 10.1

looks at ways in which language changes. Section 10.3 looks at some of the forces that give rise to changes.

10.2 How Language Changes

Where we say *How do you know that . . . ?* Geoffrey Chaucer might have said *How wostow that . . . ?* From this we can see two or three differences between the English of the fourteenth century and that of today. The verb *witen,* a cognate of German *wissen,* has disappeared, leaving only a few traces in such words as *unwittingly.* The syntax of

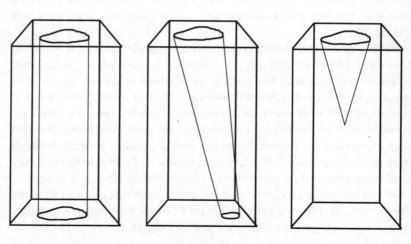

Figure 10.2   **Figure 10.3**   **Figure 10.4**

questions has changed, the inversion of subject and verb having given way to the use of *do* as an auxiliary verb. In section 7.4 we saw that Chaucer wrote 'How lyketh thee my wyf and hir beautee?' Here again we see a question being formed by the inversion of subject and verb. In this case the subject is *my wyf*, the verb *lyke* being used as we use the verb *please* today. It therefore follows that the verb is in the third person, this being indicated by the morph *-eth*. We no longer distinguish number or case for the second-person pronoun; we use *you* throughout. The pronunciation of the long vowels has changed since Chaucer's time; he would, for example, have pronounced the vowel in the word *wyf* as /iː/, as opposed to the diphthong /ai/ that most of us use today. The word *beautee* is a French import; 500 years earlier an Anglo-Saxon poet would probably have used the Germanic *fægernis*, the word that has come down to us as *fairness*. These are a few examples of a myriad of changes – semantic, phonological, morphological, syntactic – that have constituted the evolution of the living organism that is the English language.

The lexemes of a language, the cells of the vocabulary, may expand their semantic range at the expense of others. The word *fowl* once had the broad semantic range that has now passed to the word *bird*, which once denoted a young bird in particular; while the King James Bible tells us that God said that there should be 'fowl that may fly above the earth' (Genesis, chapter 1, verse 20) the New English Bible tells us that He said 'and let birds fly above the earth'. The semantic range of *fowl* has, then, been subjected to narrowing, that of *bird* to extension. The semantic range of a word may undergo a change of status; the word *knight* has been elevated, its Old English ancestor *cniht* having denoted a youth or servant (cf. German *Knecht*). A word may fall out of use altogether, as we have seen with Middle English *witen*.

The phonological form of words changes. The word *bird* has evolved from Middle English *brid*. This inversion of segments is known as **metathesis**. It is particularly common with the liquids [l] and [r]; the Latin words *periculosus* meaning *dangerous*, *marmor* meaning *marble* and *formaticum* meaning *cheese* (made in a mould) have given *peligroso* to Spanish, мрамор to Russian and *fromage* to French.

Words can change because people lose sight of where they start and finish. The word *adder* that denotes a kind of snake was known to Chaucer as *naddre* and Germans still use the word *Natter*. What has happened in English is that the phrase *a naddre* has been reanalysed as *an addre*. Similarly, the Swedish pronoun *ni*, meaning *you*, was originally *I*, the /n/ having been carried over from the verbal inflection that accompanied it. Changes that result from a misunderstanding of word boundaries in this way are examples of **metanalysis**.

In section 4.5 we saw that a sound may affect a neighbouring sound, that for example the final segment of the word *ten* becomes /m/ before the word *buns*, it becoming bilabial like the /b/. When such forces permanently affect a word, as opposed to only affecting it in certain phonological environments, they are relevant to historical linguistics. Similar **assimilation** is seen in the word *imbibe*, the prefix *in-* having become *im-* when the word was still Latin. The word *assimilation* itself exhibits assimilation, the prefix *ad-* having become *as-* before the initial sibilant of *similis* in Latin. In the case of *imbibe* the assimilation was partial, the /n/ changing to share its place of articulation with the /b/. In the case of *assimilation* the assimilation was total, the /d/ being replaced by a segment identical to that which followed. In both these cases the assimilation was regressive, a segment being dominated by a following one. The Italian equivalent of *woman*, *donna*, exhibits total regressive assimilation, it being a reflex of the Latin word *domina*. The French equivalent, *femme*, on the other hand, exhibits total progressive assimilation, the /n/ of the Latin *femina* having assimilated to the preceeding /m/.

Similarly, such forces as **palatalisation** and **nasalisation** can permanently alter lexemes. The French equivalent of *hundred*, *cent*, has been shaped by both; palatalisation has brought forward the place of articulation of the /k/ in the Latin *centum* under the influence of the following front vowel and that vowel has been nasalised under the influence of the /n/ before it disappeared from the spoken word.

Also lost, in this case from the written word as well, are the front vowels in former inflections that led to the vowels of *foot* and *food* being fronted in the plural form *feet* and the verb form *feed*. Such **mutation** is a distinctive feature of the Germanic languages.

Under the influence of neighbouring vowels consonants may be weakened. This weakening, or **lenition** (*lenis* is the Latin equivalent of *soft*), can change a voiceless consonant into a voiced one and a plosive into a fricative. Both these changes are seen in the Spanish word *vida* meaning *life* and the Danish word *vide* meaning *to know* for in both cases the intervocalic consonant evolved from /t/ to /ð/; the Spanish word is a reflex of Latin *vita* and the Danish word is a cognate of the Middle English word *witen*. A similar change accounts for the fact that it may be difficult to know whether an American or somebody from Northern Ireland is saying *writing* or *riding*.

Many phonological changes, then, are widespread, occurring commonly in particular environments. Sometimes a language experiences a wholesale shift in a large part of its phonological system. This happened to the long vowels of English in the fifteenth and sixteenth centuries, each vowel becoming more close, the highest becoming diphthongs as in the words *wife* and *house*. We call this shift the **Great Vowel Shift**. Long before, German had been subjected to a shift in its system of consonants, the **Second German Consonant Shift**. A major part of that shift was a form of lenition, the voiceless plosives becoming affricates or fricatives depending on their position in the word; thus what is *pipe* in English is *Pfeife* in German, what was *witen* in English is *wissen* in German.

With such shifts a whole series of segments generally changes to perpetuate an evenly spaced series of sounds which efficiently provides enough distinctive segments. But it may take a century or two for the symmetry to be restored. The shift may be initiated by a segment at one end of the series becoming more like its neighbour. They might coalesce or the neighbour might in turn move to maintain a distinction between the two segments, in which case a so-called **push chain** has been set in motion. If, on the other hand, the shift is initiated by a segment at one end drawing away from its neighbour and the other segments in the series move to fill the vacated domains we have a so-called **drag chain**. The vowel shift in English in the fifteenth and sixteenth centuries is often described as a drag chain shift (Potter, 1968, pp. 65–6; Barber, 1995, pp. 191–3), the most close vowels having been the first to move up.

Lexemes may in certain circumstances lose their independence and be reduced to the status of bound morphs. In the Romance languages the adverbs like Spanish *rápidamente* incorporate a bound element that was once the ablative form of the Latin word *mens*, meaning *mind*, the idea being that one is doing something in a particular frame of mind. As *mens* was of feminine gender the adverbial morph is affixed to the feminine form of the adjective. An equivalent of *I shall write to him quickly* in Spanish is *Le escribiré rápidamente*. In the future tense we again see an example of a lexeme being morphologised in the Romance languages for it originated in a construction in which the infinitive was followed by *habere*, meaning *to have*; cf. Spanish *escribir* meaning *to write* and *he* meaning *I have*. We may still see traces of the fact that the adverb and the future tense once comprised distinct lexemes. When two adverbs are used together Spanish only uses the adverbial morph in the second one; the equivalent of *I shall write to him quickly and affectionately* is *Le escribiré rápida y cariñosamente*. When a pronoun is used with the future tense in Portuguese the pronoun may be inserted between the infinitive and the future tense morph; thus *I shall write to him* may be *Escrever-lhe-ei*.

Conversely, there are many cases in which the Romance languages have developed free forms. An alternative to *escreverei* is *vou escrever*, *vou* belonging to the verb *ir*, meaning *to go*. *I have been writing the book* would be *Tenho escrito o livro* in Portuguese. With these compound tenses Portuguese, like other Romance languages, has developed functions for the verbs *ir* and *ter* that correspond closely to the way that we use *to go* and *to have* in the future tense and the perfect tense respectively. These forms are the result of slight semantic adjustments; in the future tense *to go* has lost the implication of physical movement and in the perfect tense *to have* has lost the implication of possession, the origins of this tense being in constructions like *I have the book; it is written*.

A major feature of the development of the Romance languages has been the general loss of the case system of Latin, its function having been assumed by such mechanisms as prepositions and word order. Similarly, English was not always as analytic as it is today. If we hear *Christ gives men a sign* we know who is giving the sign to whom because the convention in English that the subject should come before an indirect object is now more rigid and because the verb is in the singular. In Old English one also had the guidance of a case system; in the Old English equivalent, *Crīst ge-sweotolaþ mannum*, it is clear that it is the men who are on the receiving end because *mannum* is in the dative plural form.

This erosion of the case system facilitated the change in the use of the verb *to like* that we saw earlier in this chapter, it becoming less clear who pleases whom. A major example of syntactic change that we saw was the appearance of the verb *do* as a dummy auxiliary in questions and negated statements.

Before leaving this section, we might consider for a moment that an awareness of the ways in which lexemes change can allow us to amuse ourselves by exploring lexical labyrinths, by constructing extensive word webs that trace a wide variety of words back to a common source. Offspring that have survived the Middle English verb *witen* include the words *unwittingly* and *witness*. The semantic equivalence and an awareness of the sound shift that changed /t/ into /s/ between vowels in High German suggests that our old word *witen* is a relative of the German word *wissen*, meaning *to know*. From the node *wissen* we can link to such words as *Gewissen* which means *conscience* and has a very similar composition to this Latinate word: an element denoting knowledge prefixed by an element indicating comprehensiveness. In Scandinavia the cognate of *witen* has been digested in the equivalents of *somebody*, the original expression meaning something like *I do not know who*; this has produced, for example, *nokkur* in Icelandic. Our words *view* and *vista* are both derived from the feminine form of a Romance past participle of the equivalent of the verb *to see*, the one from French *vue*, the other from Italian *vista*. Thus they are offspring of Latin *videre* meaning *to see*. What we might find particularly surprising is that if we go far enough back we can establish a link between the web that includes *unwittingly* and that that includes *view*. We know because we see.

A word can travel abroad and, shaped by its travels, by the phonology of the language it stayed with, come back to rejoin its cousins. Old English had *weardian*, meaning *to protect*, this having developed into modern English *to ward (off)*. From a Germanic cognate of *weardian* French acquired *garder* which came into English as *to guard*. Swedish has *fällstol* meaning *folding chair* and its well-travelled cousin *fåtölj* meaning *armchair*, the latter being derived from the French lexeme *fauteuil* which in turn was derived from a Germanic lexeme for a folding chair.

10.3 Why Language Changes

We have seen that some phonological changes are widespread, occurring in many languages. The more widespread they are, the greater the justification for proposing some underlying physiological factor. In many cases such a factor may be ease of articulation. Having been introduced in chapter 4 to the mechanics of the production of speech sounds we are in a position to appreciate that certain combinations of segments are easier to articulate than others. There is a tendency for intervocalic voiceless plosives to be subjected to lenition because producing a voiced fricative between vowels requires less physiological change than does the production of a voiceless plosive. With voiced fricatives the vocal cords can continue to vibrate throughout a sequence of segments and the airstream is not interrupted by plosion. Similarly, ease of articulation lies behind assimilation and palatalisation. When saying the name *Edinburgh* it is easier to articulate the nasal segment as bilabial /m/ before the bilabial /b/ as your lips can stay in the same position for both segments (hence the French spelling of the name of this city: <Édimbourg>). When we talk of the *city of Edinburgh* we have an example of palatalisation, the initial segment having moved forward from the /k/ of Latin *civitas* so that the tongue is in a better position to move on to the front vowel that follows.

We may discard segments altogether; this may happen, for example, in a consonant cluster, as in the word *castle* that we pronounce as /kaːsl/ or /kæsl/. We may, indeed, discard a substantial part of the word, perhaps only in a colloquial context as with *bike* or generally as with *bus* (just as well when one imagines a highway engineer trying to paint the word *omnibus* across a bus lane!). And as for *veterinary surgeon*, is it any wonder that we usually settle for *vet*? The Danes reduced the word *automobil* to *bil*. The Swedes may call an electric locomotive an *ellok* and a stationmaster a *stins*, a blend contracted from *stationsinspektor*. In discussions of the omission of parts of words one may encounter such terms as **apocope**, which denotes the omission of a final element of a word, and **syncope**, which is the omission of an internal element of a word.

Simplification can proceed until the language is in danger of losing the distinctions that it requires to fulfil its function of efficient communication, communication with a minimum of misunderstanding. When there is scope for simplification linguists may talk of **redundancy**. One clear candidate for simplification is grammatical gender. In Old English the ancestor of the word *moon* was masculine, that of the word *sun* was feminine and that of the word *house* was neuter; in German the words *Mond*, *Sonne* and *Haus* are still masculine, feminine and neuter respectively. These Old English nouns took different forms depending on the case required; *sunne* and *hus*, for example, had the forms *sunnan* and *huses* in the genitive singular.

Since then English has abandoned grammatical gender for nouns and abandoned most of the case system. We retain the genitive in, for example, *the house's roof*, something that we could abandon in favour of *the roof of the house*. We retain gender and case with pronouns. We only have gender in the case of personal pronouns, *he* and *she*, and if we can get by without it in the plural we should be able to do so in the singular. As far as case is concerned, we retain it in the pronouns, but again we can argue that we can do without the distinction between *I* and *me* if *you* can serve both as subject and object. Do we need the indefinite article *a*? Welsh manages without an indefinite article. So do Arabic and Russian. The Russian equivalent of *I am not an astronaut* is as minimal as я не космонавт, literally *I not astronaut*. Steven Pinker (1994, p. 181) gives a nice illustration of redundancy by pointing out that we can understand what he is writing 'xvxn xf x rxplxcx xll thx vxwxls wxth xn "x"'. Arabic script proves the point.

We can see such redundancy causing variations in our contemporary language. I have used the object form *whom* in this chapter but it increasingly seems pedantic, at least when it does not follow a preposition. *Between you and me* alternates with *between you and I*. Judging by the misuse (if I may be so prescriptive!) of the apostrophe, it seems that it may be no more necessary to distinguish in writing between the possessive *banana's* and the plural *bananas* than it is in speech. Such variation may be indicative of change in progress.

We speak not only of *the house's roof* but also of *the sun's rays*, this despite the fact that the genitive form of *sunne* was *sunnan*. Having done away with gender, we have taken one genitive form and applied it generally. So, too, the nominative plural form of *sunne* was *sunnan*; we now say *suns*, having generalized the plural morph of such masculine words as *cnihtas*, meaning *youths*. This is an example of **analogy**, another development that can be ascribed to the minimisation of effort in that it produces a system that is easier to learn and remember. Young children go through a stage in which, having discerned a pattern, they apply it comprehensively, saying things like *The mans goed in the house*, before they discover that there are some words to which the general pattern does not apply. Irregularities tend to persist when they are so common that there is little chance of us forgetting them, as with the plural form *men* and the past tense of the verb *to go*. But occasionally an analogical form establishes itself and remains; in Old English and Middle English the past participle of the ancestors of the verb *to help* was *holpen*, it having since been regularised to *helped*.

When we have reduced the linguistic distinctions to the bare minimum we still receive guidance from the context of the utterance, from our experience of life. As we have already observed, if we read on a butcher's door *Sorry, no dogs* we do not conclude that he has run out of mongrel meat. If we read on the packaging of some product *Keep out of the reach of children* we understand that it is the product that is dangerous, not children.

But clearly the loss of distinctiveness may nevertheless reach a point where there is a danger of confusion. It has been suggested that Cinderella came to lose a glass slipper because the French word for squirrel fur, *vair*, had coincided phonologically with the word for glass, *verre*. This is an example of **homonymic clash**. Where such a clash is deemed unacceptable an alternative to one of the words may come into use. English once used the verb *to let* both in the sense of to allow and to obstruct; as these senses are so contradictory there was a real danger of confusion and *to let* in the sense of to obstruct gave way, remaining only in one or two instances such as the phrase *without let or hindrance*.

Language also changes because the communities in which it is spoken change. Different cultures come into contact, one perhaps dominating another. Society's values change. New discoveries and inventions have to be named.

The Anglo-Saxons were joined in England by Danes. These Germanic peoples spoke varieties that had not yet diverged so much that they were mutually unintelligible. But the differences in inflections caused complications. It has been suggested that contact with the Danes not only gave the English language new words such as *take* and *die*, the former ousting *niman* and the latter narrowing the semantic range of *steorfan* which became our *starve*, but also contributed to the erosion of its case system.

The arrival of the Normans in the eleventh century had a much more significant effect on English. English was much more different from Norman French than it had been from the Norse tongue of the Danes. Society was largely split between the Norman masters and the Saxon subjects, the former continuing to speak Norman French and the latter continuing to speak English. Both these factors – the great linguistic divide and the great social divide – initially limited the extent to which English was influenced by Norman French. When through time the social division broke down the English language reasserted itself. But it was now an English influenced by Norman French, particularly in those fields of activity that had been the preserve of the Norman masters: administration, the law, chivalry, hunting, and so on. Thus in the fourteenth century Chaucer wrote *jugement* as well as *doom*, *beautee* as well as *fairnesse*. The social divide is reflected in the fact that animals are generally known by the Germanic terms, the resultant meats by the French terms: the masters ate what the peasants reared. In the novel *Ivanhoe* by Sir Walter Scott we can read the following:

> 'Nay, I can tell you more,' said Wamba in the same tone: 'there is old Alderman Ox continues to hold his Saxon epithet while he is under the charge of serfs and bondsmen such as thou, but becomes Beef, a fiery French gallant, when he arrives before the worshipful jaws that are destined to consume him. Mynherr Calf, too, becomes Monsieur de Veau in the like manner: he is Saxon when he requires tendance, and takes a Norman name when he becomes matter of enjoyment.'

The lexemes derived from French, then, often co-existed with those derived from Old English, the former perhaps having narrowed the semantic range of the latter. The semantic range of a lexeme in the one language may be influenced by that of a lexeme in the other. This happened to the Middle English verb *faren* which in Old English had meant *to go*, *to travel* but came to mean *to behave* as well under the influence of what was to become the French verb *faire*; in *The Canterbury Tales* Chaucer wrote, for example, 'Ye fare as folk that dronken been of ale.' The dialect in which Chaucer wrote, East Midland, became a prestigious dialect, not because it was the dialect used by Chaucer so much as because it was the dialect of the nation's capital city, London.

In the last chapter we saw some of the social factors that are influencing the development of the language today, such factors as taboo, equality and group identity.

In conclusion we can look at a fairly widespread example of how a society's values may be reflected in its language. In the past people's wealth was closely associated with the amount of livestock that they owned and this association is seen in many languages. In Old English the word *feoh* denoted both money and cattle; it has come down to us as the word *fee* and it is a relative of the German word *Vieh* meaning *cattle*. A more distant relative, the Latin word *pecus*, denoted livestock and has given us our word *pecuniary*. (Here we can see another word web developing!) In Spanish the word for cattle, *ganado*, is also the past participle of the verb *ganar* meaning *to earn*. The Russian word for cattle, скот, once also denoted money or property, it being cognate with the German word *Schatz* meaning *treasure*.

10.4   When Language Changes

When we know what changes took place we can attempt a little linguistic archaeology to find out when they took place. We may be helped by knowing the date of a text, but sounds may be obscured by conservative spelling. The /k/ of Latin *centum* has evolved by way of /ts/ into the /s/ of French *cent* without this being reflected by any change in the character used to represent them. But if we look at German we see that the word *Keller*, meaning *cellar*, was adopted from the Latin word *cellarium* and that it was followed by the word *Zelle* with the affricate segment /ts/. English has adopted the word *chief* from Old French and its cognate *chef* from Modern French. If we can assume that the pronunciation of the initial segments has not changed since they came into English we can trace the development of Modern French /ʃ/ by way of /tʃ/ from Latin /k/ where it was followed by /a/, the source of these words being the Latin word *caput*. The assumption that a sound in a borrowed word has not changed since its adoption is, of course, hazardous. The word *fine* was adopted from French with the vowel /iː/, as was the word *machine*. Our conservative spelling has failed to reflect the fact that the vowel in the former has become the diphthong /ai/ as a result of the vowel shift in English referred to in section 10.2. Thus if we know when we started to use these two words we have an indication of when the vowel shift was initiated by the diphthongisation of the long close vowels.

The resultant form of a word can tell us whether one change happened before or after another. The French word *cent*, pronounced /sã/, now has a nasalised vowel and no nasal consonant; as the nasal consonant, /n/, caused the nasalization of the vowel, the nasalisation clearly took place before the loss of the /n/.

10.5 Divergence

At the end of section 10.2 I linked our word *unwittingly* with the German word *wissen* and I linked our words *view* and *vista*. I then suggested that if one delved far enough one could establish a relationship between all of these words. To find a lexeme that was a source of both *unwittingly* and *wissen* one might have to go back to a time before the Germanic peoples first came to England in the fifth century. One would have to go back to a similar point in time to find anything like the common ancestor of the French and Italian equivalents of *to see*. In the first case we are going back to some West Germanic tongue, in the other we are going back to Latin. To link all of these words together we need to go much further back in time in search of a source that gave rise to both the Germanic languages and Latin. The relationship between these languages can be shown in the form of a family tree (see Figure 10.5). Here, too, reality is less abrupt than our representation suggests. Synchronically, as we have seen in chapter 8, there are continua, and diachronically there is a gradual evolution; French, for example, gradually evolved from Latin rather than Latin giving birth to French. Thus the more steps we show on these two dimensions – for example Occitan on the synchronic dimension and Old French on the diachronic dimension – the truer would be the impression given. Having said this, the family tree is still very useful as a means of showing the lineage and the degree of relatedness of languages; Figure 10.5 shows clearly that Italian has

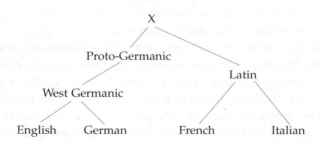

Figure 10.5

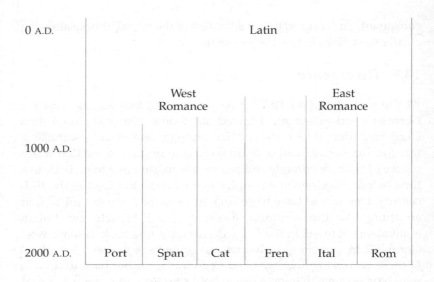

0 A.D.	Latin					
	West Romance			East Romance		
1000 A.D.						
2000 A.D.	Port	Span	Cat	Fren	Ital	Rom

Figure 10.6

evolved from Latin and that it is more closely related to French than to English. An alternative means of representing the evolution of languages is as shown in Figure 10.6.

Observing that the English word *foot* is similar to the German word *Fuß*, that the English word *father* is similar to the German word *Vater*, and concluding that the similarity could not reasonably be accounted for by coincidence was hardly a major achievement. So, too, with the French and Italian equivalents *pied* and *piede*, *père* and *padre*. The words in each pair must be derived from a common source or – less likely, particularly with terms for such basic elements of human life as parts of the body and kinship – one must be borrowed from the other. What was somewhat more laudable was the hypothesis that all these words that denote feet and fathers ultimately derive from common sources. The sound changes behind these correspondences were presented early in the nineteenth century by the Dane **Rasmus Rask** and the German **Jacob Grimm**, he who wrote fairy tales with his brother. They observed that words with /p/ in Latin tended to have /f/ in the Germanic languages; thus where Latin had *pes*, *pater*, and *pecus* English has *foot*, *father* and *fee*. They observed that, similarly, the voiceless stops /t/ and /k/ in

Latin correspond to /θ/ and /x/ in the Germanic languages. This series of correspondences became known as **Grimm's Law**.

Having established this, linguists in the nineteenth century were driven to attempt to delve into the mists of time and reveal the nature of the common ancestor of Latin and the Germanic languages, the X of Figure 10.5. This common ancestor pre-dated any written evidence. That being so, the linguists had to rely on the laws of sound change that they were developing, to decide which sound was most likely to have given rise to those in the subsequent languages. It is considered, for example, more likely that the Germanic fricatives /f, θ, x/ developed out of the plosives /p, t, k/ than that the Latin plosives developed out of the fricatives, for it is more common for consonants to weaken, to undergo lenition, than to strengthen, undergo fortition. Trask illustrates the process of reconstruction using a selection of western Romance lexemes (Trask, 1996, pp. 208–16).

Having embarked on the quest for the nature of this source language, it is natural to wonder where its speakers lived. It has been suggested that linguistic reconstruction – identifying those features of life and the environment which are denoted by related terms in the subsequent languages – supported by archaeological evidence, points towards a culture of what is now southern Russia. Common terms for flora and fauna have been adduced. But Bynon reminds us that the meaning of terms may change and concludes that the 'location of the Indo-Europeans in time and space must remain, for the time being at least, an open question' (Bynon, 1993, p. 280).

These speakers of the source language are called Indo-Europeans because they have left their mark not only on the Germanic languages and the offspring of Latin but also on most other languages in Europe and on languages as far away as India. The spread of their language may have been principally due to migrations of peoples or principally due to cultural transmission as, for example, the culture of agriculture spread. The source language is referred to as Proto-Indo-European. A family tree for all the principal **Indo-European** languages of Europe is given in the next chapter, in section 11.1.

If Proto-Indo-European produced Proto-Germanic, Latin and others, which in turn produced such languages as English and German, French and Italian, there has clearly been a process of divergence at work during the course of the several millenia since the days of Proto-Indo-European, a process similar in some ways to Darwin's theory of evolution that was launched on the world while linguists were exploring the history of the Indo-European languages. I shall conclude this section by focusing on the process that has resulted in us being unable to talk to Swedes.

Two thousand years ago there was a Proto-Germanic tongue. The Germanic people had not settled England. Those in Scandinavia had not yet developed significant linguistic differences compared to those further south. In the fifth century A.D. Germanic peoples crossed to England; the result was the variety known as Anglo-Saxon or Old English. By this time the Germanic people in Scandinavia were beginning to acquire distinctive linguistic characteristics, to develop the variety that we know as Old Norse. In an Old English text we can read such things as 'þā ge-wende Hinguar ēast mid his scipum', this meaning *Then Hinguar turned eastwards with his ships*. This shows us that at that stage English still had a case system; following the preposition *mid* we have the dative plural form *scipum*. Even today Icelandic uses the dative plural form *skipum*. It shows us, too, that English still observed the Germanic principle of word order that the verb should be the second element; as the first position in the sentence has been occupied by *þā* the subject *Hinguar* has fallen back behind the verb so that the verb can remain in the second position. Swedish has also abandoned the case system but the distance between English and Swedish today is due to changes in the former more than to changes in the latter. The Old English ancestor of our word *house* was *hūs* pronounced /hu:s/. It was of neuter gender and in the nomin- ative and accusative cases the plural form was the same as the singular form. Since then we have lost the gender distinction, this word has acquired the plural morph /iz/ by analogy with other declensions and, as we have seen, the vowel has become the diphthong /au/ as a result of the vowel shift of English. In Swedish, on the other hand, the word is still of neuter gender and it still has the same form in the plural as it does in the singular. The vowel has not been diphthongised but it has moved further forward. The Swedish phrase *mina hus* consequently resembles its 'aunt' Old English *mīnu hūs* more than the 'daughter' *my houses* does.

Not least as a result of the Norman Conquest, we have lost or marginalised a lot of the Germanic vocabulary that Swedish retains. Old English had *healm* meaning *straw*, *witan* meaning *to know*, *lǣce* meaning *(medical) doctor*, *stōl* meaning *seat*. We have lost *healm* and *witan*, we generally only use *leech* to denote the blood-sucking worm used by medieval doctors, and *stool* now denotes only the humblest of seats, the Normans prefering to use the word that has come down to us as *chair* to denote what they sat on. Allowing for changes in the real world in the course of a thousand years, Swedish still uses the words *halm*, *veta*, *läkare* and *stol* in much the same way as the Anglo-Saxons used *healm*, *witan*, *lǣce* and *stol*.

In Middle English the system of inflections was much weaker than it had been in Old English. Adjectives still added -e in the plural and following a determiner such as *this*. We have since eroded even this inflection but Swedish retains something very similar. Since Middle English we have, as we saw earlier, introduced the dummy auxiliary *do* into questions; Swedish still follows the old practice of inverting the subject and the verb, as we still do with the verb *to be* and the modal verbs.

While we say *Do you smoke?*, then, we still say *Are you rich?*, not **Do you be rich?*. There are usually some recesses that changes do not reach. While we no longer feel that we have to keep the verb in second position and while the plural form of nouns that were once neuter has long been assimilated to a common form, we still occa-sionally say things like *Never have I seen such skinny sheep*. While Swedish has abandoned the case system, the phrase *till sjöss*, meaning *at sea*, and others retain the genitive form.

10.6 Convergence

We are, then, unable to speak to Swedes because English and Swedish have generally grown further and further apart over the course of many centuries.

But Swedes now stick paper together with *tejp*, their repres-entation of our word *tape*. Industrial unrest in Sweden might result in a *strejk*. People on the move might listen to music using a *freestyle*. While we are exposed to very little Swedish in comparison with Swedes' exposure to English, we have acquired from Swedish the words *ombudsman* and *orienteering*.

So, while the languages have diverged, they have also influenced each other at a superficial level. This is particularly true in this age of aeroplanes, television and the Internet. But it is nothing new; the Danes were interacting with the English in the ninth century. They brought us words like *take* and *die*, affected our system of pronouns, and so on. As the Normans, as their name suggests, had Norse

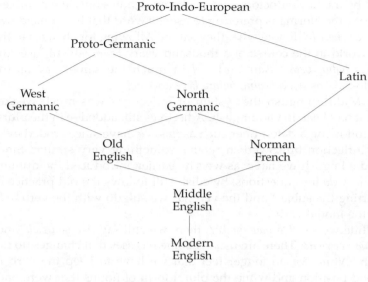

Figure 10.7

origins, the Norman Conquest brought us more Norse words by way of Norman French; *equip* ultimately comes from Old Norse *skipa*, it having undergone the French treatment of initial /s/ + consonant.

The family tree representation does not usually show interaction between branches. But it could do; the part of the Indo-European tree that is relevant to the above developments could be arranged as shown in Figure 10.7.

What cannot readily be illustrated by such a diagram is the spread of a particular feature from one language to other, perhaps very different, languages. The uvular /R/ spread from France, despite the distinction between Romance and Germanic languages, to the south of Sweden. There are Latin lexemes that spread to much of the empire, replacing older lexemes, but did not reach the extremes of the Roman world; thus, for example, as equivalents of *to eat* the Italians have *mangiare* and the Catalans have *menjar* from Latin *manducare*, but other Spaniards and the Portuguese have *comer* from the older Latin word *comedere*.

These are examples of **wave theory**. One linguist associated with this field was the Italian **Matteo Bartoli** who produced 'norme areali linguistiche' which serve as guidelines for determining the relative age of different forms which occur in neighbouring regions. Lateral areas, those with poorer communications with the centre of influence, will, for example, tend to have older forms, as we have just seen with the Romance equivalents of *to eat*. A larger region will tend to have older forms, but this norm may be overridden by the one above.

When languages share major features that transcend families it may be useful to arrange them by such features rather than by family. This is the study of **typology**. An example that is often used is the definite article in Albanian, Bulgarian and Romanian; each of these languages belongs to a different branch of the Indo-European family and yet each follows the minority practice of suffixing the definite article. This commonality has been ascribed to the heritage of Byzantium.

The significance of typology increases where it can be shown that one feature tends to co-exist with others. Languages with the word order verb–subject–object tend to put adjectives after the nouns that they qualify; this is seen in languages as different as Welsh and Mixtec, an indigenous language of southern Mexico. Languages with the word order subject–object–verb tend to place adjectives before nouns, this being true of, for example, Turkish and Japanese. The more typological correlations one can make like this, the greater our progress towards the quest for linguistic universals.

10.7 Pidgins and Creoles

As Figure 10.7 showed us, Middle English was the result of the fusion of Old English and Norman French as the Saxon and Norman societies merged. Being a language that developed to facilitate communication between two different cultures, it is considered by some linguists to be a **creole**, a creole being a language that may result when two cultures co-exist.

A creole usually develops out of a more limited **pidgin**. A pidgin is more limited in its functions and, consequently, linguistically. It may have arisen, for example, as a means of communication between traders from different cultures; the various suggested origins of the term *pidgin* include corruption by the Chinese of the English word *business* or the Portuguese word *ocupação*. Or it may have arisen in the context of slavery, as a means of communication between slave and master and/or between slave and slave. It often arose in the context of colonialism and the vocabulary is often largely based on that of the language of the colonial power concerned: English, Dutch, Portuguese, French, and so on. A pidgin typically lacks such features as grammatical gender, a copula and a passive construction. They generally lack articles and have a poorly developed system of prepositions. Pidgins have a small vocabulary, with the result that many things are denoted by circumlocution; to take an example from Romaine (1988, p. 35), hair is denoted by *gras bilong hed* in Tok Pisin in Papua New Guinea. They generally have little inflectional morphology. As a result of the small vocabulary and the lack of inflections, words are often used in what we consider to be different word classes.

Where a pidgin is spoken in a stable community such as a slave community it may become the only language of subsequent generations. Being the only language, it will need to meet all the linguistic requirements of its speakers, with the consequence that it will cater not only for such functions as receiving orders but also for such functions as phatic communion, expressing emotions, and so on. When this stage of development has been reached the pidgin has become a creole.

The development of the structure of different pidgins and creoles often follows a similar path and that path has many similarities to the course of language acquisition in children; the lack of articles and copulas in pidgins, for example, reflects the lack of such items in the speech of 24-month-old children. This has led many linguists to turn to pidgins and creoles in the hope of finding universal factors underlying language change and language acquisition.

Summary

The semantic range of a lexeme may change or a lexeme may cease to exist. Its phonological form may be changed by such processes as assimilation, palatalisation and lenition. Lexemes may become bound morphs. Syntactic changes include the widespread loss of a case system in western Europe.

Some changes are the result of minimising effort. There is some scope for this due to the redundancy that exists in language. Some changes are the result of historical or social developments.

As language has developed it has often diverged, one variety evolving in a differential way in different regions. It is generally accepted that a Proto-Indo-European language spoken several thousand years ago increasingly developed distinctive varieties leading to most of the languages of Europe. Such varieties continue, however, to influence each other after they have gone their separate ways, and features can spread between quite different languages.

Exercises

10.1 Give four reasons – one lexical, one phonological, one morpho-logical and one syntactic – why an Englishman of the tenth century might find the following question strange: 'Do the houses have a good view?'

10.2 The following is from *The Canterbury Tales*:

> And specially, from every shires ende
> Of Engelond, to Caunterbury they wende,
> The holy blisful martir for to seke,
> That hem hath holpen, whan that they were seke.

(a) The first *seke* is a verb, the second an adjective. What is the modern equivalent in each case? The adjective had the basic form *seek*; why is it inflected here?
(b) Why do we not have the word *holpen* in Modern English?

10.3 Give an example of semantic narrowing other than any given in this chapter. Can you suggest why it may have happened?

10.4 Which kind of change has taken place in the case of the following English words?
    apron < Old French *naperon*   *burn* < Middle English *brenne*

10.5 Account for the changes to the consonants in the following:
    Spanish *milagro* < Latin *miraculum*

10.6 Scots has the words *kirk* and *kist* as equivalents of standard English *church* and *chest*. What process has distinguished the initial segment of the standard English words from that of the Scots words?

10.7 Discuss the merits and limitations of a family tree diagram as a means of representing the synchronic and diachronic relationship between languages.

10.8 What arguments might be presented to support a view that Old English and Modern English are different languages?

11

The Languages of Western Europe

or
Hur Vet du att Jag inte Var Astronaut?

11.1 The Indo-European Family of Languages

Ten chapters have introduced us to the principal features of language. In this eleventh chapter I shall relate these features to the major languages of western Europe and thereby build up something of a profile of each language.

As we have seen, most of the languages of Europe are considered to have a common source, a hypothetical language spoken several thousand years ago, perhaps in what is now southern Russia. The process of evolution and differentiation since then has left us with the languages of today. The nature of this process is such that each language is more closely related to some languages than to others. French and Italian are relatively closely related, both having developed out of Latin. To find an ancestor common to both French and German or to both French and Russian one has to go much further back in time. This situation can be represented by a family tree diagram such as that shown in Figure 11.1. The Brittonic group of Celtic includes Welsh and Breton, the Goidelic group Irish and Scottish Gaelic. English, Dutch and German are West Germanic languages; Icelandic, Norwegian, Swedish and Danish are North Germanic languages. French, Catalan, Spanish and Portuguese are West Romance languages; Italian and Romanian are East Romance languages. The Baltic branch includes Lithuanian and Latvian and the Slavonic branch includes Russian, Ukrainian, Polish, Czech, Bulgarian and Serbo-Croat.

145

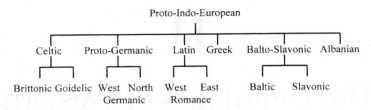

Figure 11.1

Figure 11.1 represents the principal extant Indo-European languages of Europe. There are other varieties that might be included such as Faroese, Frisian and Occitan. We shall be looking at the Germanic languages, the Romance languages and the Celtic languages, these being the groups that are relevant to western Europe. Having done that, we shall briefly make the acquaintance of one of the languages of Europe that is not a member of this family: Finnish.

11.2 The Germanic Languages

We begin with the Germanic languages, with the group of languages that includes English.

These languages grew out of the speech of the Germanic peoples in northern Europe. A change that did much to distinguish the speech of these peoples from that of other Indo-European peoples was the **First Germanic Consonant Shift**, the shift that we saw referred to as **Grimm's Law** in section 10.5. This shift changed the voiceless plosives /p, t, k/ into the fricatives /f, θ, x or ç/. Thus where Latin had *pater*, *tres* and *canis* English has *father*, *three* and *hound*. The /k/ that was retained in *canis* has also been retained by the Celtic languages. As a result the Scots Gaelic word for a dog sounds very similar to the Germanic Scots word for a cow, the one being *cù* the other *coo*. The words *cannabis* and *hemp* illustrate the Germanic development of /k/ – they are cognates which denote products from related plants. As the voiceless plosives developed into fricatives their quality was adopted by the voiced equivalents. Thus the numbers that the Romans knew as *duo* and *decem* are called *two* and *ten* by us. Our words *ignore* and *agnostic*, the one from Latin and the other from Greek, are cognates of our word *know* in which the <k> used to be heard. This shift took place well over two thousand years ago.

In the Germanic languages lexical variation is often the result of variation in the root vowel. We *ride* along a *road*, we *sing* a *song*. The German verb *klingen*, meaning *to sound, to ring*, is accompanied by the noun *Klang*. In Dutch the equivalent of *vowel* is *klinker* while the equivalent of *phonology* is *klankleer*. This is **vowel gradation** or, using the German term, **ablaut**. Gradation is seen in the strong verbs of the Germanic languages, those that form their past tense by a change of root vowel as opposed to an inflection. Thus, for example, the pattern *break – broke – broken* has similar counterparts in other Germanic languages; Dutch has *breken – brak – gebroken*, German has *brechen – brach – gebrochen*.

Another feature found throughout the Germanic languages that accounts for variations in vowels is **i-mutation**, this also being known by the German term **umlaut**. In this case the root vowel of a word has been fronted under the influence of a front vowel in an inflection. These inflections were often those of the plural forms of nouns, the comparative forms of adjectives and verbal forms. The inflection has often been lost since causing the change. Thus English has *feet* as the plural form of *foot*, *deem* as a verbal form of *doom* (which, as you may remember, was in Chaucer's day similar in meaning to *jugement*). In Swedish we find similar pairs: *fot* and *fötter*, *dom* and *döma*. It is interesting to note that this mutation links the noun *knot* and the verb *knit*.

The widespread erosion of inflections was in large part due to another feature of the Germanic languages, the fixing of stress on the initial or root syllable of the word. As was pointed out at the beginning of chapter 6, the Germanic word *manliness* has the stress on the first syllable, whereas the Latinate word *virility* does not.

The Germanic languages generally share a similar word structure. The German equivalent of *to examine* or *to investigate* is *untersuchen*, literally **under-seek*. The Dutch counterpart is *onderzoeken*, the Swedish *undersöka*.

As far as word order is concerned, the Germanic languages have a general principle that the verb should remain in second position. Thus if something other than the subject occupies first position the subject falls back behind the verb to allow the verb to remain in second position. That something may, for example, be an adverb or even a subsidiary clause. English has generally abandoned this principle but it is still seen in such sentences as *Never have I heard such a thing*.

Through time Proto-Germanic developed regional varieties that we call West Germanic, North Germanic and East Germanic. North Germanic, the Germanic of Scandinavia, for example, developed such features as the loss of initial /j/ (while English has *young* and German has *jung*, Danish has *ung*) and the addition of a determiner to the end of the noun (while English has *the boat* and German has *das Boot*, Danish has *båden*). As we have seen from the family tree of the Indo-European languages, West Germanic has given us English, Dutch and German, and North Germanic has given us Icelandic, Norwegian, Swedish and Danish. East Germanic has died out.

11.2.1 West Germanic

In the fifth century some Germanic peoples crossed to England and settled. These peoples were for the most part Angles and Saxons. The country was named after the Angles, *Englaland* (the Gaels in Scotland call it *Sasunn* after the Saxons) and the speech variety that they developed was called *Englisc*. Since that time, as we have seen, **English** has changed a great deal and we refer to their variety as Anglo-Saxon or Old English. In the late Middle Ages the English spoke Middle English and now we speak Modern English. (So how, you may wonder, will linguists of the future refer to any subsequent stage?)

Clearly there was no sudden break in the development of the language. With that understood, it is helpful to identify stages in the development. The necessarily arbitrary dates that we put on these stages are 1100 and 1500. 1100 serves to mark the transition from Old English to Middle English, a major factor in that transition being the Norman Conquest. Around 1500, when the Great Vowel Shift, the shift that raised the long vowels of English, was in progress, we have the transition to Modern English. Chaucer wrote in Middle English, Shakespeare in early Modern English.

Further details of the development of the English language have been given in chapter 10 and we now move on to its close foreign relatives.

A particularly close relative, as we might expect given that the Angles and Saxons came from north-western parts of the continent of Europe, is **Dutch**, *nederlands*. In section 8.3 we saw that a Dutchman might tell you that his book is under a clock by saying /mən buk iz ɔndər də klɔk/. That is an extreme example of similarity; if the similarity were always this great we would regard Dutch as a dialect of English or vice versa. English has, as we have seen, changed a lot since Old English; it has lost its case system, it has acquired Romance vocabulary from the Normans, it has undergone a major vowel shift. But then to some extent Dutch has followed a similar path. It too has lost the case system. It too has developed diphthongs from long close vowels; the Dutch equivalents of *five* and *house*, *vijf* and *huis*, are pronounced with /ɛi/ and /ʌy/. Although much less than English, Dutch has acquired lexemes of Romance origin; thus, for example, the equivalent of *holiday* or *vacation* is *vakantie*.

In other respects Dutch is closer to German. Both languages have, for example, so-called separable verbs, verbs with an element that is separated from the root in the present and past tenses. Thus the Dutch *afbreken*, meaning *to break off, to interrupt*, becomes *brak af* in the past tense, as in *Hij brak het gesprek af, He broke off the conversation*. In subordinate clauses the verb tends to come at the end of the clause. The past participle and the infinitive are preceded by their complements. Thus the equivalent of *He said that my dog had drunk the water* is *Hij zei dat mijn hond het water gedronken had*. Forming the past participle with the prefix *ge-* is another feature that Dutch shares with German. We still had a similar feature in Middle English; Chaucer wrote *Thou hast y-dronke so muchel hony . . .* A phonological similarity between Dutch and German is the fact that both devoice plosives and fricatives at the end of a syllable; *hond* is pronounced /hɔnt/.

Dutch, then, as one might expect from the geographical location of the region in which it is spoken, lies between English and German linguistically. Dutch nouns have gender but there is a much weaker distinction between masculine and feminine gender than there is in German; the definite article *de* is used for both. As in German the infinitive ends in <en> in the written language, but in Dutch one does not usually hear /n/ in this case. Dutch is in an intermediate position with regard to the retention of /n/ before a fricative; German retains it in *fünf* and *Mund*, English has lost it in its equivalents *five* and *mouth*, Dutch has lost it in *vijf* but retained it in *mond*. Dutch makes extensive use of the plural morph /s/.

At the end of this chapter there are sample texts to illustrate some of the distinctive features of certain major languages. They are followed by a translation into English and notes on some of the principal features. The first of these, text 11.1, represents Dutch.

Two features that distinguish **German** from both English and Dutch are its case system and its consonants. The first of these is conservative, the distinctiveness arising from the fact that German has retained a system that English and Dutch have abandoned. The second is progressive in that German experienced a major shift in its consonant system.

German has four **cases**: the nominative case that indicates the subject of a sentence, the accusative case that indicates the direct object, the genitive case that indicates possession and the dative case that indicates the indirect object. Thus in the equivalent of *The baker's child gave the teacher the letter*, *Das Kind des Bäckers gab dem Lehrer den Brief* the word *Kind* meaning *child* is in the nominative case, *Bäcker* meaning *baker* is in the genitive case, *Lehrer* meaning *teacher* is in the dative case and *Brief* meaning *letter* is in the accusative case. Only in the case of *Bäckers* does the form of the noun indicate the case. With the other nouns in this sentence only the definite articles indicate the case and even they are deficient; *das Kind* can be in the accusative case as well as the nominative case. So even Germans need to rely somewhat on word order, assisted by their experience of the world, to decipher an utterance.

The use of a particular case may be determined by a preceding preposition. Some, such as *durch* meaning *through*, are followed by the accusative case. Some are followed by the dative case, an example being *mit* meaning *with*. (You may remember that in section 10.5 we saw that *mid* was followed by the dative case in Old English.)

The shift in the consonant system that gave German much of its phonological distinctiveness took place in the south around the sixth century A.D. and subsequently pushed northwards. It is sometimes called the **Second German Consonant Shift**, the first consonant shift being that which had given the Proto-Germanic speech distinctive consonants many centuries before. It is also known as the **High German Consonant Shift**, as it helped to distinguish the High German variety of the south that came to form the basis of standard German.

This shift affected the voiceless plosives /p, t, k/. Between vowels, for example, they become the fricatives /f, θ, x (or ç)/. In initial position they stopped halfway, becoming affricates. Thus what is *pipe* in English and *pijp* in Dutch is *Pfeife* in German. Once this had happened, the vacated voiceless plosives were occupied by their voiced counterparts, with the result that what is *day* in English and *dag* in Dutch is *Tag* in German.

In more recent times the long close vowels developed into diphthongs, as in English and Dutch; the result is seen in such words as *Pfeife* and *Haus*.

These various changes to the phonology of High German have affected the north of Germany only in so far as High German serves as the standard language. The local vernacular, **Low German** or **plattdeutsch**, was not affected by them and so remains phonologically close to the other Germanic languages. In *Der Schimmelreiter* (1888), by Theodor Storm, who grew up in Schleswig, we can read the following words of wisdom:

> Hest du din Dagwark richtig dan,
> Da kommt de Slap von sülvst heran.

Dagwark would be *day's work* in English, *dagwerk* in Dutch and *Tagewerk* in High German, *dan* would be *done, gedaan* and *getan*, these illustrating the fact that Low German was not subjected to the change /d/ > /t/ that formed part of the High German Consonant Shift. We see, too, that it was not subjected to the change /p/ > /f/, *Slap* corresponding to English *sleep*, Dutch *slaap* and High German *Schlaf*. That Low German was not subjected to the later diphthongisation of the close vowel /i:/ is seen from the possessive adjective *din* which shares its form with the Scandinavian counterparts but not with the High German counterpart, that having become *dein*.

High German is illustrated by text 11.2.

11.2.2 North Germanic

We have seen that in Scandinavia the Germanic tongue developed such characteristics as a suffixed definite article and the loss of initial /j/. Thus the Swedish equivalent of *year* is *år* and the Swedish equivalent of *the year* is *året*. Similarly, the Scandinavian languages often lack an equivalent of our semi-vowel /w/ in initial position before a back vowel; the Swedish equivalent of *word* is *ord*. Another

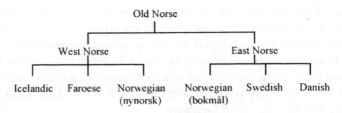

Figure 11.2

feature that helped to distinguish the languages of Scandinavia was the development of the reflexive pronoun *sik* into a verbal suffix that came to indicate passive or reciprocal action. The Swedish equivalent of *The king wrote the book* is *Kungen skrev boken*; by adding *-s* to the verb we get one of the two ways of forming the passive, *Boken skrevs av kungen* being an equivalent of *The book was written by the king*. We might note just for interest that this development has given us the verb *to bask*, its origin being in the Old Norse *baða sik* meaning *to bathe oneself*. There was fracture or breaking of the vowel /e/ that produced, for example, *jämn* in Swedish where English has *even*.

Such features had begun to give the Germanic tongue of Scandinavia a distinctive character around the fifth century A.D. This Scandinavian variety is known as Old Norse. By the eleventh century differences had emerged between Norse spoken in the west and Norse spoken in the east. Thus we can represent the development of North Germanic in greater detail as shown in Figure 11.2.

Figure 11.2 shows that Icelandic and Faroese are closely related to *nynorsk*, the variety of Norwegian that is based on the old dialects of western Norway. But since that time major differences have arisen for Norwegian, like the other continental Scandinavian languages, has undergone many changes, whereas the insular languages have changed relatively little.

Icelandic has, for example, like German, retained four cases for the nouns. It has kept its vocabulary very pure by coining words for new concepts from its own elements rather than by introducing foreign words. Thus a kitchen is denoted by the word *eldhús*, literally *fire-house*. The Icelandic word for an astronaut is *geimfari*, *geimur* being *space* and *fara* being *to travel*.

A number of reasons have been proposed for the conservative nature of Icelandic. Until modern times the isolated position of

Iceland severely limited Icelanders' contact with people other than their Danish masters and a nationalist spirit strengthened their resolve to resist contamination from Danish. It has been argued that the tradition of the sagas restrained change. It has been argued, too, that it would be difficult to adapt foreign words to the case system with its mutations and inflections.

During the Viking period, in the ninth and tenth centuries, differences began to emerge between Norse spoken in the west and Norse spoken in the east.

In the east monophthongs developed where West Norse retained diphthongs. Icelandic retains an Old Norse diphthong in, for example, its word for smoke, *reykur*, whereas **Danish** has reduced it to a monophthong in its equivalent *røg*. Icelandic, like *nynorsk*, has *haust*, which is the equivalent of our *autumn* and a cognate of our *harvest*, whereas Danish, like Norwegian *bokmål*, has *høst*. **Swedish** has *rök* and *höst*.

In the west there was more assimilation of nasal consonants before voiceless stops; thus where Danish has *synke* (and we have *to sink*) Icelandic has *sökkva*.

The Hanseatic League of the late Middle Ages, dominated by Lübeck, had a greater influence on the speech of the east than on the speech of the west. Reflecting its fields of activity, the influence of Low German on the vocabulary of Swedish was particularly marked in the case of vocabulary relating to trade, crafts and urban life. Thus while the Icelandic equivalent of *to pay*, *gjalda*, perpetuates the Old Norse lexeme, the Swedish equivalent, *betala*, came from Low German. Similarly, the Icelandic equivalent of *town* or *city*, *borg*, is perpetuated from Old Norse, whereas the Swedish equivalent *stad* owes this particular meaning to Low German.

By the time of the Hanseatic League differences had begun to emerge within East Norse, these laying the foundation for the distinctive characters of Danish and Swedish.

Danish had voiced the voiceless stops following a vowel. We have seen that Danish has *røg* where Icelandic has *reykur* (and *Reykjavík* which means *Bay of Smoke*); as we have also seen, the Swedish word is *rök*. The equivalent of *to buy* and a cognate of *cheap* is *köpa* in Swedish and *købe* in Danish. To continue the explanation of the names of Scandinavian capital cities, the Danes call theirs *København*, this meaning something like *Trading Harbour*. Further, the alveolar and velar plosives weakened to fricatives; thus where Swedish has *veta*, meaning *to know*, and *röka*, meaning *to smoke*, Danish has *vide* and *røge* pronounced /viːðə/ and /Røːɣə/. This results from the influence of the surrounding vowels. Such lenition is widespread; we see a very similar process in the development from Latin *vitam*, meaning life, to Spanish *vida*, pronounced /biːða/. An old velar fricative has become a stop in Swedish but a close vowel in Danish, /i/ after a front vowel and /u/ after a back vowel. Thus Swedish has *väg* and *lag* where Danish has *vej* (/vai/) and *lov* (/lɔu/). We can compare this development to that in English whereby Old English *weg* and *lagu* have come down to us as *way* and *law*.

The noun *røg* ends with a glottal stop that is another feature of Danish; in Danish it is called *stød*, meaning *push* or *thrust*.

The verbs *köpa* and *købe* illustrate another phonological difference between Swedish and Danish. Swedish has palatalised /k/ and /g/ before a front vowel; whereas *købe* begins with the phone /k/, *köpa* begins with the phone /ʃ/ (cf. the /tʃ/ in cheap).

Text 11.3 gives a sample of Swedish.

Also a member of the East Norse group is the more common variety of **Norwegian**, *bokmål*, literally *book speech*. It was drawn towards Danish during a long period of domination by Denmark that came to an end with the Napoleonic Wars. It has some lexemes that relate to Danish and not to Swedish, examples including *lomme*, meaning *pocket*, and *huske*, meaning *to remember*, but the phonology is closer to that of Swedish.

In the nineteenth century there was a desire to restore a variety of Norwegian that was free of Danish influence. The result was *nynorsk*, literally *New Norwegian*, a variety which, as we have seen, was developed on the basis of the old dialects of western Norway, the dialects that had once spawned Icelandic. *Nynorsk* still fights on but remains a minority variety; *haust* remains in the shadow of *høst*.

11.3 The Romance Languages

The southern part of western Europe was dominated by the Romans two thousand years ago. As a consequence Latin was spoken throughout this part of the continent. At one time Latin had been the language of Lazio in central Italy, just one of several Italic languages. But the region of Lazio includes the city of Rome and as the Roman empire grew, so too did the significance of Latin.

The eventual decline of the Roman empire did not, on the other hand, result in the decline of the Romans' speech. Generally Latin remained and evolved into the Romance languages of today.

One major feature of this evolution was the withering of the case system of Latin. Instead, the Romance languages came to rely more heavily on the use of prepositions and on a more rigid word order. The lexis of the Romance languages generally perpetuated the accusative form of nouns and adjectives; the Italian word for a bridge, *ponte*, for example, presupposes the accusative form *pontem* rather than the nominative form *pons*. As we saw in section 10.2, the Romance languages developed an adverb based on Latin *mente*, indicating that something is done in a certain mind, an example being *veramente*, the Italian equivalent of *truly*. We saw, too, that they developed a future tense on the basis of the infinitive plus *habere*, as in the Italian equivalent of *they will sell*, *venderanno*. The Romance languages developed articles, something that Latin had not had; the equivalent of the numeral *one* came to be used as an indefinite article and the demonstrative adjective *ille* provided the source for a definite article. As an example of general phonological changes, /k/ became palatalised before front vowels, such that, for example, Italian now has *cinque*, the equivalent of the numeral *five*, pronounced with the initial segment /tʃ/.

Like any other language spoken over a large area, Latin would have had regional variation. For one thing, it was not deposited on a 'tabula rasa', on a clean slate; in different regions it met with different linguistic substrata, such as the language of the Gauls. Differences would naturally arise in different parts of the empire. As we saw in section 10.6, some later Latin words like *manducare* did not reach the extremes of the empire. Another example of this is the above word *tabula* in so far as the sense of a piece of furniture at which one eats is concerned; it has given rise to the Italian lexeme *tavola*, the Catalan lexeme *taula* and the French lexeme *table*, but in the far west the lexeme is *mesa* (Spanish and Portuguese) and in the far east it is *masă* (Romanian). Further diversification resulted from a lack of centralisation when the empire collapsed and from subsequent contact with different cultures. Spanish and Portuguese have, for example, been greatly influenced by many centuries of contact with Arabs, Romanian by contact with Slavs.

In respect of certain fundamental features, developments in the west differed from developments in the east. In the east voiceless plosives between vowels or between vowel and liquid consonant remained as in Latin, whereas in the west there was lenition. Thus Latin *amicus* meaning *friend* became *amico* in Italian but *amigo* in Spanish and *ami* in French. In the west vowels following a stressed vowel are less likely to have been retained; as we saw above, Latin *tabula* has become *tavola*, a word with a stressed syllable followed by two unstressed syllables, in Italian and the shorter *table* in French. In the west the plural morphs seem to be derived from those of the accusative case of Latin, whereas in the east they seem to be derived from those of the nominative case. Thus, for example, the accusative plural of Latin *amicus*, *amicos*, resembles Spanish *amigos* while the nominative plural *amici* at least looks like the Italian word *amici*. In the west a prothetic vowel is used before /s/ plus another consonant; thus Latin *strictus* (cf. English *strict* and *strait*) evolved into *stretto* in Italian but *étroit* in French, *estret* in Catalan and *estrecho* in Spanish.

We can, then, talk of West Romance and East Romance. In the previous paragraph I used French, Catalan and Spanish to provide examples of features of West Romance and Italian to provide examples of features of East Romance. In fact the dialects of northern Italy exhibit West Romance features and linguists define this principal boundary within the Romance world with reference to a line that runs across the north of Italy, the La Spezia–Rimini line.

11.3.1   West Romance

As differentiation continued we can eventually discern varieties that we can call early forms of the Romance languages that we know today.

The first to distinguish itself was **French** which is generally traced back to the ninth century. More specifically, it is widely considered that the earliest surviving specimen of French is the Strasbourg Oaths of 842 when Charles the Bald and Louis the German met at Strasbourg to conclude an alliance against their brother Lothair. In that text we see, for example, that the intervocalic /p/ of the Latin lexeme *sapere*, meaning *to know*, has developed to the /v/ that we have in Modern French *savoir*. The word for a thing appears as *cosa*, it having lost the diphthong of the Latin *causa*.

This word is now *chose* in French; one of the developments that have distinguished French from both its 'mother' Latin and its 'sisters', the other West Romance languages, has been the palatalisation of /k/ before /a/ in Latin by way of /tʃ/ to /ʃ/. Another distinguishing feature has been the loss of /s/ before a consonant, as in the development of *tête*, meaning *head*, from Latin *testa*. The word *château*, meaning *castle*, exhibits both these developments, the Latin ancestor having been *castellum*. The segment /s/ ceased to be pronounced before a consonant around the thirteenth century but for some time afterwards the word was written as *chastel* or *chasteau* (*chasteau* developed by backformation from the plural form *chasteaus*).

There has been widespread loss of final consonants and widespread loss of final /ə/. This common reluctance of different items to stand in final position has resulted in severe erosion of the spoken word; the Latin word *pontem*, meaning *bridge*, has, for example, become *pont* in French, this being pronounced /pɔ̃/. As this phonetic transcription indicates, the vowel was nasalised by the following /n/ before it disappeared; this is another distinguishing feature of French. Yet another is the widespread development of Latin /a/ to a front mid vowel as in, for example, the evolution of Latin *matrem*, meaning *mother*, to French *mère*.

French is illustrated in text 11.4.

We have been looking at some of the principal features of standard French, a variety that evolved from the speech of the north of what is now France, more specifically from the speech of the region around Paris, a variety that is called Francien. In the south there was a variety that we know as **Occitan**. The northern and southern varieties may also be referred to as *langue d'oïl* and *langue d'oc* respectively, *oïl* and *oc* having been the equivalent of *yes* in each variety. The speech of the south was generally more conservative than that of the north. We have seen that the Latin word *causa* has become *chose* in French, the first segment having been palatalised and the second having been monophthongised. In Occitan neither of these developments happened; the word remained *causa*.

In Figure 8.5 we saw a major linguistic division running across France; that shows the northern boundary of Occitan. One should add that it is widely recognised that there is a third variety, Franco-provençal, that lies to the north of the eastern end of this boundary.

Just as High German came to dominate Low German, so, too, French increasingly established itself in the south. As we saw in section 9.2, the speech of the Paris region gained prestige as the nation state of France developed, as Paris became an ever more significant centre of power. As usually happens with the spread of a standard variety, French established itself in the towns before the rural areas and in writing before speech.

Today most people in the south speak French, whether or not they also speak Occitan. As we saw in section 9.6, people who speak Occitan will tend to do so in the home and in other informal situations; in more formal situations they will be more likely to speak French. This generalisation obscures the fact, however, that we are not dealing with a binary situation. Rather, we are dealing once again with a continuum; the more formal the situation, the closer a person's speech approximates to standard French. Typically what people speak is a southern variety of French. In the south, for example, there is less occurrence of nasalised vowels, the nasal consonant being pronounced instead. Unstressed /ə/ in final position is more often pronounced in the south. Given these two features, the word *compte*, meaning *account*, pronounced /kɔ̃:t/ in the north, will often be pronounced /kontə/ in the south.

To the north of the eastern Pyrenees, in Roussillon, one may hear the word *compte* pronounced in a similar way, the only difference being that the nasal consonant is articulated as a bilabial sound: /komtə/. This fine distinction has taken us one more step along a West Romance dialect continuum; we have now encountered **Catalan**.

Just as Occitan has been threatened for centuries by the language of the nation state of France, Catalan, spoken mostly to the south of the Pyrenees, has been threatened by the language of the state of Spain. Following the death of General Franco in 1975, however, democracy and devolution were restored in Spain, and as part of that process the Catalan language was given official status alongside Spanish in the autonomous region of Catalonia in north-eastern Spain. It now thrives.

Like Occitan, Catalan is relatively conservative, having changed less in its evolution from Latin than, say, French and Spanish have. The Catalan word for a stone, for example, *pedra*, has only voiced the /t/ of the Latin original *petra*; the French equivalent *pierre* has retained no trace of the /t/ and, like the Spanish word *piedra*, has diphthongised the stressed vowel.

There was a time in the Middle Ages when the speech of the kingdom of Castile was of no greater significance than Catalan. But, like Francien, Castilian became more significant as did the power of those who spoke it, with the result that it became the national language of the state of Spain and is better known to us as **Spanish**.

In section 5.6 we saw that the Latin word *focus* has given Spanish *fuego*, meaning *fire*, *hogar*, meaning *home*, and *hoguera*, meaning *bonfire*, and that the short vowel /ɔ/ developed into /we/ in *fuego* but not in the other two reflexes because only in the case of *fuego* was it stressed. These three reflexes of *focus* also show the widespread loss of initial /f/ in Spanish; one environment in which it remains is before the glide /w/.

Another phonological development characteristic of Spanish was the palatalisation of the initial consonant clusters /fl/, /kl/ and /pl/ as /ʎ/. Thus the Latin source of our word *flame*, *flamma*, has become *llama* in Spanish. This is a homonym of the word *llama* that forms part of the present tense of the verb *llamar*, meaning *to call*, there having been palatalisation in this case of the cluster /kl/ of the Latin word *clamare*.

The lexis of Spanish has been given a distinctive flavour by the presence of the Arabs in Iberia for several centuries. Loanwords generally accompany new concepts, and the areas in which the Arabs contributed significantly to life in Iberia and thereby to the Spanish language include administration, agriculture and furnishings; thus Spanish has borrowed from Arabic words such as *alcalde* meaning *mayor*, *aceituna* meaning *olive* and *alfombra* meaning *carpet*. As these examples show, the loanwords taken from Arabic often begin with /a(l)/, the Arabic definite article having been incorporated into the word.

It was, of course, through Spanish that many indigenous American words came to Europe; the discovery of the Andes and of the local animals by the Spaniards resulted, for example, in an addition to the set of homonyms *llama*.

Text 11.5 is Spanish.

As in Spanish, in **Portuguese** there has been palatalisation of initial /fl/, /kl/ and /pl/, the result in this case being /ʃ/. In Portuguese Latin *clamare* and *flamma* became *chamar* and *chama*. Portuguese has lost intervocalic /l/ and /n/; thus the equivalent of *to go out* is *sair* (cf. Spanish *salir*) and the equivalent of *full* is *cheio* (cf. Spanish *lleno*).

The loss of /l/ is seen in plural forms; the equivalent of *tunnels* is *túneis*. Before disappearing the /n/ often nasalised the preceding vowel; thus, for example, what was *manus*, meaning *hand*, in Latin became *mão* in Portuguese, the nasalisation being indicated in this case by the tilde, in Portuguese *til* (˜), a mark that may be seen as a vestigial <n>.

One distinctive morphological feature of Portuguese is the personal infinitive. In the Spanish text, text 11.5, we see the construction *al pasar* which, like the English equivalent *on passing*, gives no indication of the subject, of who or what was passing. Portuguese, however, can do so; as well as *ao passar* Portuguese allows, for example, *ao passarmos*, this indicating that the subject is first-person plural and so is comparable to *as we passed*. Another feature is the positioning of object and reflexive pronouns after a finite tense in affirmative utterances. As in Catalan and Spanish, pronouns are suffixed to an infinitive but in Portuguese they can also follow, for example, the present tense; a Spaniard would tell you that he is called José by saying *Me llamo José*, a Portuguese person by saying *Chamo-me José*.

11.3.2 East Romance

East Romance, represented principally by Italian and Romanian, has in many respects remained closer to Latin. As we have seen, in the east voiceless intervocalic plosives have remained voiceless; thus Latin *lupus*, meaning *wolf*, has become *lupo* in Italian and *lup* in Romanian as opposed to *lobo* in Spanish and Portuguese. Vowels that follow stressed syllables are more likely to have survived in the east. Romanian retains, albeit in a simplified form, the case system of Latin.

In the east the plural forms of nouns and adjectives reflect the nominative forms of Latin; thus the equivalent of *wolves* is *lupi* in Italian and Romanian as opposed to *lobos* in Spanish and Portuguese.

We have seen that the local speech of the north of Italy belongs to West Romance rather than East Romance. **Italian** is, indeed, quite varied. It is spoken in an area that only became a political unit in the second half of the nineteenth century, and while a standard language based principally on the variety of Tuscany has increasingly established itself, there is still relatively great variation, particularly as regards phonology and lexis. The voicing of inter-vocalic plosives in some words such as *riva*, meaning *shore*, and *lago*, meaning *lake*, reflexes of the Latin words *ripa* and *lacus*, has been ascribed to northern provenance; Italy's principal lakes are, after all, in the north!

In Italian the initial clusters /fl/, /kl/ and /pl/ have become /fj/, /kj/ and /pj/, the /l/ having become a glide. Thus, for example, the Latin word *flamma*, meaning *flame*, has become *fiamma* in Italian and the Latin word *plenus*, meaning *full*, has become *pieno*.

Another feature of Italian has been the assimilation of consonants before /t/; the Latin word *lactis*, meaning *milk*, has, for example, become *latte* in Italian.

Although it is not spoken in western Europe, I shall outline a few of the principal features of **Romanian** (alternatively written Ruman-ian) for the sake of completing our introduction to the family of Romance languages.

Romanian, as we have seen, retains the case system of Latin, albeit in a simplified form; the nominative and accusative cases have combined, as have the genitive and dative cases. The equivalent of *the door of the room* is *uşa sălii*, *uşa* being in the first of these cases and *sălii* in the second. *Uşa* is the definite form of *uşă*, the definite form being marked at the end of the word. The Romanian equivalent of Italian *il lupo*, *the wolf*, is *lupul*. The Romanian equivalent of *the devil* is *dracul*; perhaps this brings to mind the name of a certain Tran-sylvanian count?

A phonological feature of Romanian has been the tendency for different vowels to be drawn to a close central position before a nasal consonant, as in, for example, *cîmp*, meaning *field*, a reflex of Latin *campus*. Another has been the labialisation of velar consonants; Latin *lactis* has become *lapte*, Latin *noctis*, meaning *night*, has become *noapte*. *Noapte* also illustrates a characteristic diphthongisation.

There has been extensive Slavonic influence on the lexis of Romanian; the equivalent of *time*, for example, is *vreme* (cf. Russian время). In the past couple of centuries, however, there has been a strengthening of ties with the Romance world once again, not least of all under a strong French influence in the nineteenth century. One consequence was the abandonment of Cyrillic script in favour of Roman script.

11.4 The Celtic Languages

The Celtic languages are now only a shadow of their former selves. They were once spoken across Europe. Then, under the pressure of the Romans and the Germanic peoples, they were driven to the north-west fringe of Europe. There they hang on today, the native tongue of only a million or so people.

As we saw in section 7.5, one of the distinctive features of the Celtic languages is their basic word order: verb–subject–object (VSO). Thus, for example, Welsh has *Gwelodd hi gi* and Scottish Gaelic has *Chunnaic i cù*, both saying literally *Saw she dog*. Adjectives follow nouns: the Welsh equivalent of *small dog* is *ci bach*, literally *dog small*; the Welsh equivalent of *white bread* is *bara gwyn*, literally *bread white*. As we saw in section 10.6, there is a tendency for languages with the word order VSO to place adjectives after nouns. A phonological feature developed by the Celtic languages was the loss of initial /p/; the equivalents of *fish* and *father*, *piscis* and *pater* in Latin, are *iasg* and *athair* in Scottish Gaelic.

The Celtic languages are, as we have seen, split into two groups: Brittonic comprising Welsh and Breton, and Goidelic comprising Irish and Scottish Gaelic. Reflecting a distinctive phonological development, these groups are also known as P-Celtic and Q-Celtic respectively. From the labialised velar /kʷ/ P-Celtic has evolved the labial plosive /p/, whereas Q-Celtic has evolved the non-labialised velar /k/; thus the equivalents of *four* and *head* are *pedwar* and *pen* in Welsh but *ceithir* and *ceann* in Scottish Gaelic. The Welsh word *plant*, meaning *children*, is a cognate of the word *clan* that we have received from Gaelic.

The Brittonic (or Brythonic) group comprises the majority of speakers of the Celtic languages.

A major feature of the Brittonic languages is the mutation of initial consonants. We have seen that the **Welsh** equivalents of *white* and *small* are *gwyn* (feminine *gwen*) and *bach*, but the equivalent of *small white loaf* is *torth wen fach*. We have seen that the equivalent of *dog* is *ci* but that the equivalent of *She saw a dog* is *Gwelodd hi gi*. It is, incidentally, the variant *gi* that we have in the compound *corgi*. These variations are examples of one type of mutation, that which is known as soft mutation. There are also variations known as nasal mutation and spirant mutation. *Cymru*, the Welsh name for Wales, has the soft form *Gymru*, the nasal form *Nghymru* and the spirant form *Chymru*. The corresponding variants of *pen*, meaning *head*, are *ben*, *mhen* and *phen*.

The origins of the mutations are phonological. The soft mutation of initial /k/ and /p/, for example, reflects the tendency for voiceless plosives followed by a vowel to become voiced in initial position when the preceding word ends in a vowel. Over time, however, such mutations became grammaticalised, that is they came to be determined by function rather than by phonological environment. As an example, the equivalents of the possessive adjectives *his* and *her* in Welsh once had different forms, one of which gave rise to soft mutation and one of which gave rise to spirant mutation. Now, however, *ei* serves for both, with the result that the mutation alone distinguishes the gender of the owner; while *his dog* is *ei gi*, *her dog* is *ei chi*. In *Gwelodd hi gi*, meaning *She saw a dog*, the soft mutation of *ci* results from it standing as an object immediately after a subject; here, then, mutation helps to distinguish subject and object. Other circumstances in which soft mutation arises include where a feminine noun is preceded by the definite article and where a noun is preceded by one of certain prepositions; thus the equivalents of *garden* and *pound* are *gardd* and *punt* while the equivalents of *the garden* and *for a pound* are *yr ardd* and *am bunt*.

Breton, the Celtic language of Brittany in north-west France, is not a survivor of continental Celtic, of Gaulish. It was taken across the English Channel from Cornwall around the fifth century as the Saxons extended their hold on southern England. One indication of the links between Cornwall and Brittany is *Cornouaille*, the name of the region around the Breton town of Quimper.

Migrations also account for the spread of the Goidelic group for **Gaelic** was taken from Ireland to Scotland. Irish Gaelic survives, precariously, on the west coast of Ireland, in areas referred to as the Gaeltacht, and Scottish Gaelic survives on the islands off the west coast of Scotland.

In Gaelic, as in the Brittonic languages, initial segments vary. As in Welsh, there is, for example, mutation in feminine nouns following the definite article; in Irish Gaelic the equivalents of *woman* and *the woman* are *bean* and *an bhean*. The verb *bris*, meaning *to break*, becomes *bhris* in the past tense. The same thing happens in Scottish Gaelic where, for example, the equivalent of *She broke the chair* is *Bhris i an sèithear*, the initial segment of *bris* having changed from /b/ to /v/.

11.5   Finnish

And finally, Finnish. We end this chapter by looking at some of the features of Finnish, a representative of the few languages of Europe which do not belong to the Indo-European family.

Finnish, as we have seen (sections 2.1 and 6.1), is described as an agglutinating language, items that would be expressed by separate words in English being expressed by suffixes in Finnish. Thus the equivalent of *in my house* is *talossani*, *-ssa* equating to the preposition *in* and *-ni* to the possessive adjective *my*. The suffix *-ssa* is one of a number of suffixes which, like our prepositions, indicate the relationship between items. As we see, *-ssa* often corresponds to our preposition *in* and this construction may be called the inessive case. Our *on* often corresponds to the suffix *-lla* (the adessive case), our *out of* often corresponds to the suffix *-sta* (the elative case), and so on.

The case suffixes introduced above all have an alternative form with the vowel <ä>. Thus the adessive case has the suffix *-lla*, which has a vowel close to the cardinal vowel [ɑ], and the suffix *-llä*, which has a vowel close to the cardinal vowel [a]. The choice of vowel in the suffix is determined by the stem vowel of the word to which it is attached. The suffix *-lla* accompanies the back vowels represented by <a, o, u> while *-llä* accompanies the front vowels represented by <ä, ö, y> and usually <e, i>; thus *on the chair* is *tuolilla* while *on the table* is *pöydällä*. This is an example of vowel harmony, one of the distinctive features of Finnish.

Other phonological features include a traditional reluctance to admit initial consonant clusters. The Finnish word *tuoli* that we have just seen is an equivalent of the Swedish word *stol*. The equivalent of *shore* is *ranta*, a cognate of English and Swedish *strand*. The equivalent of *school* is *koulu*. Finnish has also been reluctant in the past to admit voiced plosives in initial position; thus the Finnish equivalents of *bank*, *doctor* and *gas* are *pankki*, *tohtori* and *kaasu*.

Summary

Most of the languages of Europe are considered to be derived from a single source, Indo-European.

The Indo-European languages of western Europe are grouped as the Germanic languages, the Romance languages and the Celtic languages. The Germanic languages are distinguished by such features as the First Germanic Consonant Shift, vowel gradation and i-mutation. The Romance languages are those which have evolved from Latin. The Celtic languages, the remains of a once extensive variety, are distinguished by such features as the word order verb–subject–object and extensive mutation of initial segments.

These groups may be divided further. The languages of Scandinavia, the North Germanic languages, are distinguished from the West Germanic languages by such features as their suffixed definite articles. The Romance languages are divided into West Romance and East Romance, distinguishing features including whether or not voiceless intervocalic plosives have become voiced. The Celtic languages are divided into a Brittonic group and a Goidelic group.

Finnish is an example of the non-Indo-European languages of Europe.

Texts

Text 11.1   Dutch
Source: The newspaper *De Telegraaf* (1997).

De man met het witte hondje en zijn vrouw zijn weer actief langs de doorgaande vakantieroutes in Frankrijk. Bij de politie in Arnhem, maar ook bij andere politiekorpsen in het land zijn aangiftes binnengekomen van Nederlanders die opgelicht zijn door het keurig uitziende stel. De man spreekt vakantiegangers aan met het verhaal dat zijn auto opengebroken is of dat hij bestolen is.

The man with the little white dog and his wife are active once again along the trunk holiday routes in France. To the police in Arnhem but also to other police forces in the country have come in reports from Dutch people who have been swindled by the elegant looking couple. The man speaks to holidaymakers with the story that his car has been broken into or that he has been robbed.

De man met het witte hondje (*The man with the little white dog*): Dutch has two definite articles, *de* and *het*, the latter being used with nouns of neuter gender. Dutch makes extensive use of the diminutive suffixes *-tje* and *-je*. In the diminutive form nouns take the article *het*: *de hond* but *het hondje*.

weer (*once again*): In many cases intervocalic /d/ is tending to disappear; the equivalent of *again* can be either *weder* or, as here, *weer*.

zijn aangiftes binnengekomen (*reports have come in*): As in several other European languages, the equivalent of *to be* is used to form the perfect tense in the case of verbs expressing motion or change. As in English we see the segment /s/ being used to form the plural of a noun, as in German we see a past participle formed with <ge>.

De man spreekt vakantiegangers aan (*The man speaks to holidaymakers*): *Aanspreken* is a separable verb.

dat zijn auto opengebroken is of dat hij bestolen is (*that his car has been broken in to or that he has been robbed*): In a subsidiary clause the verb tends to come at the end of the clause. Like the English equivalents *to break* and *to steal*, *breken* and *stelen* are strong verbs, the past participles showing similar vowel gradation.

Text 11.2   German
Source: *Die Verwandlung* (1912) by Franz Kafka.

Daß die Veränderung der Stimme nichts anderes war als der Vorbote einer tüchtigen Verkühlung, einer Berufskrankheit der Reisenden, daran zweifelte er nicht im geringsten. Die Decke abzuwerfen war ganz einfach; er brauchte sich nur ein wenig aufzublasen, und sie fiel von selbst. Aber weiterhin wurde es schwierig, besonders weil er so ungemein breit war. Er hätte Arme und Hände gebraucht, um sich aufzurichten; statt dessen aber hatte er nur die vielen Beinchen, die ununterbrochen in der verschiedensten Bewegung waren und die er überdies nicht beherrschen konnte.

That the change in his voice was nothing more than the precursor of a bad cold, an occupational illness of travelling salesmen, he did not doubt in the slightest. Throwing off the blanket was quite easy; he only had to puff himself up at bit and it fell off by itself. But after that it was difficult, particularly as he was so extraordinarily broad. He would have needed arms and hands to raise himself up; but instead he had only the many little legs that were continually moving in the most random fashion and that, moreover, he was unable to control.

Daß (*That*): This exhibits the consonant shift /t/ > /s/, the English and Dutch equivalents being *that* and *dat*. In the future *daß* will be written *dass*, there being a spelling reform in progress which among other things will replace <ß> by <ss> after short vowels.

die Veränderung der Stimme (*The change of the voice*): In German nouns are marked by the use of a capital initial letter. Both these nouns are of feminine gender. Here the first is in the nominative case and the second is in the genitive case to indicate possession (*of the voice*). So, too, *Verkühlung*, *Berufskrankheit* and *Reisenden* are all in the genitive case.

tüchtigen (*thorough*): This exhibits the shift /d/ > /t/, the English and Dutch equivalents being *doughty* and *duchtig*.

im geringsten (*in the slightest*): This is in the dative case; *im* is a fusion of the preposition *in* and *dem*, a dative form of the definite article.

abzuwerfen (*to throw off*): *Abwerfen* is a separable verb, this being indicated by the embedding of the element *zu* in the infinitive. *Aufblasen* and *aufrichten* are also separable verbs. The separable particles have the nature of prepositions or adverbs; *ab-* indicates movement away (cf. English *off*) and *auf-* indicates upward movement (cf. English *up*). In inseparable verbs such as *verändern* and *beherrschen* the morphs *ver-* and *be-* are less independent, being bound prefixes. *Werfen* and *blasen* are strong verbs, their past tense and past participle forms being *warf* and *geworfen*, *blies* and *geblasen*. *Werfen* exhibits the consonant shift /p/ > /f/; it is cognate with the English lexeme *warp*.

fiel (*fell*): This is the past tense form of *fallen*, a strong verb with the same alternation pattern as *blasen*: *fallen – fiel – gefallen*.

weiterhin wurde es schwierig (*beyond that it was difficult*): This illustrates the Germanic principle of word order that the verb should retain second position; as the first position is occupied by the adverb *weiterhin*, the subject, *es*, falls back behind the verb.

weil er so ungemein breit war (*as he was so extraordinarily broad*): In a subordinate clause the verb is placed at the end. The English translation uses the adverb *extraordinarily* to qualify the adjective *broad*; German rarely distinguishes between adjectives and adverbs.

hätte (*would have*): Here the subjunctive form of the verb is being used in a conditional construction. The subjunctive form of a verb generally indicates a hypothetical situation.

Hände (*hands*): This is the plural form of *Hand*. The plural form of nouns often entails mutation.

Beinchen (*little legs*): *-chen* is a diminutive suffix. As with Dutch words with the diminutive suffix *-(t)je*, words with the suffix *-chen* are of neuter gender.

ununterbrochen (*continual(ly)*): This is derived from *brechen*, a strong verb like *to break* and *breken*, its English and Dutch equivalents. *Brechen* has the same alternation pattern as *werfen*: *brechen* – *brach* – *gebrochen*. It exhibits the consonant shift /k/ > /ç/.

Text 11.3   Swedish
Source: the magazine *Vi* (1997).

> Sedan invigningen 1866 har han stått där uppe i röken från alla Vaxholmsbåtarna. På andra sidan vattnet ligger slottet han byggde, också rökskadat. Tessin håller en modell av slottet i handen. Man ser fortfarande att det är slottet fast marmorn vittrat och lösts upp så att ytlagret är bara pulver.

> Since the inauguration in 1866 he has stood up there in the smoke from all the Vaxholm boats. On the other side of the water lies the palace he built, it too damaged by smoke. Tessin holds a model of the palace in his hand. You can still see that it is the palace although the marble has weathered and disintegrated such that the outer layer is just powder.

Sedan invigningen 1866 har han stått (*Since the inauguration in 1866 he has stood*): As the sentence begins with the adverbial phrase *Sedan invigningen 1866* the subject *han* and the verb *har* are inverted to keep the verb as the second concept in the sentence.

invigningen (*the inauguration*): This is the definite form of the noun *invigning*, the suffix *-en* serving as the definite article. Other words in the definite form include *röken*, *vattnet* and *slottet*, *-en* indicating common gender and *-et* neuter gender.

röken (*the smoke*): *Rök* illustrates the monophthongisation that took place in East Norse; cf. Icelandic *reykur*.

Vaxholmsbåtarna (*the Vaxholm boats*): *Båtarna* is the definite plural form of *båt*.

vattnet (*the water*): Here we have an example of elision. The unstressed /ə/ of *vatten* is elided when the definite article *-et* is suffixed. We see the same thing happening to *ytlager*.

slottet (*the palace*): *Slott* is an example of the vocabulary acquired from Low German.

fast marmorn vittrat och lösts upp (*although the marble has weathered and been dissolved*): Swedish can omit the auxiliary of the perfect tense in a subsidiary clause.

lösts (*been dissolved*): Like *rök*, *lösa* is an example of the mono-phthongisation in East Norse. The final *-s* indicates that in this case it is in the middle voice to serve as the passive.

Text 11.4 French
Source: the novel *La Porte étroite* (1909) by André Gide.

> Elle me repoussait, m'arrachait d'elle doucement – et ce furent là nos adieux, car ce soir je ne pus plus rien lui dire, et le lendemain, au moment de mon départ, elle s'enferma dans sa chambre. Je la vis à sa fenêtre me faire signe d'adieu en regardant s'éloigner la voiture qui m'emportait.

> She pushed me away, gently forced me from her. And that was our farewell, for that evening I was unable to say anything more to her and the following day, at the moment of my departure, she shut herself in her room. I saw her at her window waving goodbye to me and watching as the vehicle that was carrying me away drove off into the distance.

Elle me repoussait (*She pushed me away*): Here the verb is in the imperfect tense which in the Romance languages generally describes what was happening at a given moment (as with *qui m'emportait, that was carrying me away*) or indicates habitual action. In Modern French a stylistic variation has developed whereby the imperfect tense may be used for a completed action.

m'arrachait d'elle (*forced me from her*): Here we have examples of simplification, the /ə/ of *me* and *de* having been elided before a following vowel. In section 5.6 we saw the suggestion that such elision may reflect a natural tendency towards consonant–vowel (CV) syllables.

doucement (*gently*): In the Romance languages adverbs are formed by adding a derivative of the Latin equivalent of *mind* to the feminine form of the adjective, the Latin word, *mens*, having been of feminine gender. This word contains an example of the nasalisation of a vowel, the vowel in the final syllable having been nasalised by the /n/ before it ceased to be pronounced; the word is pronounced /dusmã/.

ce furent là nos adieux (*that was our farewell*): *furent* is in the past definite or past historic tense. This tense is used to refer to a completed action in the past. It is used in the written language; in the spoken language the perfect tense is used for this purpose. So, bearing in mind what was said above about the use of the imperfect tense, there is some variation in the use of tenses for reference to actions in the past depending on register and style. The phrase *nos adieux* illustrates liaison, the situation whereby a final consonant is pronounced only when a vowel follows, another consequence of the preference for CV syllable structure.

le lendemain (*the following day*): Uncertainty about whether segments constitute an article or part of a noun may lead to an article being incorporated into a noun. In this way *l'endemain* (cf. Italian *indomani*) was seen as simply a noun, with the result that another article was used with it.

chambre (*room*): Here we see an example of the evolution of Latin /k/ before /a/ to /ʃ/ in French. The Latin original was *camera*.

fenêtre (*window*): Here we see an example of the loss of /s/ before a consonant; cf. Italian *finestra*.

en regardant (*watching*): *En* is the only preposition that is not accompanied by the infinitive; it is accompanied by the present participle.

Text 11.5 Spanish
Source: the novel *Nada* (1944) by Carmen Laforet.

> Salté de la cama traspasada de frío y de sueño. Tan asustada, que tenía la sensación de no poder moverme aunque, en realidad, no hice otra cosa: en pocos segundos arranqué las ropas de la cama y me envolví en ellas. Tiré la almohada, al pasar, en una silla del comedor y llegué hasta el recibidor envuelta en una manta, descalza sobre las baldosas heladas, en el momento en que Angustias entraba de la calle seguida del chófer con sus maletas y conduciendo a Gloria por un brazo. La abuelita apareció también.

> I jumped out of the bed, overcome by cold and sleep. So startled that I felt as though I was unable to move although, in fact, I did nothing else; in a few seconds I grabbed the bedclothes and wrapped myself in them. As I passed I threw the pillow onto a chair in the dining room and I arrived at the hallway wrapped in a blanket, barefoot on the frozen tiles, just as Angustias was coming in from the street followed by the driver with her cases and leading Gloria by the arm. Granny also appeared.

Salté (*I jumped*): No subject pronouns are used in this extract; the morph *-é* is sufficient to indicate the first-person singular.

la cama (*the bed*): Spanish once also had a word *cama* meaning *leg*. This homonymic clash resulted in the word *pierna* replacing *cama* as the word used to denote a leg. In Catalan, where no such clash occurred, the word *cama* still denotes a leg.

frío . . . heladas (*cold . . . frozen*): Latin /g/ has often been lost before a front vowel in Spanish. *Frío* shows a loss of intervocalic /g/, it being from Latin *frigidus*. From the same source Spanish later acquired the word *frígido*; such later borrowings, less subjected to sound changes, are often more learned in nature and are known as *cultismos* in Spanish. *Heladas* shows a loss of initial /g/ in an unstressed syllable, the verb *helar* being from the Latin *gelare*. Cf. *congelar*, also meaning *to freeze*, which has a palatal fricative sound.

sueño (*sleep*): This is a reflex of the Latin word *somnus*. It exhibits the development of /we/ from a short vowel in Latin. It also shows the assimilation of /mn/ to /nn/ and the subsequent development to /ɲ/, the sound represented by <ñ>.

moverme (*move myself*): This is the infinitive of a verb being used reflexively. The reflexive pronoun is suffixed to the infinitive in Spanish.

hice (*I did*): This is part of the verb *hacer* which is a reflex of the Latin *facere* and so illustrates the loss of initial /f/.

las ropas de la cama (*the bedclothes*): *Cama*, meaning *bed*, may be an example of a word with origins that pre-date the arrival of Latin in Iberia. *Ropa*, meaning *clothes*, came into the Romance languages from Germanic; it is related to our *to rob*, clothing being considered to be a form of booty.

la almohada (*the pillow*): This is an example of a lexeme taken from Arabic that denotes an item of furnishing.

hasta el recibidor (*to the hallway*): Most of the words taken from Arabic were nouns; *hasta*, meaning *as far as* or *until*, is perhaps the only function word that Spanish has taken from Arabic.

llegué (*I arrived*): This illustrates the palatalisation of initial /pl/, the verb *llegar*, meaning *to arrive*, being derived from Latin *plicare*, meaning *to fold* (it has been suggested that the association between folding and arriving is the folding of sails). The /pl/ is retained in the Spanish cognate *plegar*, meaning *to fold*, this word being considered to be a *semicultismo*.

en el momento en que Angustias entraba (*just as Angustias was coming in*): *Entraba* is in the imperfect tense, it serving here to describe what the situation was when the narrator arrived in the hallway.

conduciendo a Gloria (*leading Gloria*): Spanish has a personal *a* that is used when the object of an action is a person.

La abuelita (*Granny*): *-ito* (feminine *-ita*) is one of the more common of the numerous so-called diminutive suffixes that Spanish has. This suffix often implies affection rather than smallness.

Text 11.6 Italian
Source: the magazine *Oggi* (1997).

Sempre *Pioneer* ci permise di avere le prime fotografie da distanza ravvicinata di Giove, il pianeta più misterioso e più grande del sistema solare, e delle sue lune. Da quando Galileo scoprì, circa tre secoli fa, le prime quattro delle sue dodici lune, Giove è stato accuratamente studiato dagli astronomi, ma scarsissime e inadeguate sono le informazioni che siamo riusciti a ottenere sia pure attraverso i telescopi più potenti.

Pioneer always allowed us to have the first photographs at close quarters of Jupiter, the most mysterious and the largest planet in the solar system, and of its moons. Ever since Galileo discovered, some three centuries ago, the first four of its twelve moons, Jupiter has been closely studied by astronomers, but very scanty and inadequate is the information that we have managed to obtain even by means of the most powerful telescopes.

il pianeta più misterioso (*the most mysterious planet*): Here we see the development /pl/ > /pj/; *più*, meaning *more*, is a reflex of Latin *plus*.

delle sue lune (*of its moons*): In Italian possessive adjectives are generally accompanied by a definite article. Here again we see a definite article fused with a preposition.

tre secoli (*three centuries*): A comparison of *secoli* and the Spanish equivalent *siglos* illustrates three of the principal features that distinguish between East Romance and West Romance; the Italian word retains the voiceless intervocalic plosive, it retains the vowel following the stressed vowel, the first one, and in the Italian word the plural marker reflects the nominative case of Latin, whereas in the Spanish word it reflects the accusative case.

scarsissime (*very scanty*): *Scarsissimo* is an intensified form of *scarso*; thus it means *very scanty*. In Latin the morph *-issim-* marked the superlative.

siamo riusciti (*we have managed*): In Italian most intransitive verbs, verbs which are not accompanied by a direct object, form the perfect tenses with the auxiliary *essere* as opposed to *avere*. In such cases the participle agrees with the subject in respect of gender and number.

ottenere (*to obtain*): This illustrates the assimilation of a consonant immediately before /t/.

sia pure (*be it even*): *Sia* is a subjunctive form of the verb *essere*. The subjunctive generally indicates a hypothetical situation (Cf. English *even though it be*).

Exercises

11.1   In the following three sentences (a) identify three examples of significant difference between Dutch and German and (b) account for the difference in word order between the English sentence on the one hand and the Dutch and German equivalents on the other:

English	I have seen ten sheep
Dutch	Ik heb tien schapen gezien
German	Ich habe zehn Schafe gesehen

11.2   (a) Two of the following German words are derived from the Latin equivalent. Which do you think they are? Give a reason.

Latin	*English*	*German*
piper	pepper	Pfeffer
piscis	fish	Fisch
peregrinus	pilgrim	Pilger

(b) Of the two words derived from Latin, which do you think entered German first? Give a reason.

11.3   From Wittenberg Martin Luther spread his religious teachings and with them the local form of High German.
(a) Why might it seem strange that High German was spoken in a town with this name?
(b) What, would you suggest, does this illustrate about the nature of placenames?

11.4   Supply the missing Danish word:

English	Swedish	Danish
pipe	pipa	pibe
street	gata	gade
cake	kaka	

11.5   Account for the differences between the initial segments of the following words:

English	French	German
tooth	dent	Zahn

11.6   The Latin word *planus*, meaning *flat, even*, evolved into Italian *piano* (*flat, even*) and Portuguese *chão* (*floor*). Account for the phonological differences between these Italian and Portuguese words.

11.7   The French word *échelle*, meaning *ladder, scale*, has evolved from the Latin word *scalae*. Identify in this evolution three features of the phonological development of French.

11.8   (a) What are the principal phonological differences between Catalan and Portuguese as far as the consonants are concerned? Give examples.
(b) The Latin word for a moon is *luna*. What do you think it has become in Catalan and Portuguese?

11.9   (a) It is thought that the word *penguin* is derived from Breton. Using the examples of Welsh that you have been given, what feature of a bird (not necessarily a penguin!) do you think the word alludes to?
(b) The French word *baragouin* means *gibberish*, it resulting from the fact that the French could not understand the Bretons. What do you think was the meaning of the Breton phrase that gave rise to this word?

11.10   Give a pair of Finnish allomorphs.

For each of the following sentences, (a) say which language it is in and (b) translate the sentence into English.

11.11   Ao chegarmos o professor deu-nos a mão.

11.12   È il ponte più stretto della città.

11.13   Han ved at båden sank i denne havn.

11.14   La mère de mon ami est dans sa chambre.

11.15   Mijn vrouw is met de auto gekomen.

11.16   Bróðir minn gaf mér þessa orðabók.

11.17   Tha m'athair ag iasgach anns an loch.

11.18   Der Lehrer hatte das Boot des jungen Kindes gebrochen.

12

Writing Systems

or
Why Does the Coming Together of Two Women in China Result in a Quarrel?

12.1 Communication across Time and Space

We are near the end of the book and yet we have given little consideration to the visual representation of language, to writing. Back in chapter 1 we defined language as a system of communication by means of speech sounds – this reflects the emphasis that linguists place on the spoken language. The reasons for this emphasis include the fact that we acquire speech naturally while we have to be taught how to read and write, the fact that we generally speak more than we read and write, and the fact that writing develops as an adjunct to speech; some societies have no writing system and no society has developed a written language and only subsequently decided to transmit the utterances orally.

Nevertheless writing has played an important part in the development of our society. Our society requires communication to be made across space and time. Laws have to reach every part of the country and they have to endure. It would be difficult to build a power station without specifications and contracts. Almost as importantly, writing is allowing you to study the subject of language without having to travel to a particular place at a particular time to listen to me or some other linguist. Societies have often had to span space and time as best they could using such means as messengers and law-speakers, but they rarely offered the same potential that writing offers. In modern times rival means of communication, of bridging space and time, such as the telephone, the television, the tape recorder and the video have appeared, but writing still thrives.

This chapter looks at different ways in which humans communicate through writing.

12.2　Morphemic and Phonetic Script

The written representation of an object, of a concept, of an action, and so on may be a direct representation of the object itself or a representation of the word that represents the object. The characters or, more technically, the graphs <1> and <5> represent a concept directly; they are **morphemic** symbols. The written words <one> and <five>, on the other hand, are symbols of symbols; they represent the sounds that represent the concepts, they are **phonetic** symbols.

In some cases one may see in a morphemic symbol a visual representation of the object or concept that it represents. Our character <1> represents the concept of singularity by a single stroke; the same applies to the equivalent Roman numeral, <I>, and the characters used by the Arabs, <١ >, and the Chinese, < ━ >. The Roman and Chinese equivalents of <2> and <3> are similarly transparent. Our characters <2> and <3> become a little more transparent if we turn them clockwise through 90 degrees and compare them to the Arabic numerals from which they derive, <٢> and <٣>, these being the symbol <١> with the addition of one hook and two hooks respectively. But it would become increasingly cumbersome if we kept adding strokes or hooks, and eventually we use opaque characters like <5> which are linked to a particular concept only as a matter of convention, just as the sequence of sounds /faiv/ is. Thus there is no reason why a character that looks like our <7> should not represent the concept of six in Arabic, as is the case.

Phonetic systems may generally have a character for each sound segment; the written word <seven> represents the sequence of sounds /sevən/. Such a system is called an **alphabetic** system. Alternatively, phonetic systems may have a symbol for each syllable; these are **syllabic** systems. In addition to the Chinese symbols for the basic vocabulary, Japanese has other alphabets which it uses for its inflections, for foreign names, and so on. These supplementary alphabets are syllabic, this being quite adequate for a language in which the syllable structure is almost entirely consonant–vowel

(CV); it is not necessary to have separate symbols for consonants as they never occur in clusters.

The Chinese system of writing is primarily morphemic, while the system that we use is primarily phonetic. Among the more transparent symbols in Chinese are <山> and < 孑 >, simplified images of a mountain and a child respectively. Our written words <mountain> and <child> represent most immediately not the objects but the sequence of sounds that represents the objects. I have said 'primarily morphemic' because there are phonetic elements in the Chinese script. I have said 'primarily phonetic' because when we read we generally associate a visual pattern with an object or concept rather than spelling out the sounds represented by the characters. If we did spell them out the written words <child>, <one> and <five> might be as likely to have us say *chilled*, *own* and *fever*!

Like the pictograms that we see at airports around the world, morphemic symbols, symbols that represent something without the intermediate element of the spoken word, have the advantage that a written communication can be understood by people who speak so differently that they would not understand each other's spoken language. Without training we would not understand a Frenchman who says *quatre*, a Pole who says *cztery* or a Welshman who says *pedwar*, but the symbol <4> is internationally understood. Similarly, Chinese characters are understood throughout China even though the spoken language varies greatly. Given this variety, the writing system contributed greatly to the cohesion of the Chinese empire. Having adopted the Chinese script, even the Japanese understand characters that the Chinese use; the words for a mountain are mutually incomprehensible, the Chinese word, transliterated into Roman script, being *shān* and the Japanese word, similarly transliterated, being *yama*, but both write the character < 山 >.

Morphemic systems do, however, present problems in the modern age. Having a different graph for each morpheme clearly means that thousands of graphs must be used. It is easy enough for us to have a few symbols like <5, 7, +, &, => as a supplement to our alphabetic system, but imagine us having only such symbols, having to represent the words *dog*, *eat* and thousands of others by such symbols. A morphemic system introduces problems for typing and word processing. As international contact increases, the difficulty of representing foreign names without a phonetic writing system becomes more important. Foreign names may be represented by using for each syllable the graph for a word with a similar pronunciation, but this is cumbersome. To use an example given by Geoffrey Sampson (1985, p. 167), the name Tchaikovsky is represented in Chinese by five graphs, graphs which if read for their semantic content rather than their sound would convey 'firewood, suddenly, begin, this, foundation'!

Our alphabetic system has advantages of economy and adaptability. Only a modest number of graphs are needed and they can be combined to represent any permutations, to represent, for example, our various consonant clusters.

Generally speaking phonetic systems develop out of morphemic systems. When humans first wanted to convey visually the idea of an object it was natural that they should draw an image of that object rather than attempt to represent the sound of whatever word they used to denote that object. The former required no convention, no training; the latter did. Through time the image may become stylised and conventions may develop. The moon might be represented as a half moon, as a semi-circle, to distinguish it from the circle that might represent the sun.

Somewhere along the line humans passed from drawing pictures to writing with morphemic symbols. It is generally considered that the representation is writing once it can only be understood by those who are party to the culture concerned, who share the convention. Thus Sampson says that one might suggest that a key distinguishing feature of writing is that it 'communicates ideas in a *conventional* manner' (Sampson, 1985, p. 26). He proceeds to say that there is convention in art too, but the fact remains that art transcends cultural boundaries much more easily than writing does. The American practice of displaying the word <walk> at pedestrian crossings uses language, even if people who do not speak English may come to understand the message by associating it with the shape and combination of the characters. The European practice of displaying an image of a man walking is not language.

What that green walking man is is a **pictogram** or an **ideogram**. If one considers pictograms and ideograms to be different one will consider a pictogram to be more of an image, an ideogram to be more conventional. Of the icons that are displayed in railway stations, the image of a train that indicates where the trains are to be found is more of a pictogram than is the symbol <i> that indicates where one can obtain information, the latter being derived from a word. Clearly, concrete objects lend themselves to representation by pictograms more readily than more abstract concepts do. One is more likely to use the term *pictogram* for the Chinese graph for a mountain, <山>, than for that of the concept of one thing being located above another, < 上 >. But it is not easy to distinguish between pictograms and ideograms.

Whether pictograms or ideograms, images tend, as we have seen, to become stylised. A further development may be that the stylised image comes to be associated not only with a particular object but also with the initial sound of the word that denotes that object. When this happens the system has begun to develop from a morphemic system to a phonetic one. In the Middle East a graph that represented an ox's head came to be associated with the initial sound of the word for an ox, *'aleph*. It has come down to us as the letter <A>.

12.3   Chinese Script – A Morphemic System

As we have seen, the Chinese system of writing is primarily morphemic, the characters being associated directly with the object or concept that they denote rather than with the sounds of a spoken word. Images become more stylised and more angular, but in some cases one can still see a resemblance between the character and the object denoted. We have already referred to the character that denotes a mountain, <山>, and the character that denotes a child, <子>; other examples are the characters < 日 > and < 木 >, which denote the sun and a tree respectively. So, too, we can see a logic in various characters that denote abstract concepts; <上>, <下> and <中> denote the concepts of above, below and middle (the last of these is found in <中国 >, the digraph that denotes China, the Chinese referring to their country as the Central Country). Superimposing the character for a tree on that for the sun, thereby alluding to the sun rising behind the trees, gives a character that denotes the concept of east: <東>. As with the digraph for China, concepts may be represented by combining or reduplicating characters. The characters for the sun and the moon together, <日月>, denote the concept of brightness. The character for a woman together with that for a child, <女子 >, denotes goodness and love. On a more negative note, the reduplication of the character for a woman, <⼥⼥>, denotes quarrelling. These may be referred to as symbolic compounds.

When referring to the Chinese writing system I qualified the word *morphemic* with the word *primarily* for there developed a phonetic element. The character representing one concept may also come to be used to denote another concept that is denoted by a word that sounds similar. Thus it may be sound rather than concept that is the common thread linking different uses of a character. Often the semantic element, the radical, is supplemented by a phonetic element that indicates the spoken word, this specifying the sense of the semantic element. Thus, for example, the character for a woman can be accompanied by another indicating the sounds /ma/ to denote the particular kind of woman indicated by these sounds, a mother. The same phonetic element is added to the character for a mouth to denote scolding, that also being pronounced /ma/, albeit with a different tone. As with our own language, the link between a phonetic element and pronunciation may become tenuous as changes in pronunciation fail to be reflected by the written characters.

The Japanese adopted Chinese characters. We have seen, for example, that the character for a mountain is used by both. But the Japanese needed to supplement the system with graphs that would deal with such features of their language as inflections and grammatical particles. Thus the morphemic Chinese symbols (kanji) are supplemented by two syllabic scripts (hiragana and katakana).

In Japanese the Chinese characters generally represent content words, words such as nouns and verbs, while inflections and particles are represented by hiragana. Katakana is used mainly to write foreign words; America, for example, is represented by the katakana graphs for the syllables /a/, /me/, /ri/ and /ka/: <ア,メ,リ,カ>.

12.4   Roman Script – An Alphabetic System

The writing system that we use came to us from the Middle East by way of the Greeks and the Romans. It had its roots in a morphemic system, probably Egyptian hieroglyphs, but the Phoenicians, a Semitic people, associated symbols with the initial sound of certain words as well as with the objects that those words denoted. As we have seen, they associated the graph for an ox, <∆>, with the initial sound of the spoken word, *'aleph*, and, subsequently rotated, this has come to us as our letter <A>. Similarly, our letter <B> began life as the graph representing a house, the word denoting a house being *beth*, the first morph of *Bethlehem*. These words were used to denote these alphabetic graphs – hence the word *alphabetic*.

This development is as though we were to use the symbol <4> to represent the first sound of our word *four*, /f/. If we did the same with the symbols <8> and <3> we could write the word *faith* as <483>!

As in subsequent Semitic languages, the system developed by the Phoenicians represented only the consonants; the initial sound of the word *'aleph* was a glottal stop, not a vowel.

The Phoenicians were great traders and some eight or ten centuries B.C. their writing sytem was adopted by the Greeks. But the Greeks felt that they had to be able to represent vowels as well and they did so by using Phoenician symbols that were not needed for consonants; *'aleph* was one such graph. Another change made by the Greeks concerned the direction in which one wrote; the Phoenicians had written from right to left but the Greeks eventually wrote from left to right. The writing in fact became a mirror image of what it had been, for the letters were also turned round; Semitic < ∃ >, for example, became Greek <E>. This development took place by way of the practice of changing direction at the end of the line; this practice was likened to the passage of an ox ploughing a field and was consequently called boustrophedon.

The Greek alphabet passed to the Romans, probably by way of the Etruscans. Certain changes took place in the process; as the Etruscans had no voiced plosive sounds the Romans had, for example, to restore a symbol for the sound [g], which they did by amending the character <C>, the symbol for the voiceless equivalent.

Accompanying the introduction of Christianity, the Roman alphabet came to Anglo-Saxon both directly from Rome and by way of Ireland. Thus it was Roman largely influenced by the forms that the Roman characters had adopted in Ireland. Again certain amendments were required to cater for the features of the phonology; thus the symbol <þ> was adopted from the runic alphabet to represent the sound /θ/ which had been unrepresented in the Roman alphabet. The runic alphabet, called the futhork after its first six characters (<ᚠ, ᚾ, ᚦ, ᚠ, ᚱ, ᚲ>), had been another development from the Greek alphabet, it having been adopted by the Germanic peoples and adapted to facilitate carving. Particularly after the Norman Conquest, the English alphabet was increasingly influenced by continental forms.

Another branch of the development took the Greek alphabet to the eastern Slavs. Here again the alphabet accompanied Christianity. In the ninth century the faith – or, if you prefer, the 483! – and the writing system were taken to the Slavs by two Greek brothers. These missionaries were called Cyril and Methodius and the resulting alphabet is known as the Cyrillic alphabet. In this case, too, the system was altered to reflect differences in phonology; to represent /ju/, for example, the characters <I> and <O> were linked to produce <Ю>.

Some Slavs received Christianity from Rome rather than Greece and this is reflected in the alphabet used. The Polish and Russian equivalents of our word *truth* are very similar to each other, but the Poles, having received Christianity from the west, write <prawda> and the Russians, having received Christianity from the east, write <правда>.

As it is a Semitic language – like the language of the Phoenicians – Arabic uses a script that has also been developed from that of the Phoenicians. Arabic continues the Semitic tradition of writing from right to left. Furthermore, it generally only represents the consonants; in Arabic it is the consonants that indicate the semantic core of words, the vowels merely indicating derivations or grammatical variations. Whether the Arabic system is alphabetic or syllabic is debatable given that it does not represent the vowel sounds.

The spread of Islam took the use of the Arabic script to non-Semitic languages such as Persian and Turkish.

12.5 Allographs

The form of a graph may vary; instead of <h> we use <H> at the beginning of a sentence. Just as variant forms of phonemes and morphemes are called allophones and allomorphs, so, too, such variants of graphs that are determined by context or position can be called **allographs**.

The Arabic script is cursive and so graphs are often joined to each other. As a result there are different forms for each graph depending on its position in a word; the sound /b/ is represented by < ب > but

when linked the form is < ﯨ > in initial position, < ﯿ > in medial
position and < ﺐ > in final position. The word for a house, a cognate
of *beth*, illustrates the form in initial position (which, remember, is to
the right): بيت.

And that's another thing – chimpanzees wouldn't be able to write
a specification or an operating manual for a power station!

Summary

As a supplement to their spoken language societies have often
developed a system of writing so that their communication can
transcend time and space. If, like Chinese script, the system primarily represents objects and concepts directly it is morphemic; if, like
our script, it represents the sounds of the words that represent the
objects and concepts it is phonetic. Phonetic systems may be
alphabetic or syllabic. Phonetic systems generally develop out of
morphemic systems, images becoming symbols representing objects,
some symbols in turn becoming associated with a sound that
represents the object concerned.

Exercises

12.1 How and why have the Japanese supplemented the system of
characters that they inherited from the Chinese?

12.2 What are the benefits of an alphabetic system over the
alternatives? Explain with examples why these benefits are
greater in some languages than in others.

12.3 Outline the history of the letter <A>.

12.4 Give examples of how religion has influenced the alphabet that
a society uses.

Glossary

ablaut *Ablaut* is the production of variants of a lexeme by means of changes to the root vowel. Also called **vowel gradation**.

accent *Accent* is the manner of pronunciation of a speech variety.

affix An affix is a semantic or syntactic element joined to a word to make another, e.g. the *re-* in *rejoin*.

affricate An affricate is a consonant sound that begins as a plosive and ends as a fricative, e.g. [dʒ].

agglutinating/agglutinative language This is a language in which concepts that we would express using prepositions, possessive adjectives, and so on are expressed as morphs concatenated in the same word as the relevant base. An example is Finnish in which the equivalent of *in my house* is *talossani*.

agreement Agreement is the reflection in one word of the grammatical properties of a word that it accompanies. In *These books are mine* the words *these* and *are* reflect the fact that *books* is plural. Also called **concord**.

allograph An allograph is a variant form of a written character; <h> and <H> are allographs.

allomorph An allomorph is a variant form of a morph. The variation may be determined by phonological environment, as with the allomorphs /s/ and /z/ of the plural morpheme in *cats and dogs*.

allophone An allophone is a variant form of a phone that is dependent on context and cannot be functionally significant.

alphabetic script An alphabetic script is a writing system in which each phonemic segment is represented by a character. We use such a system, our segment /p/, for example, being represented by the character <p>.

alveolar ridge The alveolar ridge is the ridge behind the upper teeth which may, for example, be the place of articulation of the sound [t].

analogy Analogy is the change to one form under the influence of another, often change to an irregular form under the influence of a regular form. As an example, the Middle English past participle *holpen* became *helped*.

analytic language This is a language which tends to express each concept and function by means of a separate word. A good example is Chinese. English is also fairly analytic; cf. *We live in that white house*. Also called **isolating language**.

apocope Apocope is the loss of the final element of a word.

approximant An approximant is a consonant sound that entails a minimum of constriction of the airflow, e.g. [w].

argot Argot is a type of slang used by a group as a secret means of communication.

aspiration Aspiration is an expulsion of air as a consonant is articulated; the /t/ in *top* is aspirated and as such may be represented in phonemic transcription as /t^h/.

assimilation Assimilation is a change to a sound under the influence of another, as, for example, when the prefix *in-* became *im-* in *imprison* under the influence of the bilabial /p/.

auxiliary verb An auxiliary verb is a verb which may accompany a lexical verb. It may do so to fulfil a grammatical function, as *do* does in negating constructions such as *I do not know*. It may indicate mood, as in *I should know*, in which case it may be called a modal auxiliary.

back vowel A back vowel is a vowel produced with the tongue drawn back in the mouth, e.g. [u].

backformation Backformation is the development of a lexeme by the erroneous assumption that it formed the basis for another lexeme, e.g. the development of the verb *edit* from the noun *editor*.

bilabial A bilabial sound is a sound in which the two lips are used in its articulation, e.g. [p].

blend word A blend word is a compound word in which at least one element has been abbreviated, e.g. *motor cavalcade* becoming *motorcade*.

calque A calque is a lexeme adopted in translated form by one language from another, as the English lexeme *honeymoon* was adopted by French as *lune de miel*. Also called **loan translation**.

cardinal vowel The cardinal vowels are a set of vowels that serve as reference points for describing the vowel system of individual languages.

clause A clause is a sequence of words that incorporates a subject and a predicate. It may be a whole sentence (e.g. *He will do it today*) or part of a sentence (e.g. *. . . that he will do it today*).

clitic A clitic is a variant of a word that is reduced in such a way that it has no syllable and so is dependent on another word, such as the *-'s* in *He's asleep*.

close vowel A close vowel is a vowel produced with the tongue high in the mouth, e.g. [iː].

code-switching Code-switching is the use of different speech varieties depending on the social context.

cognate The noun *cognate* denotes a lexeme that derives from the same source as another. The adjective *cognate* similarly describes two or more lexemes that derive from the same source. Thus, for example, the Spanish word *lleno* and the Italian word *pieno* can be said to be cognates or cognate, both deriving from the Latin word *plenus*.

collocation Collocation is the conventional combination of lexemes as in, for example, *auspicious circumstances*.

componential analysis Componential analysis is the semantic analysis of a lexeme in terms of the presence or absence of distinctive features.

compound A compound is a lexeme that is composed of two or more roots, e.g. *boathouse*.

concord Concord is the reflection in one word of the grammatical properties of a word that it accompanies; in *These books are mine* the words *these* and *are* reflect the fact that *books* is plural. Also called **agreement**.

connotation Connotation is an association between a lexeme and a concept that arises from a person's attitudes, experiences, and so on, as the lexeme *school* might connote boredom for some children.

consonant A consonant is a speech sound produced with total or substantial obstruction of the airflow, e.g. [p] and [f].

constituent structure Constituent structure is the hierarchical relationship between words, phrases and sentences.

content word A content word is a word that denotes something, that has a full lexical meaning, e.g. *arrow, departure, hopeless*. A content word is opposed to a function word.

conversion The conversion of a word is the process of using it in a different word class, as when, for example, the noun *table* came to be used as a verb as in, for example, *They tabled a different proposal.*

creole A creole is a variety that has developed from a pidgin to the extent that it serves as the principal language of a community.

deep structure *Deep structure* is a term used in transformational grammar to denote the underlying structure of an utterance.

deixis Deixis is the situation in which the referent of a lexeme is dependent on the context, e.g. *until then.*

derivation Derivation is the development of one lexeme from another by affixation, e.g. the development of *shallowness* from *shallow.*

diachronic A diachronic view of language is a view over a period of time. Diachronic is opposed to synchronic.

diacritic A diacritic is a mark added to a written symbol to indicate a variation of the pronunciation of the sound represented by that symbol, as in the French word *jeté* meaning *thrown.*

dialect A dialect is a speech variety used by a community comprising some of those who speak a particular language.

dialect continuum A dialect continuum is a succession of speech varieties without major linguistic boundaries.

diglossia Diglossia is a state whereby a society has two distinct speech varieties, one being used in more formal contexts, the other in less formal contexts.

diphthong A diphthong is a vowel which glides from one position to another as in, for example, the word *house* in which the vowel rises in the course of its production.

discourse analysis Discourse analysis is the study of the dynamics of a conversation.

drag chain A drag chain is a sequence of sound changes initiated by one sound drawing away from the others. A drag chain is opposed to a push chain.

embedding Embedding is the inclusion of one clause within another, e.g. *The dog I bought last week has died.*

emotive utterance An emotive utterance is an expression of emotion, e.g. *That's fantastic!.*

euphemism A euphemism is an acceptable alternative to a taboo word.

felicity condition A felicity condition is a condition that must apply before an utterance can constitute a speech act; *I promise to* *do it tomorrow* is no promise if the speaker is unable to do what is promised or if he does not feel bound by his utterance.

focal area A focal area is the core of a dialect area.

fricative A fricative sound is a sound articulated by the constriction of the airflow in such a way that audible friction results, e.g. [f].

front vowel A front vowel is a vowel produced with the tongue pushed forward in the mouth, e.g. [iː].

function word A function word is a word that indicates a grammatical relationship between elements of an utterance, e.g. *of* and *and*. A function word is opposed to a content word.

glottal stop A glottal stop is a sound produced by a complete obstruction and release of the airflow at the larynx.

head A head is the principal element of a phrase. In the phrase *these young men* the head is the word *men*, the word *men* indicating the referent and the other words providing supplementary information.

historical linguistics Historical linguistics is the study of language change.

homograph A homograph is a lexeme that is written in the same way as another, e.g. *wind* as in *The wind is blowing* and *wind* as in *The paths wind up the hill* are homographs.

homonym A homonym is a lexeme that has the same form as another.

homonymic clash Homonymic clash is a change whereby two or more words come to have the same form, e.g. *sound* denoting something that one hears and *sound* denoting being in good condition.

homophone A homophone is a lexeme that is pronounced in the same way as another, e.g. *meet* and *meat* are homophones.

hyponymy Hyponymy is the hierarchical arrangement of lexemes whereby the semantic range of a lexeme encompasses those of two or more other lexemes, e.g. *cat* and *dog* are hyponyms of *mammal*.

i-mutation I-mutation is the fronting of a root vowel under the influence of a front vowel in a suffix. Also called ***umlaut***.

idiolect An idiolect is the speech variety of an individual.

idiom An idiom is a phrase which can only be understood as a unit, not as a summation of the meaning of each constituent word; *kick the bucket*, for example, contains little that would suggest dying.

implicature An implicature is something which has not been explicitly stated in an utterance but which has to be inferred if a communication is to be successful; *Sorry, no dogs* on a butcher's door is only correctly understood if we infer that dogs are rarely eaten in our society and that hygiene is an important consideration in a food shop.

inflecting language An inflecting language is a language which makes extensive use of inflection. An example is Spanish in which, for example, *vivimos* is an inflected root, as opposed to the analytic English equivalent *we live*.

inflection Inflection is the grammatical marking of a lexeme by means of an affix as, for example, the affix *-ed* in *waited* indicates past tense.

intonation Intonation is the variation in pitch during the course of an utterance.

isogloss An isogloss is a line on a map that delimits the area in which a dialectal feature dominates.

isolating language An isolating language is a language which tends to express each concept and function by means of a separate word. Also called **analytic language**.

labiodental A labiodental sound is a consonant sound in which the flow of air is constricted by the upper teeth being held against the lower lip, e.g. [f].

lateral A lateral sound is a consonant sound in which the airflow passes to either side of the tongue, e.g. [l].

lenition Lenition is the weakening of a consonant, often under the influence of neighbouring vowels. This may take the form of voiceless consonants becoming voiced or plosives becoming fricative; thus, for example, the Old Norse *gata*, meaning *road*, has become *gade* in Danish, the voiceless plosive /t/ having become the voiced fricative /ð/.

lexeme A lexeme is an item of vocabulary which may consist of one or more than one word, e.g. *concede, give in*. The term is often used to denote the basic uninflected form of an item; the lexeme *give* can, for example, be realised by such words as *gives* and *gave*.

loan translation Loan translation is the adoption of a lexeme from another language in translated form, e.g. the adoption of *honeymoon* by French as *lune de miel*. Also called **calque**.

loanword A loanword is a lexeme adopted by one language from another.

manner of articulation The manner of articulation of a consonant is the way in which the flow of air is constricted in its production. The manner of articulation of the segment [f], for example, is fricative.

metanalysis Metanalysis is change to a word resulting from erroneous division between words; as an example, *an adder* evolved from *a naddre*.

metathesis Metathesis is the inversion of segments of a word; as an example, Middle English *brid* became modern English *bird*.

minimal pair A minimal pair is a pair of words that are phonologically the same but for one segment, this serving to illustrate that two sounds are separate phonemes; thus the words *foal* and *vole* are a minimal pair that shows /f/ and /v/ to be contrastive in English.

mood The mood of an utterance is its status in terms of expression of fact (*She is doing it today*), expression of possibility (*She may be doing it today*), and so on.

morph A morph is the form in which a morpheme is realised; thus, for example, the segment /s/ is a morph of the plural morpheme in English.

morpheme A morpheme is a minimal unit that is of grammatical or semantic significance. A morpheme that can stand by itself is a free morpheme, a morpheme that cannot stand by itself is a bound morpheme. The word *painters*, for example, consists of three morphemes, the free morpheme *paint* and the bound morphemes *-er* and *-s*.

morphemic script Morphemic script is a writing system in which a character represents an object or concept itself as opposed to the sounds of the spoken word that denotes the object or concept.

morphology Morphology is the study of the composition of words.

mutation Mutation is change to a sound in certain morphological or syntactic contexts. Mutation produced the verb *feet* as a cognate of the noun *foot* and it is seen in, for example, the Welsh phrase *ei ben*, meaning *his head*, the basic form of the noun being *pen*.

narrow transcription A narrow transcription is a more detailed phonemic transcription whereby, for example, an aspirated [t] is represented as [tʰ].

nasal A nasal consonant is one which is produced by passing air through the nasal cavity, e.g. [n].

nasalisation Nasalisation is the change to a sound resulting from the presence of a nasal consonant as in, for example, the French word *vin*.

neo-classical compound A neo-classical compound is a compound word consisting of Latin or Greek elements, e.g. *hepatitis*.

noun phrase A noun phrase is a phrase that denotes an object, concept, and so on. It will generally include a noun and a determiner and may include one or more adjectives, e.g. *that young man*.

organ of speech An organ of speech is an organ of the body that may be used to produce a speech sound, e.g. lungs, lips, the tongue.

palatalisation Palatalisation is the movement of the place of articulation of a sound towards the hard palate under the influence of a neighbouring sound.

performative utterance A performative utterance is an utterance which is itself an act, e.g. *I declare this bridge open*.

phatic communion Phatic communion is the use of speech to maintain social relations, e.g. *Pleased to meet you*.

phone A phone is a minimal distinct speech sound, e.g. [f]. Also called a **segment.**

phoneme A phoneme is a sound that is semantically or functionally distinctive in a language system.

phonemic alphabet A phonemic alphabet is an alphabet in which there is a one-to-one correspondence between speech sounds and the characters that represent them.

phonetics Phonetics is the study of speech sounds.

phonology Phonology is the study of the sound systems of languages.

phrase A phrase is a semantically cohesive sequence of words. An example is the sequence *that old car*, this denoting a particular object.

phrase structure rules Phrase structure rules are rules which determine whether or not a sequence of words is grammatical.

pictogram A pictogram is a stylised visual representation of an object.

pidgin A pidgin is a means of communication between people with different first languages.

place of articulation The place of articulation of a sound is the place where the flow of air is constricted in the production of that sound; in the case of the sound [p], for example, this is the lips.

plosive   A plosive consonant is one that is produced by completely obstructing the flow of air, e.g. [p], [t]. Also called a **stop**.

polysemy   Polysemy is the situation in which a lexeme has two or more distinct referents.

popular etymology   Popular etymology is the process whereby a loanword is modified to make it semantically more acceptable. By this process the French word *crevisse* became *crayfish* in English.

pragmatics   Pragmatics is the study of the relationship between linguistic form and intended communication.

prefix   A prefix is a bound morph affixed infront of a root, e.g. *re-* in *rejoin*.

push chain   A push chain is a sequence of sound changes initiated by one sound approximating to another; other sounds then change to maintain their distinctiveness. A push chain is opposed to a drag chain.

redundancy   Redundancy is the situation in which an utterance contains more information than is necessary for successful communication. Given that we need to indicate the subject, it is unnecessary, as the Scandinavian languages show, to mark the third-person singular form of the verb as in *She drives*.

regional standard   A regional standard is a more formal speech variety used by speakers in part of a language area.

register   A register is a speech variety, the use of which is determined by social context.

root   A root is a morph that forms the core of a word. It may form a word by itself, it may be accompanied by another root, by an affix or by combinations of these. The root of *rejoined* is *-join-*.

segment   A segment is a minimal distinctive speech sound, e.g. [f]. Also called a **phone**.

semantic extension   Semantic extension is the extension of the semantic range of a lexeme to incorporate a new concept, e.g. the use of *mouse* to denote an object used to operate a word-processor.

semantic range   The semantic range of a lexeme is the set of objects or concepts that that lexeme denotes.

semi-vowel   A semi-vowel is a speech sound that resembles a consonant in that it must be accompanied in a syllable by a vowel but resembles a vowel in that it does not entail constriction of the airflow, e.g. [w].

slang Slang is a variety of speech that may be used to reinforce the identity of a section of society.

sociolinguistics Sociolinguistics is the study of the relationship between language and society.

sound symbolism Sound symbolism is a relationship between a sound and that which is denoted.

speech act A speech act is an action performed by means of an utterance such as *I apologise for my mistake*.

standard language A standard language is a codified norm of a language used in formal contexts.

stop A stop is a consonant that is produced by completely obstructing the flow of air, e.g. [p], [t]. Also called a **plosive** as the flow is then released in a burst.

stress Stress is the greater prominance given to a syllable by means of greater articulatory force.

suffix A suffix is a bound morph affixed behind a root, e.g. *-er* in *painter*.

suppletion Suppletion is the use of an etymologically unrelated word for a grammatically marked form of a lexeme, e.g. *went* as the past tense form of *to go*.

suprasegmental feature A suprasegmental feature is a phonological feature that applies to a unit larger than a segment.

surface structure Surface structure is a term used in transformational grammar to denote the actual syntactic realisation in a language of an utterance.

syllabic script Syllabic script is a writing system in which characters represent syllables. An example is the Japanese katakana script in which, for example, the character < カ > represents the syllable /ka/.

syllable A syllable is a phonological unit consisting of one or more segments, the basis of the unit being a nucleus, usually a vowel. The word *syllable* consists of three syllables: /si/, /lə/ and /bl/.

synchronic A synchronic view of language studies language at a particular point in time. Synchronic is opposed to diachronic.

syncope Syncope is the loss of an element within a word, e.g. the loss of the segment /i/ in the evolution from the Latin word *domina*, meaning *lady*, to the Italian word *donna*.

syntax Syntax is the study of the composition of sentences.

taboo word A taboo word is a word that is often avoided because it may cause offence.

tone language A tone language is a language in which pitch distinguishes between words that are otherwise homophones. An example is Mandarin Chinese.

transformational rules Transformational rules are rules for converting one syntactic structure into another, e.g. for converting the statement *She works here* into the question *Does she work here?*

transitional area A transitional area is an area with features of different dialects.

typology Typology is the study of features common to languages irrespective of the relationship between the languages concerned, e.g. the use of a suffixed definite article in south-east Europe.

umlaut Umlaut is the fronting of a root vowel under the influence of a front vowel in a suffix. Also called **i-mutation**. The term *umlaut* is also used to denote the mark used above vowels in German in the context of such mutation, as in *Häuser*, the plural of *Haus*, meaning *house*.

velum The velum is the soft palate at the rear of the mouth.

verb phrase A verb phrase is a phrase including a verb and accompanying items such as adverbs, e.g. *has not slept well recently*.

vocal cords Vocal cords are muscular tissue in the larynx, the vibration of which contributes to the production of vowels and voiced consonants.

voiced A speech sound is voiced if it entails vibration of the vocal cords, e.g. [g].

voiceless A speech sound is voiceless if it does not entail vibration of the vocal cords, e.g. [k].

vowel A vowel is a voiced speech sound constricted only by the shape of the tongue and the lips.

vowel gradation Vowel gradation is the production of variants of a lexeme by means of changes to the root vowel; an example is *rode*, the past tense of *to ride*. Also called *ablaut*.

vowel harmony Vowel harmony is the approximation of the vowel in a suffix to that in a root, typically such that both are front vowels or both are back vowels. This is a feature of, for example, Finnish and Turkish.

wave theory Wave theory is a theory of the principles whereby linguistic change spreads.

word class A word class is a category of words which share similar functions. The word class adjective, for example, contains words

which indicate properties of nouns. Word classes have traditionally been known as parts of speech.

word-and-paradigm morphology Word-and-paradigm morphology is morphology that treats the word as an entity rather than as
a succession of morphemes.

Guide to Exercises

1.1 The definition of the term *language* that I proposed in section 1.2 was 'Language is a form of human communication by means of a system of symbols principally transmitted by vocal sounds.' The element 'human' reflects the fact that it is generally only human communication that exhibits the productivity and the cultural transmission that is usually associated with language. 'Communication' reflects a major function of language (perhaps the major function – see question 1.3). 'System' reflects the fact that language provides a system or framework for generating utterances. 'Symbols' reflects the fact that the connection between word and thing is usually a matter of convention. 'Vocal sounds' alludes to the principal means of transmission of an utterance. What we understand by the term *language* may vary and variations on the above definition may, of course, be acceptable.

1.2 Language helps us to exchange information, to learn, to plan, to co-operate, to establish and maintain relationships. It helps us to refer to things that are removed from us in time and space.

1.3 Clearly communication is a major element of the function of human language. How major an element it is depends on one's definition of 'communication'. There can be little doubt that telling somebody that a train leaves at ten past four is an example of communication. A performative utterance such as declaring a bridge open is, on the other hand, primarily an action rather than communication, even though the utterance, together with any symbolic action such as cutting a tape, communicates to others that the action is taking place. More debatable are the likes of emotive utterances; if some frustration causes you to curse, are you communicating your frustration or relieving your tension?

2.1 Your definition should acknowledge the fact that a word is a sound or, usually, a sequence of sounds that is conventionally associated with an object, concept, and so on. To distinguish a word from a bound morpheme you should allude somehow to the independent nature of words; this may be done with reference to, for example, substitution or pausing. You should acknowledge the problem of distinguishing a word from a phrase with a similar function, e.g. *to appear* and *to turn up*; one might address the problem by arguing that, while *turn* and *up* form a unit in this sense, they can be used independently of each other in other senses.

2.2   One might refer to the form or the function of a towel. The former approach might produce a compound like *clothsquare* or extend the semantic range of the word *cloth*. The latter approach might produce something like *handdrier*. A combination of the two approaches might produce *handcloth* (cf. Swedish *handduk*) or *drycloth*. One might borrow a term from a foreign language, e.g. the French term *essuie-mains*. To make it more acceptable, this French term might conceivably be altered phonologically to *swimming*, particularly as there is a connection between the object concerned and the activity of swimming; this would be an example of popular etymology. Alternatively, the elements of the French term might be translated into English, this being another development that might produce *handdrier*; this would be an example of loan translation. The object might be given the name of a person, company or place associated with it.

2.3   The object is a crowbar.

3.1   In book titles content words are generally written with a capital initial letter while function words are not.

3.2   (a) One might distinguish between buses and cars by introducing a category such as 'public' (or, conversely, 'private').
(b) A motorcycle would be defined as +powered, +carries people, –four-wheeled, –public.

3.3   Possible hyponymy diagrams for these words include the following:

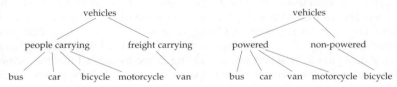

3.4   Your answer should show awareness of the variety of factors that may prevent words from being completely interchangeable. We have seen that syntax prevents *hide* and *conceal* being considered synonyms. In one context we might use either of two words but in another context we might only be able to use one, as we saw with *high* and *tall*. Two words might be distinguished by social register, one being more colloquial than the other, by whether they are associated with a positive or negative point of view, and so on.

3.5   The words *man* and *boy* are principally distinguished by age, the words *walk* and *run* by speed. The principal distinction between the words *toilet* and *loo* is one of social register. *Determined* and *stubborn* are largely distinguished by attitude – a person reluctant to give up is described as *determined* by those who sympathise and as *stubborn* by those who do not. The difference between the words *pavement* and *sidewalk* is a matter of geography, the former being used in Britain and the latter in America.

3.6 Two words with the same form may be different lexemes or may refer to different elements of the semantic range of the one lexeme. But it is often difficult to decide which is the case. One guide is the degree of similarity between the sense of the two words (consideration of foreign equivalents might help). Another guide is etymology; if the two words come from distinct sources they are more likely to belong to different lexemes. The decision of whether or not two words belong to the same lexeme is of practical significance to lexicographers as it determines whether the words should be presented under the one headword or as separate headwords.

3.7 In a situation like a bank robbery the principal intention of this utterance might be to warn. At a hunting event, on the other hand, it might be intended to convey that it is not necessary to provide a gun for somebody.

3.8 For a soldier to respond to the call *Fire!* he needs to have a gun, the call should come from a superior officer, and so on.

3.9 This sentence might be expanded to something like *Mrs Smith will try to sell the table at the market here in Winchester on Saturday 25 April*. Even this presupposes that the listener knows which Mrs Smith, which table and which year the speaker is referring to.

4.1 The words *coast* and *ghost* are distinguished by the fact that the initial segment is voiceless in the case of the former and voiced in the case of the latter. The words *ghost* and *boast* are distinguished by the place of articulation of the initial segment, /g/ being velar while /b/ is bilabial. *Boast* and *most* are distinguished by the manner of articulation of the initial segment, /m/ being nasal. *Most* and *mist* are distinguished by the fact that the former has a rounded back vowel while the latter has a spread front vowel.

4.2 [b] is a voiced bilabial plosive. [v] is a voiced labiodental fricative. [k] is a voiceless velar plosive.

4.3 The initial segment of the word *plosive* is a plosive sound, that of the word *fricative* is a fricative sound, that of the word *nasal* is a nasal sound and that of the word *liquid* is a liquid sound. (Do we possibly have examples of sound symbolism here?)

4.4 If one's nose is blocked nasal segments may be articulated like their oral counterparts. Thus the bilabial [m] may sound like [b], the alveolar [n] may sound like [d] and the velar [ŋ] may sound like [g].

4.5 As [b] is a bilabial sound, articulated with the lips, it is more difficult for a ventriloquist to conceal what he is doing.

4.6 The vowel of the word *cheese*, /iː/, is produced with the lips spread, this resembling a smile.

4.7 There is a glide from a relatively open back position towards a close front position, the lips changing from rounded to spread.

4.8 One can say that consonants need to be accompanied by a vowel, that they cannot be maintained, that they are articulated with audible friction. The distinction is, however, blurred by the fact that some consonants are more 'vowel-like' than others; the liquid consonant [l], for example, can stand in a syllable without a vowel and it can be maintained.

4.9 auə sʌn wɔz drʌŋk twais last mʌnθ.

4.10 The words *surface* and *service* only differ in that the former has a voiceless /f/ while the latter has a voiced /v/.

4.11 Plosive sounds are represented by straight strokes, fricative sounds by curved strokes. Labial sounds are represented by strokes that fall to the right, alveolar sounds by verticle strokes. Voiced sounds are represented by heavier strokes.

5.1
o/ɔ (torta/tɔrta)	n/r (tʃɛnto/tʃɛrto)
o/a (tɔrto/tɔrta)	t/d (kwanto/kwando)
(konto/kanto)	t/k (tanto/kanto)
n/l (konto/kolto)	t/p (kolto/kolpo)

5.2 Voiced plosives become voiceless in syllable-final position.

5.3 /id/, /d/, /t/, /id/. /id/ follows another alveolar plosive. Otherwise, /d/ follows voiced consonants and /t/ follows voiceless consonants, there being voicing assimilation.

5.4 köpte, byggde, levde, lekte

5.5 <s> represents /s/ in initial position, /ʃ/ in final position and before consonants and /z/ between vowels. This applies irrespective of word boundaries.

5.6 grawl, tritch

5.7 strike, splash, square, etc. Only /s/ can occur in first position. The second segment must be a voiceless plosive (/p, t, k/). The third must be a liquid or a semi-vowel (/l, r, w, j/). Not all of these combinations would be possible; as question 5.6 showed, the combination /stw/, for example, is not permissible.

5.8 The sequence /ŋkl/ bridges two syllables.

5.9 Finnish tends to avoid consonant clusters. It has traditionally avoided beginning words with a voiced plosive sound.

5.10　This is an example of i-mutation/ *umlaut* in the comparative form of the adjective.

5.11　conflict, confine, abstract, and so on.

5.12　In adjectives ending in *-ic* the stress moves to the following syllable, in adjectives ending in *-ful* it does not.

5.13　The first utterance implies that John was unable to do what he wanted. The second implies that he was only able to do something else. The third implies that he was only able to do it some other day.

6.1　(a) The *-er* and the *-'s* of *teacher's* are bound morphemes, the former being derivational, as it produces a lexeme that denotes the person who does an action, the latter being an inflectional morpheme, as it indicates possession. The *-ed* of *considered* is inflectional, indicating that the action took place in the past. The *im-* of *impossible* is derivational, producing a new lexeme that denotes the opposite of *possible*.
(b) In the word *project* one can identify two elements that had a meaning in Latin, *pro-* and *-ject* indicating movement forwards and throwing respectively. But neither element can stand by itself, neither is a free morpheme.

6.2　waited, waded　　/id/　(/d/ would merge with another alveolar
　　　　　　　　　　　　　　　　plosive if not separated by a vowel.)
　　　　waved　　　　　/d/　(voiced /v/ is followed by voiced /d/)
　　　　wiped　　　　　/t/　(voiceless /p/ is followed by voiceless /t/).

6.3　(a) *barn*, meaning *children*. (b) The singular definite article as in *bilen* and the plural definite article as in *barnen*.

6.4　Suppletion

6.5　It is grammatically unmarked. Height and high belong to different word classes. Its form is unpredictable (cf. *tallness*). Its meaning is unpredictable (cf. *highness*). Any inflection would be more peripheral, e.g. *heights*.

6.6　*Haven't* illustrates a clitic, a form that might be considered to be a separate word or an affix. Does *inspect* consist of one morpheme or two (cf. *project*)? How does one describe the realisation of the plural morpheme in the case of the word *mice*?

7.1　The distinction between morphology and syntax may presuppose that the structure of a word is substantially different to the structure of longer utterances. Such a distinction is undermined by the fact that semantically similar utterances may consist of one word or more than one word.

7.2　Possessive adjective, noun, adverb, verb, preposition, pronoun.

7.3　Examples might include *a large selection*, *four very rich men*, *my young sons*, *this hat* and *the hat that I prefer*, the last of these incorporating a clause.

7.4 (a) The black dog sleeps in the garden.

(a)

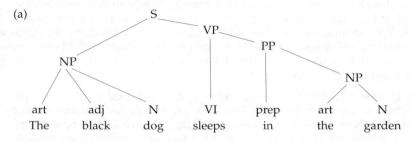

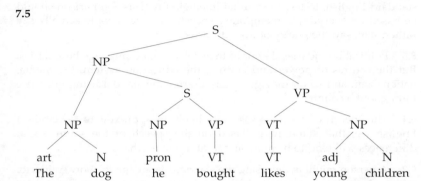

7.6 In the case of (a) the prepositional phrase *in the car* would be an immediate constituent of the verb phrase *bit the man in the car*. In the case of (b) it would form part of the noun phrase *the man in the car*.

7.7 In the case of (a) there has been a fall in the value of copper shares while in the case of (b) a policeman is having to wash in the same sink as somebody else.

7.8 Examples might include *The very old fear of death persists to this day* and *The very old fear the young in this city*.

7.9 (a) *Us* is an object pronoun and *she* is a subject pronoun. This sentence consequently contravenes the word order subject–verb–object. (b) *You*

7.10 (a) *My youngest son* (b) *the ball* (c) *the white dog*.

8.1 The significance of a regional dialect depends on how well-defined it is. This involves such factors as the number of features that are approximately coterminous.

8.2 A dialect continuum makes it difficult to establish boundaries between speech varieties. It undermines mutual intelligibility as a criterion for determining whether two varieties belong to different languages.

8.3 Mutual intelligibility is generally considered to be a principal criterion for determining whether or not two varieties belong to the one language. But it has faults. Mutual intelligibility is a matter of degree, not least as dialect continua may increase intelligibility for those close to a language boundary. The degree of intelligibility may not be mutual. Intelligibility may be increased by speakers avoiding the less standard features of their variety. It may be increased by context.

8.4 One might firstly consider what a Scots language would comprise. Would it necessarily be all the Germanic varieties of Scotland and nothing else? Is there a prestigious variety that might serve as a standard? One might then compare this Scots to other Germanic varieties, particularly standard English, to test for mutual intelligibility. This comparison should be based on everyday contemporary speech, on what people actually say rather than, say, the poetry of Robert Burns.

8.5 Political boundaries do not of themselves make language boundaries. But the centres of power and culture, the education system, the media, nationalism, and so on may gradually exert some standardising influence throughout a country.

9.1 The speech of a surgeon is more likely to approximate to standard English. As that standard is based on the speech of the south, social differences will tend to be more apparent in the north.

9.2 A person might avoid using the standard language to show solidarity with a particular regional or social community. Using too formal a register might give the impression that the speaker feels superior to the people he or she is speaking to.

9.5 We are likely to be less polite when talking to a brother than when talking to most other people. In this case the respective utterances might be something like *Shut the window* and *Would you mind shutting the window, please?*

10.1 A lexical difference is the word *view* as this would only have arrived with the Normans. The word *houses* is both phonologically and morphologically different; the diphthong /au/ resulted from the Great Vowel Shift and in Old English the word *hūs* made no distinction between the singular and plural forms in the nominative and accusative cases. A syntactic difference is the use of the auxiliary *do* to form a question.

10.2 (a) The first *seke* is a cognate of *seek*, the second a cognate of *sick*. The latter is inflected because it is in the plural. (b) *Holpen* has become *helped* by analogy.

10.4 The word *apron* has undergone metanalysis. The word *burn* has undergone metathesis.

10.5 The /r/ and /l/ have been inverted (metathesis) and the intervocalic /k/ has been voiced (lenition).

10.6 The words *church* and *chest* have undergone palatalisation; the Scots equivalents have not.

10.7 A family tree diagram shows the lineage of a language and the degree of relatedness of different languages. But it suggests abrupt transition rather than gradual evolution over time and synchronically it suggests distinct entities rather than continua, the former only being relevant for the standard language. The family tree diagram does not generally illustrate interaction between branches.

10.8 They are not mutually intelligible; we would not understand King Alfred and he would not understand us. Direct lineage does not necessarily mean that two varieties belong to the same language; we do not usually consider Latin and Italian to be varieties of one language. Indeed, in many respects (e.g. the case system) Old English is closer to modern Icelandic than to modern English.

11.1 (a) The German words *ich* and *Schafe* have the fricative sounds /ç/ and /f/ where the Dutch equivalents have the plosive sounds /k/ and /p/. The German word *zehn* has the affricate /ts/ in place of the plosive /t/ of the Dutch word *tien*. These differences are accounted for by the High German Consonant Shift.
(b) In Dutch and German the past participle of a perfect tense is placed at the end of a clause.

11.2 (a) The words *Pfeffer* and *Pilger* are derived from Latin. Unlike *Fisch*, they do not exhibit the First Germanic Consonant Shift.
(b) *Pfeffer*: it was adopted early enough to be subjected to the High German Consonant Shift, whereas *Pilger* was not.

11.3 (a) If subjected to the High German Consonant Shift the intervocalic /t/ in the name *Wittenberg*, meaning *white hill*, would have become /s/.
(b) This may illustrate the conservative nature of placenames.

11.4 kage

11.5 The French word *dent* retains the segment /d/. As part of the First Germanic Consonant Shift this segment became /t/ in the Germanic languages, as in the English word *tooth*. In High German, as part of the High German Consonant Shift, the plosive /t/ became the affricate /ts/ in, for example, initial position; hence the /ts/ in the German word *Zahn*.

11.6 In Italian the initial cluster /pl/ has become /pj/, while in Portuguese it has become /ʃ/. In the Portuguese word there has also been nasalisation caused by /n/ and then the loss of that /n/.

11.7 The word *échelle* acquired a prothetic vowel before /s/ + consonant.

It then lost the /s/. The /k/ before /a/ palatalised to /ʃ/. That /a/ became a front mid-vowel.

11.8 (a) In Catalan initial /l/ has been palatalized to /ʎ/. In Portuguese there has been palatalisation of the initial clusters /fl/, /kl/ and /pl/ to /ʃ/ and there has been a loss of intervocalic /l/ and /n/.
(b) In Catalan *luna* became *lluna*, in Portuguese it became *lua*.

11.9 (a) A white head. (b) White bread.

11.10 The case suffixes *-ssa* and *-ssä* constitute a pair of allomorphs, the form that the realisation of the morpheme takes depending on the stem vowel of the word to which it is attached. Similarly, the suffixes *-lla* and *-llä*, *-sta* and *-stä* constitute pairs of allomorphs.

11.11 Portuguese When we arrived the teacher shook us by the hand.

11.12 Italian It is the narrowest bridge in the town/city.

11.13 Danish He knows that the boat sank in this harbour.

11.14 French My friend's mother is in his/her room.

11.15 Dutch My wife has come in the car.

11.16 Icelandic My brother gave me this dictionary.

11.17 Scottish Gaelic My father is fishing in the loch.

11.18 German The teacher had broken the young child's boat.

12.1 The Japanese have introduced syllabic characters (hiragana and katakana) to represent inflections and grammatical particles and to deal more efficiently with foreign names.

12.2 An alphabetic system allows any permutations of segments to be represented with a relatively small set of symbols. A word not encountered before can be decoded. Languages with a simple syllable structure (e.g. Japanese with its CV structure) have less need to represent segments. Languages without inflections (e.g. Chinese) have fewer problems with a morphemic system.

12.3 The letter <A> began as a representation of an ox's head in the Middle East. The Phoenicians associated the symbol with the initial sound of the word for an ox, *'aleph*. The Greeks applied the symbol to a vowel.

12.4 Christianity brought the Roman script to Britain. Along with Christianity the Slavs received the Roman script or the Cyrillic script, depending on whether they received Christianity from Rome or Greece. The spread of Islam took the use of the Arabic script to Persian, Turkish, and so on.

Bibliography

General

Aitchison, Jean, *Linguistics* (Hodder & Stoughton, 1992 [1978]).
Bloomfield, Leonard, *Language* (Henry Holt, 1933).
Crystal, David, *Linguistics* (Pelican Books, 1989 [1971]).
Fromkin, V. and Rodman, R., *An Introduction to Language* (Harcourt Brace, 1993 [1974]).
Hockett, Charles F., *A Course in Modern Linguistics* (Macmillan, 1958).
Jennings, Gary, *Personalities of Language* (Victor Gollancz, 1967).
Lyons, John (ed.), *New Horizons in Linguistics* (Penguin Books, 1973 [1970]).
Lyons, John, *Language and Linguistics: An Introduction* (Cambridge University Press, 1992 [1981]).
Migliorini, Bruno, *Linguistica* (Felice Le Monnier, 1972 [1970]).
Pinker, Steven, *The Language Instinct* (Penguin Books, 1994).
Potter, Simeon, *Modern Linguistics* (André Deutsch, 1960 [1957]).
Potter, Simeon, *Language in the Modern World* (Penguin Books, 1968 [1960]).
Robins, R. H., *General Linguistics* (Longman, 1990 [1964]).
Sapir, Edward, *Language: An Introduction to the Study of Speech* (Harcourt, Brace & World, 1921).

Animal Behaviour

Hinde, Robert A., *Ethology* (Fontana, 1982).
Manning, Aubrey, *An Introduction to Animal Behaviour* (Edward Arnold, 1979).

Semantics

Berlin, B. and Kay, P., *Basic Color Terms: Their Universality and Evolution* (University of California Press, 1969).
Leech, Geoffrey, *Semantics* (Penguin Books, 1974).
Levinson, Stephen C., *Pragmatics* (Cambridge University Press, 1983).
Mott, Brian L., *A Course in Semantics and Translation for Spanish Learners of English* (Promociones y Publicaciones Universitarias, 1993).

Ogden, C. K. and Richards, I. A., *The Meaning of Meaning* (Ark Paperbacks, 1985 [1923]).
Palmer, F. R., *Semantics* (Cambridge University Press, 1981 [1976]).
Ullmann, Stephen, *Semantics: An Introduction to the Science of Meaning* (Blackwell, 1962).
Yule, George, *Pragmatics* (Oxford Universiy Press, 1996).

Phonetics and Phonology

Abercrombie, David, *Elements of General Phonetics* (Edinburgh University Press, 1967).
Carr, Philip, *Phonology* (Macmillan, 1993).
Catford, J. C., *A Practical Introduction to Phonetics* (Oxford University Press, 1988).
Katamba, Francis, *An Introduction to Phonology* (Longman, 1992 [1989}).
Ladefoged, Peter, *A Course in Phonetics* (Harcourt Brace, 1993 [1975]).
Mott, Brian L., *A Course in Phonetics and Phonology for Spanish Learners of English* (Promociones y Publicaciones Universitarias, 1991).
O'Connor, J. D., *Phonetics* (Penguin Books, 1991 [1973]).

Morphology and Syntax

Anderson, Stephen R., *A-Morphous Morphology* (Cambridge University Press, 1995 [1992]).
Bauer, L., *Introducing Linguistic Morphology* (Edinburgh University Press, 1988).
Brown, Keith and Miller, Jim, *Syntax: A Linguistic Introduction to Sentence Structure* (Routledge, 1996).
Carstairs-McCarthy, Andrew, *Current Morphology* (Routledge, 1992).
Chomsky, Noam, *Aspects of the Theory of Syntax* (MIT Press, 1965).
Culicover, P., *Syntax* (Academic Press, 1982).
Katamba, Francis *Morphology* (Macmillan Press, 1993).
Matthews, P. H., *Morphology* (Cambridge University Press, 1991 [1974]).
Matthews, P. H., *Syntax* (Cambridge University Press, 1992 [1981]).
Radford, Andrew, *Syntax: A Minimalist Introduction* (Cambridge University Press, 1997).

Regional Variation

Chambers, J. K. and Trudgill, P., *Dialectology* (Cambridge University Press, 1980).
Francis, W. N., *Dialectology: An Introduction* (Longman, 1983).
Petyt, K. M., *The Study of Dialect* (André Deutsch, 1980).
Trudgill, Peter, *On Dialect* (Blackwell, 1983).

Social Variation

Ager, Dennis, *Sociolinguistics and Contemporary French* (Cambridge University Press, 1990).
Clyne, Michael, *Language and Society in the German-speaking Countries* (Cambridge University Press, 1984).
Downes, William, *Language and Society* (Fontana, 1984).
Hudson, R. A., *Sociolinguistics* (Cambridge University Press, 1996 [1980]).
Sanders, Carol (ed.), *French Today: Language in its Social Context* (Cambridge University Press, 1993).
Trudgill, Peter, *Sociolinguistics: An Introduction to Language and Society* (Penguin Books, 1995 [1974]).

Historical Linguistics

Aitchison, Jean, *Language Change: Progress or Decay?* (Cambridge University Press, 1995 [1991]).
Bynon, Theodora, *Historical Linguistics* (Cambridge University Press, 1993 [1977]).
Romaine, Suzanne, *Pidgin and Creole Languages* (Longman, 1988).
Mühlhäusler, Peter, *Pidgin and Creole Linguistics* (Blackwell, 1986).
Trask, R. L., *Historical Linguistics* (Arnold, 1996).

The Languages of Western Europe

Ager, Dennis, *Sociolinguistics and Contemporary French* (Cambridge University Press, 1990).
Barber, Charles, *The English Language: A Historical Introduction* (Cambridge University Press, 1995 [1993]).
Brachin, Pierre, *The Dutch Language: A Survey* (E. J. Brill, 1985).
Clyne, Michael, *Language and Society in the German-speaking Countries* (Cambridge University Press, 1984).
Comrie, Bernard (ed.), *The Major Languages of Western Europe* (Routledge, 1990).
Donaldson, B. C., *Dutch: A Linguistic History of Holland and Belgium* (Martinus Nijhoff, 1983).
Harris, M. and Vincent, N. (ed.), *The Romance Languages* (Croom Helm, 1988).
Haugen, Einar, *The Scandinavian Languages: An Introduction to their History* (Faber & Faber, 1976).
Keller, R. E., *The German Language* (Faber & Faber, 1978).
Lockwood, W. B., *A Panorama of Indo-European Languages* (Hutchinson, 1972).
Maiden, Martin, *A Linguistic History of Italian* (Longman, 1995).
Mattoso Camara, J., Jr, *The Portuguese Language* (University of Chicago Press, 1972).

Migliorini, Bruno, *The Italian Language* [*Storia della lingua italiana*] (Faber & Faber, 1984 [1966]).

Penny, Ralph, *A History of the Spanish Language* (Cambridge University Press, 1995 [1991]).

Potter, Simeon, *Our Language* (Penguin Books, 1968 [1950]).

Priebsch, R. and Collinson, W. E., *The German Language* (Faber & Faber, 1966 [1934]).

Rickard, Peter, *A History of the French Language* (Routledge, 1993).

Russell, Paul, *An Introduction to the Celtic Languages* (Longman, 1995).

Sanders, Carol (ed.), *French Today: Language in its Social Context* (Cambridge University Press, 1993).

Writing Systems

Jensen, Hans, *Sign, Symbol and Script* (George Allen & Unwin, 1970).

Sampson, Geoffrey, *Writing Systems: A Linguistic Introduction* (Hutchinson, 1985).

Index